The Soviet Union and the Origins of the Second World War

The Making of the 20th Century

Series Editor: GEOFFREY WARNER

The Soviet Union and the Origins of the Second World War

Russo–German Relations and the Road to War, 1933–1941

Geoffrey Roberts

St. Martin's Press   New York

St. Martin's Press, College Division,
175 Fifth Avenue, New York, N.Y. 10010

First published in the United States of America in 1995

Printed in Malaysia

ISBN 0–312–13259–X (pbk.)
ISBN 0–312–12603–4 (cloth)

Library of Congress Cataloging-in-Publication Data
Roberts, Geoffrey K.
The Soviet Union and the origins of the Second World War : Russo
–German relations and the road to war / Geoffrey Roberts.
p. cm.
Includes bibliographical references and index.
ISBN 0–312–13259–X (pbk.) — ISBN 0–312–12603–4 (cloth)
1. World War, 1939–1945—Causes. 2. Russia—Relations—Germany.
3. Germany—Relations—Russia. I. Title.
D741.R53 1995
327.47043'09'043—dc20   94–46862
                                                              CIP

For Mother

Contents

Preface

This book about the USSR and the Origins of the Second World War concentrates on the story of Soviet-German relations in the period from the rise of Hitler to the launch of Operation Barbarossa in June 1941. There is, of course, much more to the Soviet role in the events leading to war than just the USSR's relationship with Germany. Relations with Great Britain, France and other countries, the Soviet response to the threat from Japan in the Far East, the role of the Communist International – all would need to figure in a comprehensive treatment of the subject. However, the Russo-German relationship is, arguably, the central part of the story. It is certainly the most controversial, and the subject on which recent releases from the Russian archives have been most revealing. In this connection readers should note that although this book is largely based on Soviet archival sources I have not had the benefit of direct access to the archives, which remain effectively closed to western researchers. No doubt when the Russian archives are finally opened up many of the interpretations and conclusions in this book will have to be revised. However, I am confident, given the wide range of published archival material now available, that the main lines of the story told here will be revalidated.

Thanks are due to John Erickson and Philip Windsor for valuable comments on a PhD thesis on which this book is in part based. Teddy Uldricks' supportive role as a kindred spirit in a fiercely contested field of research has been of inestimable value. Thanks to Brian Girvin, my colleague in the UCC History Department, for his intellectual companionship over the past two years. As ever, the most thanks to Celia Weston, my intellectual, emotional and practical partner in this and all my other projects.

The present book draws substantially on my previously published work: 'The Soviet Decision for a Pact with Nazi Germany', *Soviet Studies* (January 1992); 'The Fall of Litvinov: A Revisionist

View', *Journal of Contemporary History* (October 1992); 'Infamous Encounter? The Merekalov-Weizsäcker Meeting of 17 April 1939', *Historical Journal* (December 1992); 'Military Disaster as a Function of Rational Political Calculation: Stalin and 22 June 1941', *Diplomacy and Statecraft* (July 1993); 'A Soviet Bid for Co-existence with Nazi Germany, 1935–1937: The Kandelaki Affair', *International History Review* (August 1994); and *The Unholy Alliance: Stalin's Pact with Hitler* (London, 1989).

Finally, I would like to thank Geoffrey Warner, who commissioned the book, and to acknowledge the inspiration I derived from the publisher's anonymous referee who described the manuscript as 'highly entertaining and instructive ... an original account, packed with controversial theses and extravagant with disputatious as well as disputable asides'. I hope that other readers find the book equally interesting and controversial. Needless to say, I accept full and sole responsibility for its contents.

1 Introduction: Conflicting Views on the USSR and the Origins of the Second World War

For more than 30 years historical debate on the outbreak of the Second World War has centred on one book: A. J. P. Taylor's *The Origins of the Second World War*.[1] In the various controversies generated by the *Origins* attention has focused mainly on Taylor's depiction of Hitler as a tactical improviser in foreign policy rather than a fanatical ideologist bent on war, and on his sympathetic treatment of British and French appeasement of Germany.[2] Generally ignored in these debates is Taylor's authorship of an equally controversial and contentious interpretation of the Soviet role in the origins of the Second World War.[3]

The main thrust of Taylor's account of the USSR's participation in the events leading to war in 1939 was that Moscow, fearful of the threat to Soviet security posed by Nazi expansionism, sought an anti-German alliance with Britain and France. Throughout the 1930s Moscow manoeuvred for an anti-Hitler front in Europe. These efforts came to a head in 1939 with a proposal for a Soviet-British-French triple alliance which would call a halt to German expansion in Europe and, if necessary, fight a joint war against Germany. Having tried and failed to negotiate a suitable treaty of alliance with the British and French, and fearing an Anglo-French design of involving them in a war with Germany which they would have to fight alone, the Soviets turned to a deal with Hitler. The Nazi-Soviet non-aggression pact of 23 August 1939 – notwithstanding its secret clauses establishing Soviet-German spheres of influence in Eastern Europe – was for Moscow a matter of security not expansion. It was signed not with the intention of giving a green light to a German invasion of Poland but with a view to securing the Soviet position in the event of some kind of Munich deal over the return of Danzig to Germany.

Taylor emphasised that there was nothing altruistic about the Soviet struggle for collective security against the German menace in the 1930s; it was purely a question of what policies, agreements, and joint actions suited Soviet security interests. Moreover, in pursuing collective security against the German threat Moscow always acted with caution since the Soviet leadership were fearful and suspicious of the other capitalist great powers as well as Hitler. At many points in his exposition Taylor alludes as well to the improvisory character of Soviet foreign policy. Moscow, not knowing what the future held, reacted in an ad hoc manner to the unfolding events that constituted the origins of the Second World War. Stalin was as much an opportunist and tactician in foreign policy as Hitler. Finally, we should note Taylor's defence of the Soviet decision to sign a pact with Nazi Germany: 'However one spins the crystal and tries to look into the future from the point of view of 23 August 1939, it is difficult to see what other course Soviet Russia could have followed.'[4]

Taylor's interpretation of Soviet policy and action was neither remarkable nor unique. It was not even particularly novel. Official Soviet historians had for years been propounding a more ideological and less truthful version of the same story.[5] Taylor was, however, one of the pioneer western historians of the 'collective security' school of thought on the Soviet role in the origins of the Second World War. The touchstone of this interpretation of Soviet foreign policy in the 1930s is, quite simply, that Moscow's campaign for collective security was genuine.[6] Defining a historical school by its belief in the obvious may appear strange, but consider the contrast between the collective security view and that of a second school of thought on Soviet policy in the runup to the Second World War: the 'German' interpretation.

The 'German' school of thought can be defined in terms of, firstly, the focus of these historians on Soviet-German relations; secondly, the reliance placed on German archives for the interpretation of Soviet policy; and, thirdly, their argument that Soviet foreign policy in the 1930s was characterised by an orientation not to collective security but to an alliance with Nazi Germany. According to this interpretation, before the Second World War the USSR struggled not for an alliance against Hitler but for the reconstruction of the 'Rapallo' relationship between Germany and Russia

Following the signature of the Rapallo Treaty in April 1922 Soviet Russia and Weimar Germany had entered a period of extensive economic, military and political co-operation. Despite some ups and downs this Soviet-German alliance flourished throughout the 1920s and constituted a major axis of post-First World War international relations. The basis of this entente lay in the benefits of trade and military co-operation, in the joint desire to counter the political weight of the Franco-British combination, in mutual enmity to the newly created Polish state which occupied former German and Russian territories, and in common opposition to the Treaty of Versailles. In addition, for Moscow the Rapallo relationship with Germany acted as a guarantee against the re-emergence of the anti-Bolshevik capitalist coalition that had attempted to overthrow the new Soviet regime during the period of revolution and civil war.[7]

The Rapallo relationship between Germany and Russia collapsed following the Nazi seizure of power in 1933. However, according to the 'German' school of thought, Moscow remained unceasing in its efforts to renew the 1920s alliance. Collective security masked a preference for a deal with Hitler – an objective that was finally achieved with the signature of the Nazi-Soviet pact in August 1939. To the extent that the pact encouraged Hitler to go ahead with his attack on Poland, the USSR bears a major responsibility for the outbreak of the Second World War.[8]

The conflict between the 'collective security' and the 'German' school interpretations is one that in the end can only be settled by an analysis of the evidence. And, as we shall see, a major theme of this book is a sustained and detailed refutation of the 'German' school and a defence of the 'collective security' approach. Pending that, some general comments are in order.

Firstly, as Teddy Uldricks has pointed out,[9] the Rapallo orientation interpretation rests on a very large contention: that in pursuing its collective security campaign in the 1930s the USSR expended vast political and diplomatic effort on aims that it didn't really seek to achieve. As we shall see for the 'German' school, what is important are a few intermittent, largely informal diplomatic contacts in which the possibility of a Soviet-German détente was raised. Relatively unimportant are the USSR's entry into the League of Nations in 1934, the Soviet pacts of mutual assistance with France and Czechoslovakia in 1935, Moscow's anti-German campaign in the Munich crisis of 1938, the triple alliance negotiations of 1939, and the consistent and persistent fight for collective security and anti-fascism. It is the type of contention that in most areas of history would require some pretty impressive evidence to gain any credence at all. The 'German' school interpretation rests, however, on the flimsiest of evidential bases. In truth it is no more than a series of speculations that benefited from the absence of Russian archival evidence and drew strength from the cold war atmosphere that pervaded post-war western Soviet Studies.

Secondly, the credibility of the 'German' school is very much tied to the argument that the culmination of the USSR's continuing Rapallo orientation in the 1930s was the signature of the Nazi-Soviet pact and the period of German-Soviet détente and co-operation which followed. This argument collapses, however, if it can be shown that the Soviet turn to a pact with Nazi Germany represented a radical departure from the previous policy of collective security. The evidence from the Soviet archives that this was indeed the case – strong even in A. J. P. Taylor's day when only western and public sources were available – is now of overwhelming weight. Such a counter to the 'German' interpretation is buttressed by an analysis of Soviet policy after the pact, in the period before Hitler's attack on the USSR in June 1941. Although a period of Soviet-German rapprochement, 1939–41 was far from being a simple return to Rapallo. The main theme of Soviet foreign policy in this period was the same as in the 1930s: defence against the German threat. A search for security against Nazi aggression and expansionism was the great continuity in Soviet policy from 1933–41, not a quest for alliance with the future enemy.

A final point of general criticism to be levelled against the 'German' school is that it misidentifies the character of Soviet foreign policy in the 1930s. For these historians it is anomalous that whilst publicly urging collective security and an anti-German alliance with the west the USSR maintained normal diplomatic relations with the Nazi regime, attempted to strengthen trade and economic links, engaged in friendly political discourse from time to time, and even proclaimed its willingness to coexist peacefully with Hitler. Such anomalies are explained, we are told, by the existence of a secret foreign policy line that contradicted the ostensible objectives of the Soviet state.

From the perspective of the present this duality in Soviet policy towards Germany does indeed seem odd. However, from the perspective of the 1930s Moscow's active resistance to Hitler's policy combined with action and efforts to maintain peaceful coexistence with the German state (and with Italy and Japan, for that matter) was unexceptional and considered so at the time.[10] For those, like Soviet decision-makers, who didn't know what happened next in history, who didn't know what Hitler was going to do and how long his regime would last, and who were unsure of the likely outcome of their efforts to contain and confront the Nazi threat, there was nothing strange about keeping open all the options – particularly if there were additional political or economic benefits to be gained from so doing. Their behaviour was like that of all states at all times in the history of peacetime international relations. Furthermore, the collective security strategy itself politically and ideologically sanctioned such a modus operandi. The Soviet embrace of collective security arose from the perceived need for the USSR to make common cause with other states in opposition to Hitler's expansionist foreign policy. That didn't mean the disappearance of traditional Soviet fears and suspicions regarding other capitalist powers. Nor did it mean a neglect of the USSR's own strength, independence and particular security interests. Collective security and opposition to Hitler was not a moral crusade against fascism, but a weapon in the USSR's foreign policy armoury – one to be deployed judiciously and with due regard to the danger of Soviet isolation in a world of capitalist states that Moscow continued to view with suspicion, fear and hostility.[11]

These last considerations are also relevant to a third group of historians with a distinctive interpretation of Soviet foreign policy in the 1930s: the 'internal politics' school of thought. The 'internal politics' school with its emphasis on the domestic political dimension of the making of Soviet foreign policy represents an important contribution to the debate on the USSR's role in the origins of the Second World War. Its advocates propose an interpretation that neatly ties together three apparently incongruous aspects of Soviet policy: the undoubted reality and centrality of the collective security campaign; evidence of pro-Rapallo sentiments and policy initiatives on the part of Soviet diplomats and leaders; and, importantly, the fact that the climax of pre-war Soviet foreign relations was not the expected triple alliance with Britain and France but a pact with Nazi Germany.

Their argument is that throughout the 1930s there was an internal struggle within Soviet decision-making circles over the policy of collective security. The struggle for collective security abroad was paralleled by a struggle for collective security at home, a struggle between the pro-western Soviet Foreign Minister Maxim Litvinov, the architect and main advocate of the collective security strategy, and his opponents in Moscow and Berlin who favoured some kind of Rapallo-type orientation. One concrete expression of this internal conflict was the contradictory and ambivalent character of Soviet policy towards Germany in the 1930s, another was the signature of the Nazi-Soviet pact in 1939 – which is seen as representing, at least in part, the final victory of an anti-collective security trend in Soviet foreign policy.[12]

Again, the validity of the 'internal politics' argument rests not on the fact that it is highly plausible and makes for a good story, but on the evidence. Unlike the case of the 'German' school interpretation, as far as the evidence is concerned the jury remains out on the extent, depth and character of internal Soviet differences over foreign policy. We need much more material from Soviet archives before we can come to definitive conclusions. However, as I shall argue in detail later in the book, the evidence that is available indicates that the 'internal politics' school exaggerates the differences and, more importantly, misinterprets who and what inspired them. What differences there were lay not in some fundamental split over collective security but in the realm of tactical and political calculation. Internal disputes revolved around differences of assessment of the situation which were in turn rooted in real-world events of diplomacy and foreign policy. In the mid-1930s, for example, Litvinov came into conflict with proponents of a more conciliatory line towards Nazi Germany. However, Litvinov's opponents were not motivated by some abstract pro-Rapallo orientation but by the fact that they were the recipients of German overtures for a political and economic détente and because they thought there were advantages to be reaped from a positive response to the prospect of a normalisation of Soviet-German relations.

Another example of internal Soviet divisions over foreign policy was in relation to Japan. In this case the roles were reversed, with Litvinov arguing for conciliation and compromise while others urged confrontation with Japanese aggression and expansionism in the Far East. Needless to say there was nothing pro-Japanese about Litvinov's stance. It was merely that he attached priority to dealing with the German threat in Europe and thought there were possibilities for encouraging moderate elements in Japanese government and politics. Others disagreed and thought that Japan would back down in the face of a strong Soviet stand. Again, the difference was one of assessment and calculation. Litvinov was no more an 'appeaser' in relation to Japan than the so-called Rapalloites were in relation to Germany.[13]

A further defect of the 'internal politics' interpretation is that much of what it identifies as expressing contradictions between conflicting policy lines was in fact a function of internal tensions within the collective security policy itself. Alliance on the one hand, self-reliance on the other. The strategic principle of anti-fascism, the tactical expediency of peaceful coexistence with the Nazis. The unfulfilled hope of unity with Britain and France, the reality of Anglo-French appeasement of Hitler. The political will to achieve collective security and ideological doubt that it would prove to be possible. Given the existence of such tensions it is no wonder that Soviet policy in the 1930s was multi-dimensional and multi-faceted. Such diversity, however, was contained within a single foreign policy line. As T. J. Uldricks puts it:

There was only one foreign policy line, both before and after 1933 and, for that matter, after August 1939. That line included the assumption of hostility from all imperialist powers and, therefore, the need to keep them divided. It mandated a balance of power policy which motivated the USSR to make common cause with Germany against a perceived British threat before the rise of Hitler, and thereafter to seek Anglo-French co-operation against an even more menacing Third Reich. Throughout the decade, suspicion of all imperialist powers and a desperate search for security remained constant. Stalin may be faulted for a great many mistakes in attempting to carry out the Collective Security line, but the line itself seems indisputably genuine.[14]

To reject the 'internal politics' view as ill-founded is not to reject the methodological approach that it embodies. It reminds us that foreign policy is not made by abstractions we call 'states' and 'governments', nor can it be simply analysed and read off from grand strategies and ideologies. Foreign policy is made by individuals in discussion and contention with each other, individuals acting in real situations, responding and deciding upon action on a day-to-day basis. This process of decision-making typically contains elements of both consistency and contingency – patterns and trends flowing from overall ideology and strategy combined with the specific reactions, calculations and decisions resulting from the assessment of particular situations. In the case of Soviet foreign policy in the 1930s we find both these things, together with a perhaps more surprising feature of decision-making: its uncertain, uncalculated and ad hoc character. As A. J. P. Taylor intuited back in the 1950s the great untold story of the USSR's role in the origins of the Second World War is the haphazard and accidental nature of much of Soviet policy and action. This was nowhere more the case than in relation to Germany, as Moscow struggled for almost a decade in a highly complex situation to frame a response to a state that threatened the very existence of Soviet Russia.[15]

2 From Co-operation to Confrontation: The End of Rapallo and the Turn to Collective Security, 1933–1935

At the moment of Hitler's accession to power in January 1933 the Rapallo relationship between Soviet Russia and Germany was still largely intact. Over the next 12 months, however, a decade of political, military and economic co-operation between the two states was liquidated. Military co-operation was terminated, trade began to plummet, and in December 1933 the USSR embarked on an anti-German policy of 'collective security' – a quest for a grand alliance of states to contain Nazi aggression and expansionism. In pursuit of this quest the USSR joined the League of Nations in September 1934, participated in negotiations for a regional defence agreement in Eastern Europe and, in May 1935, signed mutual assistance pacts with France and Czechoslovakia. All of these Soviet actions were directed against Germany. Germany, the USSR's most important ally in the capitalist world in the 1920s, had become the object of Soviet encirclement and confrontation.

This dramatic and fateful turn in Soviet foreign policy was not provoked by the coming to power in Germany of a virulently anti-Bolshevik political movement nor by the anti-communist terror campaign launched by Hitler shortly after he became Chancellor. It was the perception that Hitler was intent on the active pursuit of his anti-sovietism in the field of foreign policy that prompted the abandonment of the Rapallo relationship and the development of a new foreign strategy. As Litvinov put it:

> We have our own opinion about the German regime, and of course we sympathize with the sufferings of our German comrades, but we as Marxists are the last who can be reproached with allowing sentiment to prevail over policy. The whole world knows that we can and do maintain good relations with capitalist states whatever their regime, even if it is fascist. That is not

the point. We do not interfere in the internal affairs of Germany or of any country; our relations with Germany are determined not by its internal policy but by its external policy.[1]

The ending of Rapallo and the turn to collective security did not happen overnight. Hitler's appointment as Chancellor prompted anxiety in Soviet circles, but the perspective, initially at least, was one of the continuation of the Rapallo relationship in some form. 'We want the present government to keep to a friendly position in relations with us', wrote Deputy Commissar for Foreign Affairs, Krestinsky, to Khinchuk, the Soviet ambassador in Berlin, on 23 February 1933. 'We are counting on this – that the Hitler government is dictated by the necessity of not breaking with us and, at least, maintaining previous relations.'[2]

In line with this perspective the main objectives of Soviet diplomacy towards Germany during the early weeks of the Nazi regime were to secure a public declaration of good intent towards the USSR and the ratification of a 1931 protocol prolonging the 1926 Berlin treaty of neutrality for a further five years. Both these aims were in fact achieved. In a speech on 23 March Hitler declared that relations with the USSR would continue as before and on 5 May Germany ratified the 1931 protocol.[3]

Notwithstanding its relative optimism about the immediate future of Soviet-German relations Moscow's longer term outlook was dominated by forebodings about the menace posed by Nazi foreign policy. Of particular concern was the danger of the emergence of a Franco-German coalition directed against the USSR. The fear of such an eventuality had begun to take shape even before Hitler came to power and it was a spectre that the Russians were to raise many times with the Germans in 1933.[4] On 1 March 1933 Litvinov told Neurath, the German Foreign Minister:

Naturally, we have no intention of altering our relations with Germany but we certainly cannot look kindly upon the prospect of an anti-Soviet bloc involving Germany. Until now it appeared possible to forestall such a bloc by exerting pressure on Berlin but, if this, however, turns out to be insufficient, we will of course not hesitate to exert pressure on Paris.[5]

This theme also dominated Litvinov's meeting with Dirksen, the German ambassador, ten days later. Dirksen reported to Berlin that the Soviet Union:

> considered a German-French alliance contrary to its interests and would seek to prevent it. But while the Soviet Government had in the past sought to prevent a German-French alliance by bringing influence to bear on the German side, it would now endeavour to attain the same objective through closer relations with France.

On the other hand, Litvinov had declared:

> emphatically that the Soviet Government would never enter into any alliance with France and in any way confirm the Treaty of Versailles; it would merely seek to develop its relations with France.[6]

There were also more general expressions of concern about the Nazi threat, including the following letter from Alexandrovsky, a political counsellor in the Berlin embassy, on 18 April 1933:

> Every other government in Germany, except Hitler's, could have striven for a gradual improvement in its international position, for a slow swaying of the foundations of Versailles, for the destruction of the brick wall surrounding Germany, for the gradual rehabilitation of its government in the international arena. ... Reality will make the severest amendments to the foreign policy fantasies of the Nazis, but it cannot change one thing – Hitler cannot exist without a big foreign policy and ... this means extreme, including military adventurism and, ultimately, war and intervention against the USSR.[7]

Similarly, on 19 May Krestinsky wrote to Khinchuk that even if Nazi Germany normalised its relations with the USSR it would not signify 'a final reorientation of the Hitler government, its repudiation of its former conception. It would mean for us a definite breathing space, which the longer it is, the more favourable it will be to the international position of the USSR.'[8]

In public, Moscow's apprehensions concerning the German threat were aired in the columns of *Pravda* in an article by the Soviet publicist Karl Radek who denounced Hitler's demands for revision of the Versailles Treaty:

> The path of revision ... leads through a new world war. All attempts by interested parties to represent the matter of revision merely as a peaceful resettlement of old treaties cannot deceive anyone. The diplomatic talk concerning the revision of the Versailles Treaty is simply a means of preparing for war...The word 'revision' is simply another name for a new world war ... This program of the seeking of the revision of the Versailles Treaty is the foreign policy program of German fascism.[9]

Such fears about Nazi adventurism came to a head in June 1933 when at the World Economic Conference in London, Hugenberg, the German Economics Minister, submitted a memorandum on international economic development which the Russians interpreted as a German demand for 'living space' in the USSR.[10] The USSR protested to the German government about the memorandum and Hugenberg resigned a few days later, but the incident proved to be a turning point in the breakdown of Soviet-German relations in 1933.

In a letter to Khinchuk on 27 June, Krestinsky – in the 1920s a strong supporter of Rapallo – argued that:

> The 'Hugenberg Memorandum' shows us that the present government, notwithstanding the repeated declarations of Dirksen, Neurath, Goering and Hitler about their determination to keep to a friendly policy towards the USSR, have actually not given up the foreign policy ideas which the National Socialists developed in theory and actively worked for in all the years of their struggle for power. The German government is prepared to participate in a military coalition against us, is prepared to expand its military power for war with us, and requires only two things: armaments freedom and compensation at the expense of the USSR ... We must all, first and foremost, remember that the friendly assurances of the German government are not to be believed, that in the further estrangement are the political

plans of Germany to enter into war with us and that the present position is only a temporary respite.[11]

The Hugenberg incident coincided with the ending by the Soviets of military co-operation with Germany[12] and was followed in October 1933 by Germany's withdrawal from the League of Nations Disarmament Conference and from the League itself, an action which *Izvestiya* roundly condemned: 'German fascism declares to the entire world that it has decided to take the path of preparation for war'.[13]

At this point the gradual breakdown of the Rapallo relationship became entwined with another crucial development on the Soviet foreign relations front: the blossoming of a détente with France, which was to eventually lead to the Franco-Soviet mutual assistance pact of May 1935.

A Franco-Soviet détente had been growing gradually in 1932–3[14] but it only began to develop real impetus following Germany's withdrawal from the League of Nations. A few days later there occurred the first of a series of French approaches to the Russians concerning Franco-Soviet co-operation in face of the German threat, including Soviet membership of the League of Nations. With an eye to the dangers of a Franco-German rapprochement in the absence of a Franco-Soviet one, Moscow responded positively to these proposals.[15]

In response to the détente with France on 12 December 1933 the Central Committee of the Soviet communist party passed a resolution in favour of collective security in Europe. What this meant concretely was spelt out in a series of Politburo proposals on collective security endorsed on 20 December 1933. The two key Soviet commitments were (a) to join the League of Nations and (b) to participate, together with France, in an East European-based regional defence agreement directed against Germany.[16]

These were truly revolutionary decisions. The USSR had committed itself to participate in collective action against its erstwhile partner Germany, and within the framework of the League of Nations – an organisation the Soviets had hitherto shunned as embodying the imperialist peace of Versailles.[17]

No public announcement of this radical shift in foreign policy was made but in a speech to the Central Executive Committee of the Supreme Soviet on 29 December 1933 Litvinov expounded the thinking that lay behind the new collective security policy. 'If it is possible to speak of diplomatic eras, then we are now without doubt standing at the junction of two eras', he told the CEC. An era of bourgeois pacifism had come to an end and a new era of wars of imperialist redivision was just beginning. Moreover, continued Litvinov, peaceful coexistence with all states was no longer enough to ensure Soviet security:

> We think that even hostilities which do not begin directly on the frontiers of our Union may threaten security ...
>
> The ensuring of peace cannot depend on our efforts alone; it requires the collaboration and co-operation of other States. While therefore trying to establish and maintain relations with all states, we are giving special attention to strengthening and making close our relations with those which, like us, give proof of their sincere desire to maintain peace and are ready to resist those who break the peace.

This theme of Litvinov's – the need to supplement the traditional Soviet policy of peaceful coexistence with a strategy of collective security – was nothing new. It had been a leitmotif of his statements on foreign relations since the beginning of 1933. Until now, however, Litvinov had restricted himself to generalities, evading the critical question – collective security against whom? In this speech Litvinov launched into a denunciation of German foreign policy, leaving no doubt about the inspiration behind the policy of collective security:

> In the past year our relations with Germany have become, it may be said, unrecognisable ... The reason for this was that when the change of government occurred in Germany in 1932 a politician came into power ... who at the time when our relations with Germany were at their best came out openly against them, preaching rapprochement with the West with the object of making a combined attack on the Soviet Union ... Then followed the revolution which brought a new party to power in Germany, preaching the most extreme anti-Soviet ideas. The founder of this party devoted a book to developing in detail his conception of German foreign policy. According to this Germany was not only to reconquer all the territories of which

it had been deprived by the Versailles treaty, not only to conquer lands where there was a German minority, but by fire and sword to cut a road for expansion to the East, which was not to stop at the Soviet frontier, and to enslave the Soviet peoples. ... But perhaps these people, on coming to power and occupying responsible posts, would disown these ideas. We understand very well the difference between doctrine and policy. It does happen that an opposition, on coming to power, tries to forget the slogans which it used in its fight against its political opponents. But in the given case this did not happen ... Only six months ago a member of the German Government elaborated the same idea of a conquest of the East in a memorandum submitted to the London international conference.[18]

Litvinov's speech sounded the death-knell of Rapallo. Yet for all his intransigence and militancy Litvinov was careful to keep open the door to peaceful coexistence between Nazi Germany and Soviet Russia. 'We want to have the best relations with Germany, as with other countries. Nothing but good can come from such relations', he also said in his speech. All that was required was a change in German policy towards the USSR.[19] This was a theme that Stalin took up in his speech to the 17th Party Congress in January 1934:

Some German politicians say that the USSR has now taken an orientation towards France and Poland; that from an opponent of Versailles it has become a supporter of it ... That is not true. Of course we are far from being enthusiastic about the fascist regime in Germany. But it is not a question of fascism here ... Nor is it a question of any alleged change in our attitude towards the Versailles Treaty. It is not for us ... to sing the praises of the Versailles Treaty. We merely do not agree to the world being flung into a new war on account of this treaty. The same must be said of the alleged new orientation taken by the USSR. We never had any orientation towards Germany, nor have we any orientation towards Poland and France. Our orientation in the past and our orientation at the present time is towards the USSR and towards the USSR alone. And if the interests of the USSR demand rapprochement with one country or another which is not interested in

disturbing peace, we adopt this course without hesitation. ...
No, that is not the point. The point is that Germany's policy
has changed.[20]

The importance for Moscow of keeping open the possibility of co-
operation with Berlin was underlined by some disturbing developments in relation to Poland and the Baltic States.

The independence and security of the Baltic States had always
been considered by Moscow as vital to Soviet defence. The fear
that the Baltic States could act as a launchpad for an attack on the
USSR was lent added piquancy by the Nazi takeover in Germany.
In October 1933 Izvestiya drew attention to the fact that: 'The or-
ganisers of anti-Soviet intervention have always regarded the
Baltic states as springboards for attacking the Soviet Union. The
present trumpeters of German nazism are looking at them in
exactly the same way ... That is why the Soviet Union cannot, of
course, remain indifferent in the face of intensified Nazi activities
in the Baltic states.'[21]

To counter this threat in the Baltic in December 1933 the
Russians proposed to the Poles that they issue a joint declaration
on co-operation to deal with threats to the Baltic States. The Poles
refused the proposal and, not only that, proceeded to sign a declaration of non-aggression with Germany in January 1934.[22] The
Soviet interpretation of this declaration was that it 'secures for
Germany Poland's neutrality in the event of German aggression
... This means not only will Poland assume neutrality in the event
of a German invasion of Austria, but also in the case of German
aggression against Lithuania and the East in general.'[23]

This pessimistic view was confirmed during a trip to Moscow by
Beck, the Polish Foreign Minister, in February 1934. Litvinov's
conclusion from his conversations with Beck was that there was
no possibility of collaboration with Poland against Germany in the
near future, nor any prospect of a joint agreement to safeguard
the Baltic States.[24]

Stymied by the Poles and suspicious of Warsaw's intentions,
Moscow turned to Berlin for an agreement that would enhance
Soviet security in the Baltic. On 28 March Litvinov approached
Nadolny, the German ambassador, with the idea of a joint Soviet-
German guarantee of the independence and integrity of the
Baltic States. Litvinov and other Soviet officials went to great

pains to persuade Berlin of the merits of the proposal, stressing, in particular, the importance of such an agreement for the betterment of Soviet-German relations in general.[25] In April, however, the Germans rejected the proposal on the ground that since there was no threat to the Baltic States there was no need for such a guarantee.[26] Berlin did not reject the prospect of an improvement in Soviet-German relations, but to the Russians the whole episode served only to confirm that the Rapallo era was definitely over.

The Baltic guarantee episode was followed by a period dominated by the negotiations for an 'Eastern Locarno' or an 'Eastern Pact' – a regional defence pact covering Eastern Europe under which the signatories would commit themselves to aid each other in the event of attack.[27] The idea of such a pact grew out of Franco-Russian discussions in autumn 1933 and was originally conceived by both sides as an anti-German front in Eastern Europe. However, in April 1934 Paris proposed that this regional mutual assistance pact should include Germany as well. Moscow went along with this French proposal but throughout the ensuing negotiating process the Soviet priority was not German participation but any workable and worthwhile agreement which would embody the collective security idea of mutual defence against aggression. In Soviet eyes the Eastern Pact was viewed as part of a universal collective security system, one of a whole series of regional defence agreements that would replace traditional diplomatic instruments such as bilateral military alliances, balance of power politics and non-aggression agreements.[28]

At stake in the 'Eastern Locarno' negotiations of 1934–5 was the whole strategy of collective security and the Soviets waged a desperate struggle for a successful outcome to the talks. Predictably, their main opponent was Germany. Berlin had no intention of restricting its freedom of action in relation to Eastern Europe, or of facilitating the emergence of a Franco-Russian alliance (which would underwrite any Eastern Pact).

The German response to the Eastern Pact proposal was a combination of outright opposition and attempts to dilute the agreement into a regional non-aggression pact.[29] The latter tactics caused particular consternation in Moscow which was determined that collective security in Eastern Europe would be based on binding mutual assistance agreements. The importance of this issue to Moscow is illustrated by Stalin's personal intervention in the matter. The occasion was a meeting with Eden, British deputy Foreign Minister, in Moscow in March 1935. At this meeting, Stalin's first with a foreign statesman, the Soviet dictator said:

> You told Litvinov that the German Government objected to the Eastern Pact of mutual assistance. She only agrees to a pact of non-aggression. But where is the guarantee that the German Government, which so easily violates its international agreements, will adhere to a pact of non-aggression? No guarantee whatsoever. Therefore, we cannot be content with a pact of non-aggression with Germany. To secure peace we need a real guarantee and the only such guarantee is an Eastern pact of mutual assistance.

To illustrate his point, Stalin delivered the following homily on collective security:

> There are here in this room six people, imagine that between ourselves there is a pact of mutual assistance and imagine that, for example, Comrade Maisky [Soviet ambassador to Britain] wanted to attack one of us – what would happen? We would all join forces to beat Comrade Maisky ... It is the same with the countries of Eastern Europe.[30]

The end result of this Soviet-German diplomatic struggle was a draw. In the face of German (and Polish) opposition to an Eastern Locarno, Moscow was forced to abandon the project of a general regional security pact in Eastern Europe but it did manage to secure the signature, in May 1935, of mutual assistance pacts with France and Czechoslovakia.[31] The Soviets were under no illusion that these pacts represented more than a modicum of success in their campaign for collective security. As Litvinov commented on the treaty with France:

> One should not place any serious hopes on the pact in the sense of real military aid in the event of war. Our security will still remain exclusively in the hands of the Red Army. For us the pact has predominantly a political significance, reducing the chance of war on the part of Germany and also Poland and Japan.[32]

Moscow had also succeeded in consolidating France's opposition to Germany on the political-diplomatic level and it had assuaged its nightmare of a Franco-German coalition directed against the Soviet Union.[33] In pursuing these objectives the Soviets had nailed their colours firmly to the mast of the collective security strategy and set a course for confrontation with Nazi Germany. There were no qualms in Moscow about this outcome because the conviction continued to grow that the danger of Nazi aggression and expansionism left the USSR no alternative. One public expression of this conviction was Premier Molotov's speech to the 7th Congress of Soviets in January 1935:

We cannot close our eyes to the changes that have taken place in Soviet-German relations with the coming to power of the National Socialists. With regard to ourselves it can be said that we have never had any other desire than to continue in good relations with Germany. Everybody knows that the Soviet Union is imbued with a profound desire to develop relations with every state, not excluding states in which a fascist regime prevails. However, serious difficulties in the path of Soviet-German relations have recently arisen.

Of course, the obstacle to the development of Soviet-German relations is not the super-nationalist racial theories which assert that the German people are the lords of creation. ... it is not a question of these theories, but of what lies at the basis of the foreign policy of present-day Germany ... I refer to the statement regarding Russia made by Herr Hitler in his book *My Struggle*, which is being widely distributed in Germany ... Does the statement of Herr Hitler remain in force – the statement that it is necessary to pass to 'a policy of territorial conquest' in Eastern Europe and that 'when we (National Socialists) speak of new lands in Europe today we can only think in the first instance of Russia and her border states'? Apparently this statement does remain in force, because it is only this assumption that can explain many things in the present attitude of the German Government towards the Soviet Union and towards the project for an eastern pact.'[34]

Molotov's attack on Hitler's foreign policy was followed in March by a major article in *Pravda* by Tukhachevsky, Deputy

Commissar for War and commander-in-chief of the Red Army. Published in the wake of Germany's reintroduction of conscription the article exposed Nazi militarisation and denounced Hitler's plans to attack both the Soviet Union and France.[35] In July 1935 the 7th World Congress of the Communist International opened in Moscow. Convened to endorse the Comintern's new strategy of constructing people's fronts against fascism, the Congress acted as a forum for yet more denunciations of Germany and its anti-Soviet plans.[36]

By summer 1935 the battlelines between Russia and Germany were firmly drawn. The bulwark of anti-fascism and the champion of collective security versus the aggressor state. The aspiring organiser of a peace coalition versus Nazi expansionism. The citadel of anti-militarism versus Hitler's war machine. Such a public polarisation between the two erstwhile allies was to remain in place for the next four years. Not until the Nazi-Soviet pact of August 1939 was there to be any significant deviation from the confrontation which developed in 1933–5.

That, however, was only on the surface. Behind the scenes Soviet-German relations were much more complicated than the public record of political and diplomatic conflict. One sign of this complexity was the following curious episode. In May 1935, immediately after the signature of the mutual assistance pact with France, the Russians approached the Germans with the suggestion that there should be negotiations for a general East European non-aggression and consultation pact.[37] This idea was originally a German one – an idea to which Moscow had for nearly a year counterposed the policy of binding collective security and defence agreements. Berlin did not respond to Moscow's change of heart and neither did the Soviets seriously pursue it any further. But what it indicated was that despite the breakdown of Rapallo, despite their fears concerning Nazi expansionism, and despite their ardent pursuit of collective security, the Russians were still interested in the possibility of peaceful coexistence with Germany. The exploration of that possibility was to be a major theme of Soviet relations with Germany over the next two years. It has also proved to be the source of one of the most intriguing historical controversies about Soviet foreign policy in the 1930s.

3 Confrontation versus Compromise: Dilemmas of Coexistence with Nazi Germany, 1935–1937

By the middle of 1935 Soviet-German relations were in as bad a state as they had ever been. Moscow's view of the cause of this state of affairs was summed up in a letter from Litvinov to Suritz, the Soviet ambassador in Berlin, on 3 June 1935: 'Hitler continues to fight against all efforts to organise collective security, for the basis of his policy remains, in accordance with his book "My Struggle", the building of power and preparation for aggression, in the first instance in a South-Eastern and Eastern direction.'[1]

In line with this perspective, the next two years were to be a time of high tension in Soviet-German relations – a period of political polemics, of diplomatic conflicts, and even a sort of Nazi–communist war by proxy. These were the years of Soviet-German clashes over the Soviet treaties with France and Czechoslovakia, which the Nazis denounced as anti-German pacts encirclement; of Soviet efforts to strengthen the League of Nations as an instrument of collective security; of German support for Italy in the Abyssinian war; of Hitler's remilitarisation of the Rhineland in March 1936; of the outbreak of civil war in Spain; of the launching of an anti-Bolshevik crusade at the Nuremberg rally of September 1936; and, in November 1936, the announcement by Mussolini of the Rome–Berlin Axis and the signature of the German-Japanese anti-Comintern pact.

Behind these public confrontations, however, another story of Soviet-German relations was unfolding, for during this very same period Soviet embassy officials in Berlin made a number of confidential approaches to their German counterparts about the possibility of improving relations between their two countries, leading, perhaps, to some kind of rapprochement.

A key figure in these contacts with the Germans was David Kandelaki, the Soviet trade representative in Berlin 1935–7. Under the guise of trade negotiations Kandelaki made at least two major political overtures to the Germans and it is likely that he

21

was involved in a number of other diplomatic soundings concerning the possibility of a Soviet-German détente. Despite the fact that Kandelaki fell victim to the purges following his recall to Moscow in spring 1937, there have also been many rumours and reports that during his sojourn in Berlin he operated as a special agent of Stalin and Molotov. For example, according to Yevgeny Gnedin, the Press Secretary of the Soviet embassy in Berlin during this period:

> Kandelaki clearly gave us the impression that he had confidential instructions from Stalin personally and the power to go beyond economic subjects in talks with the Germans. The trade representatives and embassy workers were aware that Kandelaki was close to Stalin ... and that he was actively attempting, irrespective of Litvinov and his co-workers, to 'build bridges' between the Soviet and Hitler governments.[2]

What are we to make of the 'Kandelaki affair'? Among historians there have been three schools of thought. According to one view Moscow's secret soundings in Berlin give the lie to its commitment to the policy of collective security. What the Russians wanted all along was a political deal with Hitler's Germany – a deal they eventually got with the signature of the Nazi-Soviet pact in 1939.[3] Another interpretation is that the concurrence of the campaign for collective security and Kandelaki's activities in Berlin exemplify deep divisions within the Soviet leadership around Litvinov's anti-German foreign policy strategy.[4] Finally, there is my own argument, in *The Unholy Alliance: Stalin's Pact with Hitler* (1989), that Moscow's soundings in Berlin were essentially tactical in nature, generated by perceptions of an economic and political crisis in Germany and aimed at exploiting perceived divisions in the Nazi power bloc over Hitler's anti-Soviet foreign policy.[5]

With the aid of some new evidence from Soviet archives[6] it can now be argued with some confidence that all three interpretations are inadequate. The cold war view that Kandelaki's activities constituted some kind of prelude to the Nazi-Soviet pact cannot withstand a detailed scrutiny of the available evidence on Soviet-German relations during this period. There were indeed internal Soviet splits over policy towards Germany, but these were complex, ambiguous and fluctuating – legitimate differences of situational assessment and tactical calculation rather than deep divisions over the collective security strategy. The idea that the Soviet approaches were prompted by an analysis of domestic instability and political division within Nazi Germany remains valid in general terms, but more important than the overall policy context was the impact of the day-to-day specifics of diplomatic relations between the USSR and Germany during this period.

The key to understanding Soviet policy in this period – something that historians have hitherto failed to appreciate – is that Moscow was confronted with numerous *German offers* of a substantial expansion in trade, all of which were accompanied by hints and promises of a commensurate development in the political sphere. These *German offers* touched a series of raw nerves in Soviet foreign strategy in the 1930s. From 1933–4 onwards the USSR pursued an anti-German policy of collective security, but alongside this ran a continued commitment to the tactical and strategic benefits of peaceful coexistence with all states – a commitment which had deep roots in the Soviet diplomatic outlook and practice. Moscow wanted alliances with Britain and France but at the same time was deeply suspicious of Anglo-French motives and aspirations, not least of their appeasement of Nazi Germany. The Russians believed in the policy of collective security but put their ultimate faith in the USSR's independent strength and resources to safeguard Soviet security.[7] The tensions between these different strands in Soviet foreign policy found expression in an internal debate around the question of trade and political relations with the Nazi regime.

Economic considerations aside, the internal arguments on policy towards Germany centred on two sets of issues. Firstly, there was the question of the prospects for a normalisation of Soviet-German political relations. If there were no such prospects then it made no political sense to qualitatively expand commerce with a state pledged to topple the Soviet regime. On the other hand, if there was a realistic chance of some kind of political détente then trade could be the lever to open the door to it. The resolution of these issues lay in an assessment of the strength of opposition in Germany to Hitler's anti-Soviet foreign policy and the prospects for a change in that policy. It was around this question that much of the Soviet debate on policy raged.

Secondly, there were issues connected to the general question of which strategy and tactics would best serve the USSR's need to contain the Nazi German threat to its security. Should the policy be one of permanent confrontation with putative Nazi aggression and expansionism or should the emphasis be on the search for compromises that would encourage German acceptance of the benefits of coexistence with Soviet Russia? Both approaches had their problems. The confrontationist stance closed down all the short-term options in relations with Germany and, given the lack of enthusiasm of Britain, France and other states for Soviet collective security proposals, it carried with it the grave danger of Soviet political isolation and exposure to German attack. The coexistence approach was more tactically sound in that it kept open the possibility of a return to normalcy in relations with Germany and matched the appeasement manoeuvres of the western powers in Berlin. But strategically the coexistence option undermined the need for policies and actions that contributed to the creation of conditions favourable to a long-term resolution of the aggressive threat posed by Hitler. In the short term, at least, the USSR had to coexist with the Nazis, but was coexistence at the expense of a grand alliance against fascism in the long run worth it?

In relation to the inner Soviet debate on these issues it is easy to identify one side of the argument. Litvinov and his lieutenants in the foreign ministry consistently opposed any big increase in Soviet-German trade, denied the reality of a substantial German opposition to Hitler (and, hence, the possibility of a détente), and emphasised the political priority of building international opposition to Nazi Germany.

With regard to the opponents of the so-called 'Litvinosty' the picture is much less clear. Kandelaki, it is certain, was an advocate of an expansion of Soviet-German trade and it appears that he and his associates believed that there were important groups and individuals in Nazi Germany that opposed Hitler's policy towards the USSR and favoured some kind of détente with the Soviets. But what were Kandelaki's motives? Was it just that Kandelaki had a natural interest in greater economic intercourse with Germany? He was, after all, the Soviet trade representative and Germany was, after Britain, the USSR's most important trading partner. Or was he a 'Rapalloite' whose aim was a return to the Soviet-German political entente of the 1920s? Was he a sophisticated political operator or was he the gullible recipient of German advances designed to maximise the Soviet economic contribution to Nazi reconstruction and rearmament?

The picture is further complicated by the fact that Kandelaki was, it seems, involved in a minor power struggle with Litvinov over the determination of trade policy. The institutional roots of this struggle over 'turf' stemmed from the Soviet state monopoly of foreign trade and the functional responsibilities of the People's Commissariat of External Trade for foreign commercial and economic relations. What this meant was that trade representatives like Kandelaki had a separate legal status from that of other Soviet diplomats and that they formally reported back to their own People's Commissariat rather than to or through Litvinov's Narkomindel.[8] It is obvious that when trade issues overlapped with questions of politics and diplomacy there was scope for conflict over policies, roles and responsibilities. This certainly seems to have been the case with Kandelaki and Litvinov. The evidence from Soviet sources, both new and old, provides intermittent glimpses of Litvinov struggling, on the one hand, to control trade policy, and, on the other, to resist Kandelaki's meddling in foreign policy. To what extent, then, were the Kandelaki–Litvinov differences a result purely of personal and bureaucratic competition?

What was the response of the Soviet leadership (i.e. Stalin, Molotov and the politburo) to the conflicts and dilemmas created by repeated German economic and political overtures? As we shall see, the concrete policy response was changing and variable, very much a case of reacting to the ebb and flow of events and circumstances and the to and fro of the internal debate. There were, however, some important threads of continuity in Soviet policy – or perhaps one should say threads of contrariety.

Moscow never fully embraced Litvinov's hardline policy towards Germany, but neither at any time did it discard it in favour of the softer stance represented by Kandelaki's activities. Litvinov's opposition to negotiating a large-scale trade and credit agreement with Germany was overruled by the politburo, but these discussions were quickly abandoned when they ran into technical and political difficulties – while at the same time the door to their resumption was never completely shut. Confronted with differing assessments of the internal opposition to Hitler and of the prospects for détente the politburo decided to explore what the actual position was. Hence the well-known Soviet diplomatic probes and political soundings of this period – overtures to the Germans which were not so much purposeful as in search of a purpose. And all the while Litvinov was allowed the luxury of maintaining virulent opposition to politburo decisions. What all this amounted to was a relatively open and indeterminate policy towards Nazi Germany, a policy with two faces: a strategic face of opposition, confrontation and containment and a tactical face of coexistence and compromise.

The traditional start-point for the story of Soviet-German relations 1935–7 is a meeting in July 1935 between Kandelaki and Hjalmar Schacht, President of the Reichsbank and Minister for Economic Affairs. It was at this meeting that the first recorded Soviet political overture of the period was made. To assess the character and significance of this political overture to Germany it is necessary to examine first the background to the meeting.

Kandelaki's primary task on arriving in Berlin at the end of 1934 was to conduct negotiations for a new credit agreement which would finance Soviet imports from Germany. These negotiations had begun in May 1934 and culminated in a credit treaty signed in April 1935 under which the USSR was granted a loan of 200 million marks repayable over 5 years at 2 per cent interest.[9] It was in the context of these negotiations that there occurred the first of many, many German overtures for a qualitative improvement of economic relations between the USSR and Germany, combined with hints about a more general rapprochement between the two states. For example, on 12 April 1935 Bessonov, a counsellor in the Soviet embassy in Berlin and Kandelaki's aide in the economic negotiations, reported to Moscow that Schacht:

spoke a lot about the necessity of further economic rapprochement between the USSR and Germany. He said that it will be hard to keep to the course of improving relations with the Soviet Union, in which rapprochement he saw a guarantee of the prosperity of both countries ... Returning to the question of the necessity of rapprochement with the USSR Schacht reiterated, to both me and Comrade Kandelaki, that his course of rapprochement with the USSR was being carried out with the consent and approval of Hitler.[10]

This was not the first sign from the German side of an interest in the possibility of a future détente between the two countries founded upon economic relations, nor was it to be the last.[11] In June 1935 these approaches took a new turn with a proposal from Schacht for a massive loan to the Soviets to purchase German goods: a billion marks, repayable over 10 years, in return for oil and raw materials from the USSR. Kandelaki proposed that Moscow should seek a written confirmation of such a loan proposal. Litvinov, however, described the proposal as a 'German manoeuvre' and felt constrained to inform the French about it. Kandelaki was instructed to avoid further discussions with the Germans about a new credit agreement and to point out to them the obstruction by their officials of the implementation of the existing 200 million mark loan.[12] This was the first sign of a divergence between Litvinov and Kandelaki over trade policy towards Germany.

Kandelaki had returned to Moscow for consultations about the German loan proposal. By July he was back in Berlin and at the meeting with Schacht on the 15th he relayed Moscow's response.

Only Schacht's report of this meeting is available. According to Schacht, Kandelaki told him that Moscow approved of the idea of further large-scale credits but wanted to postpone negotiations until the 200 million mark programme had been completed. Schacht

observed that M. Kandelaki had told me this some weeks earlier, whereupon, after some embarrassment, M. Kandelaki expressed the hope that it might also be possible to improve German-Russian political relations. I replied that we had indeed already previously agreed that a brisk exchange of goods would be a good starting point for the improvement of general relations, but that I was not able to enter into political negotiations. If these were desired, then it would be necessary to approach the Foreign Ministry through the Russian Ambassador. Upon M. Kandelaki again suggesting that perhaps I could nevertheless help a little, I asked him what kind of help he expected me to give. M. Kandelaki then stammered out something about the Eastern Pact, whereupon I asked him what he meant. After a good deal of embarrassed circumlocution on his part, I finally concluded this part of the conversation by remarking gravely that in such matters the Soviet Government must approach the Foreign Ministry through their Ambassador, adding that I would inform the Foreign Ministry of our conversation of today.[13]

Schacht's report has been quoted at some length because it contains a number of points of interest. First, was Kandelaki acting under instructions when he inquired about the possibility of an improvement in political relations? Was it an early example of what a later Soviet ambassador to Germany was to describe as the 'tactical line of linking as closely as possible the problem of improving economic relations between Germany and ourselves with the question of a real normalisation of political relations'?[14] The answer to this question is probably, yes it was. For a start it seems likely that when the German proposal was being discussed in Moscow Litvinov made what was to become his oft-repeated objection to greater trade relations with Germany: what was the point of co-operation in the economic sphere when the Nazi regime was pursuing an anti-Soviet foreign policy and there was no prospect of a change in that situation? What is likely is that Litvinov won the day as far as the loan proposal was concerned, but the politburo also sanctioned an enquiry about the prospects for political relations, including the possibility of working with Schacht to this end. As we shall see, this was precisely the approach that was to be pursued with vigour by the Soviet embassy as a whole from December 1935 onwards. Still, it remains possible that Kandelaki was acting on his own initiative at this particular meeting with Schacht and it was not until later that he won the Soviet leadership's backing for such political soundings.

The second point of general interest concerns the veracity of Schacht's report. There is no reason to doubt that Kandelaki made some kind of political approach but are we to believe that he made such a hash of it and that Schacht cold-shouldered him in the way he describes? If this was the case then it is hard to see why Kandelaki was subsequently so insistent on pursuing the matter of political relations. Moreover, Schacht's depiction of his lofty tone and brusque handling of Kandelaki is inconsistent with numerous other reports from Soviet sources of his friendliness towards the Russians. It is much more likely that quite a different conversation transpired on 15 July and that Schacht's official report to Neurath, the German Foreign Minister, aimed to cover it up. What that conversation was and what Schacht's game was we may never know, but his actions and words must have suggested to some on the Soviet side that there were possibilities of co-operation with him against Hitler.

Kandelaki's interchange with Schacht in June–July 1935 prefigured the following pattern in Soviet-German relations: a German offer on trade and credit terms, Kandelaki's return to Moscow for consultations, a Soviet political initiative. In the case of Kandelaki's approach to Schacht in summer 1935 the initiative was somewhat insipid. This was certainly not the case in December 1935 when the Soviets launched a full-scale diplomatic offensive designed to probe German intentions, to feel out the strength of the different currents in German policy towards the USSR, and, most important of all, to strengthen Moscow's hand in the trade and credit negotiations.

The Soviet soundings of December 1935 were prefaced by a meeting between Schacht and Kandelaki on 30 October 1935. The meeting was convened to discuss the implementation of the April 1935 credit agreement and the future shape of German-Russian commercial relations. Schacht again raised the question of large-scale and long-term credits for Soviet imports from Germany. Kandelaki left for Moscow the same day.[15]

Another returnee to Moscow in November 1935 was Ambassador Suritz. But by the end of the month he was back in Berlin and in the process of implementing Moscow's new game-plan. It is in a letter from Suritz to Litvinov on 28 November 1935 that we get our first glimpse of what this was:

In accordance with the directives given to me I started to activate contacts with the Germans immediately upon my return to Berlin. I made use of every possible opportunity and managed to see quite a crowd during this relatively short period of time. Besides Neurath ... I met a great number of eminent 'Nazis', including Goebbels and Rosenberg. I have also planned a number of receptions of my own, to which I invited, among others, Schacht and Blomberg [Minister of Defence]. All my contacts with the Germans have only strengthened my earlier conviction that the course against us, on which Hitler has embarked, will remain unchanged and that we cannot expect any serious alterations in the immediate future. All my interlocutors were unanimous in this respect. For example, I was told that Hitler has three obsessions: hostility to the USSR (towards communism), the Jewish question and the Anschluss; hostility towards the USSR flows not only from his ideological attitude towards communism, but also constitutes the basis of his tactical line in foreign policy.

Hitler and his entourage are firmly convinced that only if it adheres to its anti-Soviet course can the Third Reich realise its aims and gain allies and friends. The calculation here assumes that the further development of the world crisis will inevitably lead to a deepening of the contradictions between Moscow and the rest of the world. They consider that the only means of influence available to us at present to soften the anti-Soviet course is Germany's interest in the establishment of normal economic relations with us, more exactly, in receiving our raw materials. ... I repeat that it's more obvious to me now than at any time before that Hitler and his entourage will not voluntarily change their course as far as relations with us are concerned. The only impulse for this could be some far-reaching events within the country (which, it seems, cannot be expected in the near future), or the strengthening of the anti-German international front. ... There is nothing we can do, it seems, but wait patiently and continue to strengthen and develop our economic work. Strengthening of economic ties on the basis of Schacht's latest proposals suits both sides (this and only this explains the blessing to Schacht given by Hitler). Implementation of the new agreements will set interested commercial circles in motion and bring them closer to us, it will doubtless strengthen our 'base' in Germany and will make a turn in the political course considerably easier when the present German leadership is forced to it by subsequent events.[16]

So, Suritz's brief was to explore the possibility of a change in German foreign policy vis-à-vis the USSR. Suritz did not think this was at all likely and had evidently already argued that case to Moscow. The fact that he felt able to devote most of his report to arguments reinforcing his opinion is indicative of (a) the exploratory character of his political soundings in Berlin and (b) that there was an unfinished debate going on about Soviet policy towards Germany. With regard to the connection between his diplomatic activities and the trade talks of Kandelaki, Suritz alludes to this in his concluding remarks on the potential political spin-offs of the economic negotiations with Germany. In a subsequent letter to Litvinov on 18 December 1935 this connection was made explicit:

> From Kandelaki's report you probably know about the results of his first business contact with Schacht. They support the information that was passed on to us earlier that the circumstances for the coming talks are becoming more favourable. Bessonov will inform you in greater detail about the preliminary steps taken in this direction.
>
> As far as it depends on us, we are not interrupting the efforts to widen our German contacts.[17]

It is unlikely that Suritz's 28 November letter arrived in Moscow before early December. Yet already on the 3rd of the month Litvinov had seized on the letter and penned a confidential note to Stalin which picked out from Suritz's long dispatch the point that no change in Germany's anti-Soviet foreign policy could be expected. Litvinov then continued:

> The same impression, as reported by Comrade Suritz, has been gained from Schulenburg, the German Ambassador in Moscow, currently in Berlin.
>
> Initially, I regarded with some scepticism the Tass report from Geneva of Schacht's statement ... about the intention of Germany to divide the Soviet Ukraine with Poland. I instructed Comrades Potemkin and Rozenberg to check this report. The results of this investigation leave no doubt whatsoever about the reality of the aforesaid statement by Schacht. *Thus, Schacht, who not very long ago Comrade Kandelaki offered our support against Hitler, is supporting Hitler's aggressive strivings in the East.*
>
> Comrade Suritz suggests, however, the continuation of our economic work in Germany. I am in full agreement with him. A break in economic relations could lead to a break in diplomatic relations. However, in view of the utter hopelessness of an improvement in political relations, I would consider erroneous the gearing to Germany of all or most of our foreign orders in the coming years. This would be mistaken because we would be rendering important support to German Fascism, now

experiencing the greatest difficulties in the economic sphere, and also because we would, without any political benefits, in the coming years weaken economic interest in the USSR more advantageous for our country.

I propose, independently of the conclusions of the commission of the People's Commissariat of Heavy Industry, a limitation of credit orders to Germany to 100 or a maximum of 200 million marks.

The Hitlerites' anti-Soviet campaign is not only not slackening, it is taking on Homeric dimensions ... almost all German press organs without exception day by day are conducting a systematic anti-Soviet campaign ... In spite of this the Soviet press in relation to Germany has adopted a kind of passive, Tolstoyian position ... I consider that this position is wrong and propose to give our press a directive to open up a systematic counter-campaign against German fascism and fascists. Only this way can we force Germany to stop or decrease its anti-Soviet performance. (emphasis added)[18]

The first point to comment on about this note is that its summary of Suritz's report on German foreign policy and Litvinov's linked comments on trade and credit relations reveals the centrality of this dual issue in inner Soviet discussions about relations with the Nazi state. Clearly, the proposition under debate had been whether to accept the German offer of a massive new loan. Presumably a number of practical economic arguments in favour had been put by Kandelaki and others, but their rationale also included a certain assessment of German internal politics. It was the latter that Litvinov was most concerned to attack. Litvinov's points concerning the political inadvisability of an expansion of economic relations with Germany were to become a recurrent theme of his over the next year or so.

Secondly, there are Litvinov's comments on Kandelaki and Schacht. Even allowing for polemical exaggeration on Litvinov's part, there was obviously more to the Kandelaki–Schacht conversations than hitherto revealed by the latter's reports. Further, Litvinov's evident concern to discredit both Kandelaki and Schacht reveals the role played by the former's reports in Moscow's discussions.

Finally, there is the remarkable character of the note as a whole. Here is Litvinov expressing active opposition to a policy initiative only just launched by the politburo. This could only have been possible in the context of a tentative, exploratory policy towards Germany. Moreover, the aggressive tone of the note and its emotional appeal to anti-Nazi sentiment makes it highly unlikely that Stalin was a particular supporter of the Kandelaki line.

We do not know what Stalin's reply to Litvinov's note was, if any. But the next day, 4 December 1935, Litvinov replied to Suritz's letter of 28 November. 'The conclusions which you draw on the basis of intensified contacts with the Germans, don't surprise me at all ... I never had any illusions in this respect.' Litvinov agreed with Suritz about the necessity for further economic work in Germany but he was against the USSR taking the bulk of its imports from Germany to the detriment of those of other countries. 'There is no point in strengthening present-day Germany too much. It is enough, in my view, to maintain economic relations with Germany only at a level necessary to avoid a complete split between the two countries.' This was Litvinov's view and, he told Suritz, it was as far as he could gather the view of the government.[19]

Whatever Litvinov's view – and what he gathered to be the government's view – the initiative launched by Suritz's return to Berlin was by now in full swing. On 2 December at a meeting with Roediger, the Deputy Director of the German foreign ministry's Eastern Department, Bessonov broached the question of Soviet-German relations, saying that efforts should be made to achieve a détente in these relations.[20] On 10 December Twardowski, the recently returned chargé d'affaires in the German embassy in Moscow, filed a report on meetings with Bessonov and Suritz. Bessonov raised the question of an improvement in German-Soviet relations and linked this issue, as he had done at the previous meeting with Roediger, to success in the economic negotiations. Suritz, too, was interested in improving Soviet-German relations and asked how the 1926 Soviet-German friendship treaty could be developed. Suritz also said that he was under 'strict instructions to do everything in his power to bring about, at least outwardly, an improvement in mutual relations' and 'repeatedly emphasised that the idea that M. Litvinov was an opponent of Soviet-German relations was entirely mistaken'.[21] At a reception on 11 December 1935 Gnedin spoke with an official of the Nazi party's foreign political office. The German reported that Gnedin told him that he had been sent to Berlin with 'instructions to work energetically for an improvement of Soviet-German relations' and that 'Gnedin declared himself a "sincere supporter of the Rapallo policy"'.[22] Finally, we have a report by Roediger of another meeting with Bessonov, this time on 20 December 1935, at which the Soviet counsellor put forward the idea of a bilateral non-aggression treaty between Russia and Germany.[23]

The foregoing is a summary of what we know of Soviet overtures in Berlin from German records. The tenor of these German reports is one of Soviet political initiatives courteously but firmly rebuffed by their recipients. Exactly what one would expect from officials of the anti-communist Nazi regime. The impression gleaned from Soviet reports of their encounters with the Germans during the same period is somewhat different. For a start these contacts were far more extensive than those revealed by German records. More importantly, the Soviets drew some very positive conclusions from their meetings with German counterparts.

The most active suitor of the Germans was political counsellor Bessonov, Kandelaki's co-worker in Berlin. Between 1 and 12 December he had a series of meetings: with Roediger, Twardowski, Schpalke (of the war ministry), Milch (State Secretary in the Ministry of Aviation), Brinkman (chief adviser to Schacht) and Herbert Goering (Hermann's cousin and an official in Schacht's office). On the basis of these meetings Bessonov wrote two letters to Moscow on 'Perspectives on Soviet-German Relations' and the 'Mood in the Reichswehr in Relation to the Red Army'. For Bessonov these meetings confirmed the 'presence in Germany of sections and groups which for a variety of reasons are interested in a normalisation of relations with the USSR'. These circles – military, industrial, diplomatic (but not the leaders of the Nazi party) – were gratified that the USSR was not opposed to a normalisation of relations because this helped their internal struggle for their political line.[24]

Bessonov was not the only one to send such reports to Moscow. On 13 December Suritz wrote to Litvinov:

> The problem of relations with us is presently arousing much more attention and, it seems, is becoming the subject of discussion in circles close to the top leadership. As far as it is possible

to judge from private conversations (mine and other comrades) the official anti-Soviet course is being criticised not only from the side of the Reichswehr, Schacht and the foreign ministry but also from sections of the [Nazi] party itself.

Four days later Suritz wrote to Krestinsky, Litvinov's deputy, that although there had been no improvements in Soviet-German relations, there was in 'Reichswehr and industrial circles a growing belief in the unproductiveness and erroneousness of National Socialism's anti-Soviet course'.[25]

This, of course, was not what Litvinov wanted to hear. On 19 December he wrote to Suritz:

> Concerning your reports and those of your colleagues about the allegedly noticeable turn in German policy towards the USSR I am somewhat sceptical ... It is no surprise that some Reichswehr circles, industrialists and some people from culture adhere to a slightly different line [from Hitler]. This could have been expected earlier and we have never had any doubts about it. Thanks to more intensive personal contacts we managed to hear things that we had presumed before. There is nothing new and unexpected about it.[26]

Three weeks later Krestinsky, Litvinov's deputy, wrote to Suritz in a similar vein:

> As far as the question of the Germans changing their political position in relation to us is concerned, neither in Berlin nor in Moscow, nor in any other quarter of the globe are there any indications of any changes in this direction.[27]

While all this was going on in the diplomatic sphere Kandelaki, who returned to Berlin in mid-December 1935, was busy with the Soviet-German economic negotiations. Contrary to Litvinov's advice Moscow had decided to take up the German offer of an expanded and extended credit agreement. A negotiating figure of 500 million marks was agreed by the two sides and the Soviets were initially confident that a credit agreement of that dimension would be achieved. However, the negotiations floundered in wrangling about, on the one hand, German demands for gold and hard currency payments to meet existing Soviet debts and, on the other hand, Soviet complaints about German restrictions on the type of exports (e.g. military equipment) allowed to go to the USSR.[28] Despite these difficulties it appears that the two sides came near to reaching some kind of agreement. However, following the German reoccupation of the Rhineland on 7 March 1936 Moscow suspended the negotiations.[29] A new credit agreement was signed in April 1936 but it dealt only with arrangements within the existing credit limit of 200 million marks.[30]

This outcome to the Soviet-German economic negotiations suited Litvinov. He welcomed the new credit agreement on the practical ground that it would facilitate Soviet payments to Germany but was politically opposed to negotiations for a larger-scale credit arrangement. As he argued in a letter to Suritz on 19 April 1936 the German offer of bigger credits wouldn't go away and the USSR could have them when it wanted. Litvinov agreed with Suritz that there was no point in causing an economic rupture with Germany but, on the other hand, the USSR must not renounce its efforts in the struggle against German policy. Large-scale credit negotiations would strengthen Germany's hands internationally but there would be no corresponding political compensation for the USSR. Soviet policy should be, Litvinov argued, to abstain from such negotiations in order to add to international pressure on Germany to arrive at a general agreement (about a new peace settlement to replace Versailles).[31]

Litvinov's priority was clear: to do everything possible to further the struggle against Hitler, including refusing large-scale credits. Was this view shared by the rest of the Soviet leadership? The answer is yes and no. They had, of course, overruled Litvinov on the question of entering into the credit negotiations and launched the *ballon d'essai* of December 1935. It is reasonable to assume that the politburo was attracted to the economic inducements on offer and gave some credence to the idea of a change in German foreign policy leading to the normalisation of political relations. But Moscow had also agreed to abandon the economic negotiations, presumably for political reasons, and this stance was not reversed – despite badgering by the Germans to resume negotiations. Opposition to Nazi Germany on the one hand, a willingness to engage with the possibilities of coexistence on the other. Both these policy strands were present in Molotov's keynote speech to the Central Executive Committee of the Supreme Soviet in January 1936.

Molotov's speech was much like the one he had delivered a year earlier and he began the section of his speech dealing with Soviet-German relations on a conciliatory note:

> I must say quite frankly that the Soviet Government would have desired the establishment of better relations with Germany than exist at present. This seems to us unquestionably expedient from the standpoint of the interests of the peoples of both countries. But the realisation of such a policy depends not only on us, but also on the German Government.

This was followed by a long diatribe against Hitler's foreign policy:

> And what is the foreign policy of the present German Government? I spoke of the principal trend of this foreign policy at the Seventh Soviet Congress [in January 1935], when I quoted Herr Hitler's book *Mein Kampf* ... In this book Herr Hitler speaks explicitly of the necessity of adopting a 'policy of territorial conquest', and makes no bones about declaring: 'When we speak of new lands in Europe today we can only think in the first instance of Russia and her border States.'
>
> Since these statements were read from the rostrum of the Congress of Soviets, the German Government has not made any attempt to disown these plans of aggrandizement at the expense of the Soviet Union; on the contrary, by its silence it has fully confirmed that they still retain their validity. ...
>
> Everybody knows that German fascism is not merely confining itself to elaborating plans of conquest, but is preparing to act in the immediate future. The German fascists have openly transformed the country which has fallen into their hands into a military camp, which, owing to its position in the very centre of Europe, constitutes a menace not only to the Soviet Union ...

All this constitutes a growing menace to the peace of Europe, and not of Europe alone.

In conclusion Molotov returned to the theme of conciliation and coexistence, harping particularly on the differences within Germany over policy towards the USSR:

> How contradictory the situation in present-day Germany is can be seen from the following:
>
> Side by side with the reckless anti-Soviet foreign policy of certain ruling circles in Germany, on the initiative of the German Government an agreement between Germany and the USSR was proposed and concluded on 9 April 1935, for a five-year credit of 200 million marks. ...
>
> During the past few months representatives of the German Government have suggested a new and larger credit, this time for a period of ten years. Although we are not chasing after credits ... we have not refused, and are not now refusing, to consider this business proposition.
>
> The development of commercial and economic relations with other States, irrespective of the political forces that are temporarily ruling in those countries, is in conformity with the policy of the Soviet Government. We think that it is also in keeping with the interests of the German people, and it is the business of the Government of Germany, of course, to draw practical conclusions from this.[32]

Another public expression of this confrontation–coexistence dualism in Soviet policy towards Germany in this period can be gleaned from contrasting interviews given by Stalin and Molotov in March 1936. In Stalin's interview with the US journalist Roy Howard the confrontation theme was most evident:

> In my opinion there are two centres of war danger, the first is in the Far East, in the Japanese zone ... The second danger spot is in the German zone ... Up to now the danger centre in the Far East has been most active. It is possible however that the emphasis may shift to Europe. There are indications of this in the interview recently given by Herr Hitler to a French newspaper. In that interview he tried to say pacific things, but his pacifism

is so thickly sprinkled with threats against France and the Soviet Union that nothing remained of it. Even when he wants to talk of peace, Hitler cannot avoid uttering threats. That is symptomatic.[33]

In Molotov's interview with a *Le Temps* journalist the emphasis was quite different. Asked about opinion in the USSR regarding the possibility of rapprochement with Germany, he replied:

There is a tendency among certain sections of the Soviet public towards an attitude of thoroughgoing irreconcilability to the present rulers of Germany, particularly because of the ever repeated hostile speeches of German leaders against the Soviet Union. But the chief tendency, and one determining the Soviet Government's policy, thinks that an improvement in Soviet-German relations is possible.[34]

Molotov's statement has typically been treated by historians as revealing of internal divisions over policy towards Germany. But why he should choose to make such a startling revelation to a French journalist has never been satisfactorily explained. In truth, Molotov was just stating what Soviet policy was: to respond positively to hints of détente from elements in Germany. It was to them that the message in his remarks – that Moscow was willing to explore an improvement in relations provided there was some quid pro quo – was directed.

This was the state of play in Soviet policy in early 1936 when Stalin and Molotov sat somewhere in the middle of the Soviet internal debate: wavering between confrontation and compromise, unwilling to give up the chance of a normalisation of relations but cautious in their pursuit of the openings presented to them by the Germans. By the middle of 1936, however, Litvinov's hardline stance on Germany was in the ascendancy. But there were limits to Moscow's embrace of a confrontationist policy and the door to compromise with Nazi Germany always remained open. Indeed, in January 1937 the USSR made its one and only formal offer to Germany during this period of political negotiations to normalise relations. But the fleeting nature of this return to the Kandelaki line in Soviet policy reveals that there were conditions and limits to Moscow's inclination to compromise as well.

As we have seen, Soviet-German negotiations about new and larger credits had stalled following the Rhineland crisis. However, on the occasion of the signing of the April 1936 credit agreement the Germans began a new series of approaches about an expansion in trade with the USSR. Writing home on 29 April Bessonov reported that Schacht had asked Kandelaki when discussions about a big credit could begin again. The April credit agreement provided the basis for a big growth in Soviet-German trade. Schacht was also keen to exclude politics from the discussions which, he said, got in the way of business.[35]

The Russians in Berlin, however, were not so keen to exclude politics. At a luncheon given by Kandelaki on 4 May Bessonov and Gnedin spoke to Hencke of the German foreign ministry's Eastern Department. They told Hencke that they had the impression that Schacht was once more prepared to enter into new credit negotiations. The development of Soviet-German economic relations was desirable, they said, but political problems were sure to get in the way of negotiations. 'They further gave it as their personal opinion', reported Hencke, 'that the Soviet Government – despite increasing scepticism in Moscow – still saw the possibility of achieving a political détente.'[36]

In May 1936 Hermann Goering had entered the scene of Soviet-German economic relations. His involvement stemmed from two sources. Firstly, his appointment in April 1936 as head of a new Raw Materials and Foreign Exchange Office. Secondly, from the fact that his cousin Herbert worked for Schacht and was intimately involved in discussions with Kandelaki, Bessonov and others about trade and credit deals. It was under Herbert's auspices that a meeting between Hermann Goering and Kandelaki and his deputy Friedrikson was held on 13 May. According to the German report of this meeting Goering told the Russians that he was pleased the new credit agreement had been signed, which would be a 'pacemaker on the road to further political understanding'. Further:

All his efforts were directed towards making closer contacts with Russia again, politically too, and he thought that the best way would be through intensifying and expanding mutual trade relations ... He was convinced that the time was ripe to set in train more friendly relations between Russia and Germany all along the line, in both the economic and political sphere.[37]

But did Moscow think the time was 'ripe' for an improvement in relations? After his meeting with Goering, Kandelaki returned once again to Moscow for consultations. Despite what we can assume to be Kandelaki's best efforts no real change in Soviet policy on trade with Germany occurred. On 4 August 1936 Krestinsky wrote to Suritz in Berlin that 'German affairs have not been discussed here for a relatively long time'. However, continued Krestinsky, 'the prospects for Soviet-German relations are viewed in the same way as earlier ... Germany does not conceal its definitely hostile attitude in relation to us'. With regard to the economic negotiations Krestinsky said that 'the Germans do not, of course, renounce their credit proposals and they would be ready to sign with us a credit agreement for a half billion or even a billion marks right away. But, as you know, they would do it not for political but exclusively because of economic considerations. ... I think that under these circumstances we will not proceed with the resumption of the credit negotiations ... We have no motives for supporting the Germans politically.' Krestinsky concluded by saying that he would like to emphasise that there had been no decision on the loan matter, not even a detailed consideration of it. However, 'this is mine [and Litvinov's] point of view and it seems in any case to a considerable degree to coincide with the views of leading comrades.'[38]

A week later Krestinsky informed Suritz that the 'other day' there had been a discussion on the so-called 500 million credit and that the decision had been unfavourable.[39] On 19 August Litvinov wrote to Suritz that Kandelaki had been instructed to tell the Germans that, in the event of a positive reply to Soviet demands for the import of German military equipment, it would be possible to raise again the question of a new credit agreement.[40]

So, in contrast to the autumn of 1935, in summer 1936 Moscow decided not to bite at German loan proposals; only to hold out the carrot that it might if it got some of the products it wanted from Germany. The reversal of the previous policy had been occasioned by Hitler's Rhineland move and political circumstances continued to lend weight to Litvinov's arguments against resuming the economic negotiations: the popular front victory in the July elections in France raised Soviet hopes for the development of a collective security alliance against Hitler; the outbreak of civil war in Spain and the beginning of Nazi-fascist aid to Franco set the USSR on a potential collision course with Germany; and in August the first of the great Show Trials had opened in Moscow. This trial of Zinoviev, Kamenev and others, who were accused of involvement in a Gestapo–Trotskyist conspiracy, had a distinctly anti-Nazi theme. Then there was the fact that earlier Soviet overtures regarding a normalisation of political relations had come to nothing. It may be, too, that there were practical reasons for ignoring the German loan offer; the Soviets were having trouble utilising the 200 million marks already at their disposal, let alone 500 million or a billion.[41]

However, a passive acceptance of Litvinov's opposition—confrontation policy was one thing, the active pursuit of it was quite another. The difference is evident from Moscow's response to the Nuremberg rally of September 1936. At the rally Hitler and other Nazi leaders launched a major anti-communist propaganda campaign, replete with references to Bolshevik-Jewish conspiracies and the need to construct an international anti-Soviet bloc (the anti-Comintern pact with Japan was signed in November). On 11 September Suritz telegrammed to Moscow proposals that in response a note of protest should be issued, that there should be a public statement from a Soviet leader, and that the supplies of some raw materials should be suspended. Krestinsky replied on 19 September. The decision was that there would be no note of protest, the Soviet response would be restricted to press articles, and Suritz was to raise the question sharply with political leaders in Germany.[42]

It is possible that this weak reaction to the anti-Soviet rantings of Nuremberg was a sound, tactical one. As Suritz himself argued in subsequent dispatches, the diplomatic aim of Nuremberg was to isolate the USSR internationally by frightening off potential collaborators with Moscow. Nuremberg was a sign of Nazi weakness not strength, of the regime's internal and external difficulties. Since it was likely that Nazi attacks on the USSR would be restricted to propaganda it made no sense to play into the hands of Germany's political game, to add fuel to the anti-Soviet flames of the Nazis, commented Suritz.[43] It is more likely, however, that Moscow's rejection of Suritz's initial hardline proposals was motivated by a general desire not to take any step that would precipitate a break in relations with Germany and a particular concern that this should not happen at a time when Soviet policy of aiding the Republican side in the Spanish Civil War, and thereby breaking the international non-intervention agreement, was bringing the USSR into conflict with Britain and France.[44]

The last quarter of 1936 – the time of Nuremberg, Spain, the Anti-Comintern Pact, and Mussolini's announcement of a Rome–Berlin 'Axis' – was a conflict-ridden period in Soviet-German relations. But this did not deter the Germans from continuing their efforts to entice the Soviets into a new trade agreement. Contacts between Kandelaki, Schacht, and the two Goerings continued throughout the autumn, with discussions centring on Soviet demands for the lifting of military and technical restrictions on their imports from Germany.[45]

In December these Soviet-German contacts took a new tack with an invitation from Hermann Goering to Suritz for a meeting at which there would be an open-ended exchange of views. Moscow agreed to the meeting and it took place on 14 December. According to Suritz's report the meeting took the form of a monologue by Goering. During the course of this meeting Goering reiterated Schacht's commitment to the further development of Soviet-German economic relations and stated that a normalisation of political relations was also desirable. However, said Goering, what happened in the political sphere depended in the first instance on what happened in the economic sphere.[46]

There was also a second meeting of political note that December. On the 24th Kandelaki met with Schacht. According to a retrospective report submitted by Schacht to Neurath in February 1937 what happened was that 'in the course of the conversation I said that the only possibility I could see of a more active development of trade between Russia and Germany would be if the Russian Government were to make a clear political gesture, and that the best thing would be for them to state through their Ambassador here that they would refrain from communist agitation outside Russia. M. Kandelaki, apparently involuntarily, let it appear that he sympathized with my view.'[47] As in the case of his report of the July 1935 meeting with Kandelaki it is highly likely that Schacht was being economical with the truth.

We don't have Kandelaki's report of the meeting, but in a letter to Krestinsky on 27 January 1937 Suritz characterised the conversation as one in which Schacht was sounding out the possibility of direct political discussions with the Soviets. Suritz also recalled that from talks with Kandelaki and Friedrikson about their various meetings with Schacht he had gleaned that among the latter's favourite themes were Soviet withdrawals from Spain (i.e. of its aid and advisers to the Republican Government) and France (i.e. from involvement in the popular front government via the French communist party) and an end to the policy of encirclement of Germany.[48] In view of the important development that followed it is far more likely that there was a discussion with Kandelaki along the lines suggested by Suritz rather than that reported by Schacht.

Following the meeting with Schacht, Kandelaki returned to Moscow to report. On the basis of his report a 'draft oral reply', dated 8 January 1937, was drawn up for the politburo by Litvinov for transmission by Kandelaki to Schacht. The reply stated:

> The Soviet government has never avoided political negotiations with the German government, at one time it even made a definite political proposal. The Soviet government by no means considers that its policy must be directed against the interests of the German people. It has therefore no objection to now entering into negotiations with the German government in the interests of improving general relations and peace in general. The Soviet government does not refuse to negotiate through official diplomatic representatives: it agrees also to respect confidentiality and not to make publicly known our recent conversations, or future talks, if the German government insists on this.[49]

In a letter to Suritz on 14 January Litvinov commented on politburo decisions. Apparently, the only change to the initial proposals that Litvinov had made to the politburo was the inclusion of provision for Kandelaki–Schacht talks to continue, although in view of Kandelaki's lack of diplomatic experience he would not be solely charged with the negotiations.[50]

The politburo-agreed Kandelaki statement was the first formal Soviet political overture to Nazi Germany since spring 1935. It is clear from this fact, from the character of the statement itself, and from Litvinov's comments to Suritz that Moscow thought that it was faced with a major political opportunity to bring about a significant change in the character of Soviet-German relations. The kind of thinking at the base of this assessment is revealed in a letter from Suritz to Krestinsky on 27 January 1937. Noting that German diplomacy had embarked upon a new period of activity, Suritz reminded Krestinsky that when this was discussed in Moscow 'we generally agreed, you will recall, that the Germans are probably trying to smooth out the sharp points in their foreign policy line'. The reasons for this, according to Suritz, were Germany's serious economic problems and its lack of preparation for war which was pushing the country to seek compromises with other nations, including the USSR.[51] The key point to note here is Suritz's reference to 'compromises with other countries' for it is likely that it was Moscow's fears around this time that some kind of deal between Britain, France and Germany might be in the offing that impelled it to grasp the straw offered by Schacht.[52]

Kandelaki returned to Berlin at the end of January 1937 and on the 29th he delivered the politburo's message to Schacht. According to Schacht, his response was:

> I told M. Kandelaki in reply that this information was certainly of interest but I pointed out that I had said during our December conversations that the only possible channel was via the Ambassador. I was, I said, obliged to request this time too that these declarations should be made through the Ambassador directly to the Foreign Ministry. To this M. Kandelaki agreed but all the same he asked me to ascertain first of all whether there was any prospect of entering into conversations in accordance with the Russian declaration ... He would then cause the requisite action to be taken.[53]

On 4 February Litvinov reported to Stalin. His version of Schacht's reply was that the German had indeed suggested further conversations should be between Neurath and Suritz, but that he had also said that he would arrange some dinner to which Neurath, Suritz and Kandelaki would be invited. Putting the boot into Kandelaki, Litvinov further reported that Schacht had 'expressed some bewilderment in relation to the last part of our statement where it speaks of confidential conversations' and that the German was 'not inclined to give the conversations a confidential character'. Indeed, Schacht was striving to give the conversations an open character. The reason for this, Litvinov argued to Stalin, was that Germany was being forced to seek financial aid from Britain and France and Soviet-German relations were being used as part of a game associated with this aim. Litvinov concluded his report with a comment on a proposal from Kandelaki that he and Suritz should return to Moscow for further consultations: 'so far as our decision to restrict ourselves to hearing out German proposals, there is no need for Suritz and Kandelaki to come [home]. It was explained to both of them when they were in Moscow that the initiative on any proposal must be left to the German side.' All that was required, suggested Litvinov, was that Suritz be given a directive that authorised open negotiations, the only proviso being that there should be time to inform the French and Czechoslovak governments about them. Stalin and Molotov agreed and on 7 February Litvinov telegraphed Suritz his new instructions.[54]

Having made their play the Soviets sat back to await developments. Nothing happened. Kandelaki's statement to Schacht was reported in February by Neurath to Hitler. The German leader rejected the idea of political conversations with the Russians.[55] On 21 March 1937 Schacht told Suritz that he saw no prospects for any change in Soviet-German relations.[56] And that was that. The Soviets took no further political initiatives in Berlin.

As if to signal the end of an era in Soviet-German relations many of the principals involved in the so-called Kandelaki affair of 1935–7 disappeared from the scene. Kandelaki's fate of purge, prison and death was shared by his deputy in Berlin, Friedrikson. Bessonov was another victim of Stalin's repression, although in his case prison and then execution in 1941 was prefaced by a starring witness role in the Bukharin show trial of March 1938. Gnedin returned to Moscow to serve as the Narkomindel's press secretary. He was purged, and then sent to a labour camp, in May 1939. Suritz was recalled in April 1937 and posted to the Paris embassy. Schacht resigned in December 1937.

Between 1935 and 1937 Soviet policy-makers confronted a series of acute and interlocking dilemmas in relation to Nazi Germany. On the face of it relations with Germany should have posed no particular tactical and strategic problems. The USSR was committed to a policy of collective security – to the construction of a system of alliances with other states designed to curb Nazi aggression and expansionism – and was set on a course of confrontation with Germany. In no other country was the leadership as firmly convinced of the threat of Hitler as that in Moscow. This consensus embraced Stalin and Molotov as well as Litvinov. However, the collective security policy achieved only limited successes during this period. The French resisted Soviet efforts to transform the Franco-Soviet pact into a real military alliance. The League's failure to curb Italian expansionism in Africa exposed that organisation's limits as an instrument of collective security. Most important of all, Anglo-French appeasement of Germany continued apace. Hence alongside Moscow's hopes for co-operation with the great powers against Hitler ran the fear and suspicion that their leaders were manoeuvring for a deal with Nazi Germany directed against Soviet interests.[57]

When faced with repeated German offers of an improvement in relations and reported signs of a change in German foreign policy, Moscow felt it had little choice but to explore the possibilities, no matter how slim the chance of success. Such an inclination was reinforced by the extent and importance of Soviet-German economic ties and by the fact that, in the short term at least, the USSR had to coexist with Nazi Germany. This stance, however, contained its own set of dilemmas. One of these was that the Germans had their own economic and political agenda and Moscow had no interest in serving its purposes. Another was that Soviet action in the collective security field tended to cut across a policy of peaceful coexistence with the Nazis.

Moscow dealt with these contradictions and tensions in an ad hoc and haphazard manner. Litvinov wanted to cut through all these dilemmas by subordinating everything to a long-term strategy of the confrontation and containment of the German threat. For Litvinov many of these dilemmas were illusory anyway, since he believed that German hints of détente were a ruse and that the internal opposition to Hitler's anti-Soviet line lacked substance. For much of the 1935–7 period Litvinov was able to limit or avert the tactical tendency towards compromise with Germany. He was not always successful since the Soviet leadership was prepared at times to listen to other voices, including that of Kandelaki. It did not really matter. In the end nothing came of Moscow's willingness in 1935–7 to explore the possibilities of coexistence and compromise with Nazi Germany. The next occasion on which Moscow made such a diplomatic foray was in summer 1939. As in the mid-1930s that too was in response to German overtures for détente. In 1939, however, the circumstances were very different and so too was the result.

In examining the zigzags of Soviet policy towards Germany it is important to bear in mind A. J. P. Taylor's dictum about history: that events now in the past were once in the future. In the mid-1930s Moscow was uncertain about what the future held – about what would become of German overtures for détente, about the long-term fate of the Hitler regime, about the prospects for the anti-Nazi opposition in Germany. In the face of uncertainty the Soviet leadership attempted to keep the options in Russo-German relations open. When their tentative manoeuvres to this end failed they recommitted themselves to Litvinov's apocalyptic vision of the future and resumed the course of confrontation with Germany mapped in 1933–4. Indeed, the year 1938 saw the development of a crisis over Czechoslovakia that was to bring the two states to the brink of war.

4 To the Brink of War: The Czechoslovakian Crisis of 1938

Russia's involvement in the Czechoslovakian crisis of 1938 stemmed from two sources. Firstly, the USSR's commitment to collective resistance against Nazi aggression and expansionism – a policy which Litvinov had affirmed time and time again in public statements in 1936–7.[1] Secondly, there was the Soviet-Czechoslovak mutual assistance treaty of 1935 under which the Soviet Union pledged military aid to Czechoslovakia in the event of an attack on that country by a third party. Soviet assistance was, however, conditional upon France, which also had a mutual assistance treaty with Czechoslovakia, simultaneously fulfilling its aid obligations – a clause inserted in the Soviet-Czechoslovak treaty of 1935 at the suggestion of Benes/ , the Czech President.[2]

The story of the Soviet role in the events leading to the Munich 'betrayal' of Czechoslovakia in September 1938 is a simple one. From the beginning to the end of the crisis the Soviets campaigned for international resistance to Hitler's designs on Czechoslovakia, urged the Czechs to stand firm, made it crystal clear that they would fulfil their mutual assistance obligations, and agitated for France to do the same.

There were, of course, limits to Moscow's determination to defend Czechoslovakia. The Russians were very reluctant to be left fighting the Germans on their own while Britain and France stood on the sidelines and throughout the crisis they hedged on the crucial question of whether or not they would aid Czechoslovakia come what may. Such hedging was natural in view of, firstly, a suspicion that the British and French wanted to direct German expansionism eastwards, secondly, the logistical difficulties involved in rendering military assistance to Czechoslovakia, and thirdly, the Soviet conviction that in the face of a united front of all the great powers Hitler would back down. This last point is particularly important, for it was Moscow's view that what would save Czechoslovakia and the peace was a determined stand by the USSR, Great Britain and France. This stance carried with it the risk of war with Germany but it was a risk the Soviets were more than willing to share.[3]

The 1938 crisis opened with a speech by Hitler in February in which he spoke of the 10 million Germans living in adjacent states – most of them in Austria and Czechoslovakia – and claimed the right of the Reich to protect their interests.[4] This was followed in March by the events leading to the German takeover of Austria. The Anschluss came as no surprise in Moscow. As early as July 1936 Krestinsky had predicted that 'in several months or in a year or two, when the ground in Austria is sufficiently prepared, Germany will simply annex Austria'.[5] Earlier still, in March 1935, Litvinov had argued that Austria's fate seriously affected Soviet security interests. 'We cannot be indifferent toward it, no matter how aggravating it may be to Hitler's Germany.'[6] When the Anschluss actually took place Litvinov warned the Soviet party central committee that 'the annexation of Austria is the greatest event since the World War and is fraught with the greatest dangers, not least to our Union'.[7] But, in the absence of action by Britain and France, the USSR was powerless either to prevent or to reverse Germany's takeover of Austria. It could only wage a virulent protest campaign through its own press.[8]

Although Hitler made no immediate demands concerning the Sudeten Germans, it seemed obvious that Czechoslovakia would be his next target. Moscow, for its part, assumed the worst and on 17 March Litvinov issued a public statement about the 'menace' to Czechoslovakia:

> The present international situation places before all peace-loving States ... the question of their responsibility for the destinies of the peoples of Europe ... The Soviet Government is cognizant of its obligations ensuing from the League Covenant, from the Briand–Kellogg Pact, and from the treaties of mutual assistance with France and Czechoslovakia. I can therefore state on its behalf that so far as it is concerned it is ready to participate in collective actions, which would be decided upon jointly with it and which would aim at checking the further development of aggression and at eliminating the increased danger of a new world war. It is prepared immediately to take up in the League of Nations or outside of it the discussion with other powers of the practical measures which circumstances demand. It may be too late tomorrow, but

today the time for it is not yet gone if all states, and the Great Powers in particular, take a firm and unambiguous stand in regard to the problem of the collective salvation of peace.[9]

A few days later the Soviet ambassador in Prague was recalled to Moscow for consultations about the political situation in relation to Czechoslovakia. Alexandrovsky was instructed to tell President Beneš that the Soviet Union was prepared, in combination with France, to take all necessary measures relating to the security of Czechoslovakia.[10]

On April 26 Kalinin, the Chairman of the Supreme Soviet, gave a speech in which he hinted that the USSR might aid Czechoslovakia even if France didn't.[11] That, however, was a deviation from the otherwise consistent line of Soviet policy that France should fulfil its mutual assistance obligations to Czechoslovakia and so too would the USSR. At a League session in Geneva in mid-May Litvinov had the opportunity to probe Bonnet, the French Foreign Minister, on France's policy. The discussion was not very encouraging. In response to Bonnet's question as to what the USSR would do if France mobilised on behalf of Czechoslovakia Litvinov replied that Soviet aid to the Czechs would depend on the attitude of the Baltic States, Poland and Romania. He urged diplomatic action to deal with this problem and proposed military staff talks between France, Czechoslovakia and the USSR. Bonnet's only response was that Poland and Romania were emphatically opposed to the transit of Soviet forces over their territory. Litvinov also spoke with British Foreign Secretary Halifax while in Geneva and came away with the impression that an effective Anglo-French alliance in support of Czechoslovakia was doubtful.[12]

On the weekend of 20–22 May Czechoslovakia took fate into its own hands. Upon receiving reports of German troop concentrations along the border, the Czech Cabinet ordered a partial mobilisation. In fact, these reports of German troop movements were untrue. Nevertheless, Hitler appeared to back down in the face of a determined Czech stand.[13] The lesson could not have been lost on the Soviets who had consistently argued that successful resistance to Hitler short of war was possible. Litvinov took up this theme in an important speech in Leningrad at the end of June:

Before our very eyes is now being unwound the entire skein that had been wound twenty years ago ... Without firing a single shot, without any agreement with the authors of the Versailles and other treaties, Germany has already succeeded in nullifying nearly all the results for which the west European powers waged the world war ... The spectre of Germany's military and industrial hegemony has once more risen before its opponents in the world war, inspiring them with greater fear than they ever felt prior to that war. The entire diplomacy of the Western Powers in the last five years resolves itself into an avoidance of any resistance to Germany's aggressive actions, to compliance with its demands and even its caprices, fearing to arouse its dissatisfaction and disapproval even in the slightest degree.

Such tactics of non-resistance naturally encourage Germany to further aggression and to an intensification of its efforts to reconquer as quickly as possible the territories which it had to cede to other states. There is no doubt that in the more or less near future Germany will take practical steps to restore its pre-war frontiers. ...

Germany is striving not only for the restoration of rights trampled underfoot by the Versailles treaty, not only for the restoration of its pre-war boundaries, but is building its foreign policy on unlimited aggression, even going so far as to talk of subjecting to the so-called German race all other races and peoples. It is conducting an open, rabid, anti-Soviet policy ... and publicly abandons itself to dreams of conquering the Ukraine and even the Urals. ... threats, blackmail, and bluff are [the aggressor states'] favourite weapons of foreign policy. They see that with the help of these methods they have succeeded in intimidating and terrorizing other countries to such an extent that they obtain their ends practically without firing a shot ... It remains to be seen whether they will risk launching a war if they have grounds to expect serious resistance, and if they are opposed by states with equal forces, to say nothing of countries with superior forces.

In relation to Czechoslovakia Litvinov stated the following:

Apart from rendering assistance in the event of war, our pacts with France and Czechoslovakia are also designed to avert or diminish the danger of war in certain parts of Europe ... It must be said that, while promising to assist the victim of aggression, the Soviet Government does not use this help as a means of bringing pressure to bear on the victim in order to urge it to capitulate to the aggressor ... viewed from the international standpoint Czechoslovakia is a country that is defending itself, and ... the responsibilities for the consequences, in any event, will be borne by the attacking side.[14]

Two days after this speech Litvinov telegrammed Alexandrovsky with instructions to tell Beneš that his words above gave a 'precise definition of our attitude to the Czechoslovak-German conflict'.[15]

The summer of 1938 saw a lull in the developing international crisis, punctuated only by Britain's dispatch of the Runciman Mission to Czechoslovakia to investigate the conditions of the Sudeten Germans. Meanwhile, the Russians kept up their diplomatic pressure in London, Paris and Berlin on behalf of the Czechs. On 22 August 1938, for example, Litvinov told the German ambassador in Moscow that 'the Czechoslovak people would fight like one man for their independence and that France, in the event of an attack on Czechoslovakia would take action against Germany, that Britain, whether Chamberlain wanted it or not, could not leave France without help and that we would also fulfil our obligations to Czechoslovakia.'[16]

The Czechoslovakian situation exploded into a full-blown international crisis in September 1938 when Hitler at the Nuremberg rally proclaimed his support for the Sudeten German struggle for autonomy – a declaration which carried with it the definite threat of war. From Moscow's point of view this final phase of the crisis opened at the beginning of September. The first move came from Paris. On 31 August Bonnet cabled Payart, the French chargé in Moscow, with instructions to ascertain what Russian aid to Czechoslovakia could be expected, given the opposition of Poland and Romania to Soviet troop movements across their territory.[17] Payart saw Potemkin the next day[18] and on the following day received an answer from Litvinov. The USSR was determined to render Czechoslovakia assistance provided France did likewise. With regard to Polish and Romanian intransigence Litvinov suggested that this could be overcome, or at least undermined, by a

League decision against aggression towards Czechoslovakia. Litvinov further proposed joint Franco-Soviet-Czech military talks and revived the idea, first raised in March, of a conference to discuss and issue a declaration on Czechoslovakia.[19]

It seems that Litvinov sensed the French wanted an indecisive response to their questions, which would let them off the hook of their commitments to Czechoslovakia.[20] This view of the purpose of the French initiative was confirmed by a telegram from Suritz, the Soviet ambassador in Paris.[21]

On 5 September Payart returned to clarify some points of the Soviet answer. The Soviet position remained the same as before.[22] Potemkin reiterated the Soviet position in a formal statement to Payart of the policy previously outlined by Litvinov, emphasising in particular 'the determination of the USSR, in the event of Germany attacking Czechoslovakia, to carry out, together with France, all its obligations as laid down in the Soviet-Czechoslovak Pact'.[23]

What Moscow made of these equivocal approaches by France is unclear. However, by the end of the mid-September session of the League in Geneva, Litvinov (who had had further talks with Bonnet in Switzerland[24]) was certain that 'Czechoslovakia will be betrayed'. The question was 'only whether Czechoslovakia will reconcile herself to this'.[25]

From Prague on 17 September Alexandrovsky telegraphed that 'the situation in Czechoslovakia is extremely tense, but there is no panic. The wave of resistance is mounting.'[26] This tension had been sparked off by Chamberlain's conference with Hitler at Berchtesgaden two days earlier.[27] On 19 September Britain and France presented Czechoslovakia with proposals that those Sudeten districts with a majority of Germans should be transferred to Germany.[28] Beneš asked Alexandrovsky if the USSR would follow France in fulfilling its commitments to Czechoslovakia and whether the Soviet Union was prepared to support a Czech appeal to the League for aid.[29] Within 24 hours Potemkin had telegraphed the politburo's unqualified yes to both questions:

1. To Beneš' question, whether the USSR will, in accordance with the treaty, render immediate and effective aid to Czechoslovakia if France remains loyal to it and also renders

aid, you may in the name of the Government of the Soviet Union give an affirmative answer.

2. You may also give an affirmative answer to Beneš' second question: Will the USSR assist Czechoslovakia, as a member of the League of Nations, in accordance with Arts. 16 and 17, if, in the event of attack by Germany, Beneš requests the Council of the League to apply the above-mentioned articles.

On receipt of the telegram Alexandrovsky telephoned the reply to the Czech Cabinet, then in session.[30] Czechoslovakia rejected the Anglo-French proposals on the evening of 20 September.[31] A few hours later the British and French diplomatic representatives in Prague delivered a virtual ultimatum that the Czechoslovak government should accept the proposals or be abandoned by the western powers. The Czechs duly submitted on 21 September.[32]

Meanwhile, Litvinov had returned to Geneva to hear rumours that France's cautious stand on Czechoslovakia was due to Soviet passivity in the face of the crisis. These rumours prompted a speech by Litvinov to the League Assembly on 21 September[33] in which he revealed publicly the Soviet stance on Czechoslovakia:

> We intend to fulfil our obligations under the pact and, together with France, to afford assistance to Czechoslovakia by the ways open to us. Our War Department is ready immediately to participate in a conference with the representatives of the French and Czechoslovak War Departments, in order to discuss the measures appropriate to the moment. ... It was only two days ago that the Czechoslovak Government addressed a formal enquiry to my Government as to whether the Soviet Union is prepared, in accordance with the Soviet-Czech pact, to render Czechoslovakia immediate and effective aid if France, loyal to her obligations, will render similar assistance, to which my Government gave a clear answer in the affirmative.[34]

In another speech to the League two days later Litvinov attacked the idea that Moscow was hiding behind the clause in the Soviet-Czech pact that made Russian assistance conditional on that of France. Litvinov pointed out that it was the French and Czechs that had insisted in 1935 on two mutual assistance pacts rather

than a single Franco-Soviet-Czechoslovak pact and that the conditional clause had been inserted in the Soviet-Czech treaty at the
latter's request. Further, that the Czechoslovak government had
not raised the issue of unilateral Soviet assistance. The USSR
might render such assistance but that would be in virtue of a vol-
untary Soviet decision, not a matter of duty.[35]

While all this was going on in Geneva Soviet military units along
the USSR's western border were put on alert – the first stage of a
partial mobilisation of Soviet armed forces which continued until
the end of the month and amounted to the equivalent of mobilising some 90 divisions.[36] The Soviet military build-up was partly inspired by reports received in Moscow on 22 September that
Poland had begun to assemble its forces along the Czechoslovak
border in anticipation of an opportunity to grab Teschen – an
area with a large Polish population (a territory which Poland did
indeed grab following the Munich agreement). The next day the
Soviet Union warned Poland that its intervention in
Czechoslovakia would result in Moscow's repudiation of the
Soviet-Polish Non-Aggression Treaty.[37]

On 23 September Litvinov, in Geneva, met De La Warr and
Butler from the British Foreign Office and suggested a British-
French-Soviet conference to discuss the Czechoslovak crisis.[38]
However, Moscow itself responded negatively to this initiative by
Litvinov,[39] which perhaps explains why on the same day the
People's Commissar telegraphed home advocating a stronger line:

> Although Hitler has committed himself to such an extent that it
> is difficult for him to turn back, I still think that he would turn
> back if he was certain beforehand of the possibility of joint
> Soviet-French-English action against him. No joint declaration or
> conferences even can now make any impression. A determined
> stand is necessary. Believing that a European war into which we
> would be drawn is not in our interests and that we need to do
> everything necessary to prevent it, I pose the question: should we
> not declare even partial mobilisation and carry on such a cam-
> paign in the press that would force Hitler and Beck to believe in
> the possibility of a major war involving ourselves? De La Warr
> told me that the mood in Paris is stiffening. It is now possible
> that France will agree to a simultaneous declaration of partial
> mobilisation with us. It is necessary to act quickly.[40]

Litvinov's urging of a Soviet declaration of partial mobilisation and his reference to the possibility that France might declare one simultaneously is interesting. Moscow had already ordered a partial mobilisation but had yet to declare it publicly. Only when France declared its partial mobilisation on 24 September did Moscow let it become known that it had done the same. It seems likely that the Soviets' diffidence about their preparations for war (which included instructions to diplomats in Germany and Eastern Europe to destroy secret documents and codes[41]) stemmed from a fear of being left to face the Germans alone if they went out on a limb. This did not mean they were unwilling to face that eventuality, if necessary. But why invite it by a declaration of unilateral action? On the other hand – and this was Litvinov's point – a Soviet declaration of partial mobilisation might have a sobering effect on Hitler and it might also encourage the French to take a stand. Moscow, however, chose to play its cards closer to its chest by, publicly at least, keeping in step with the French and the British.[42]

On the way back to the hotel after meeting De La Warr and Butler, Maisky asked Litvinov about his proposals at the meeting:

'What you proposed to the British just now means war ... Has it been seriously considered in Moscow and decided in earnest?'

'Yes, it's been decided in earnest', Litvinov said firmly. 'When I was leaving for Geneva, we had started concentrating troops on the Romanian and Polish border. It's nearly a fortnight since then, and I would say we have at least 25 to 30 divisions there now ...'

'Suppose France backs out and doesn't act?' I asked. 'What then?'

'Doesn't matter', Litvinov grunted with an angry shrug.

'What about Poland and Romania? Will they let us through?'

'Poland won't, of course', he replied, 'but Romania is another matter. We have information that Romania will, particularly if the League of Nations pronounces Czechoslovakia a victim of aggression. Not even unanimously, but by a big majority ...' He was silent for a moment, then said: 'The main thing is how the Czechs behave ... If they fight, we'll fight alongside them.'[43]

Litvinov's comment to Maisky about the possibility of Romania allowing Soviet forces to cross its territory throws into relief one of the more obscure episodes of the Munich crisis, one that generally has been ignored by historians.

Romania, it should be remembered, was allied to Czechoslovakia through the Little Entente, established in 1929. This was an alliance of those two states, together with Yugoslavia, dedicated to the maintenance of the status quo in central and south-eastern Europe. Negotiations about the passage of Soviet forces took place between Litvinov and Comnene, the Romanian Foreign Minister, in Geneva between 9 and 13 September. Romania eventually agreed to the passage of Soviet forces on 24–25 September.[44] However, the Romanian concurrence was hedged about with provisos and, had it come into effect, would have severely restricted Soviet military aid to Czechoslovakia via Romania. For example, the Romanians insisted the Soviets could move only 100,000 men through their territory and that this had to be done within six days – an extremely difficult task in view of the state of Romania's transportation network.[45]

The Romanian concessions to the Soviet Union were, however, a side-issue in the crisis compared to the position being taken up by France and Great Britain. At the Godesberg Conference with Britain and France on 23–24 September Germany rejected the Anglo-French proposals for a compromise over the Sudetenland.[46] Hitler's rebuff led to a temporary hardening of the Anglo-French stance in the Czechoslovak crisis. It did not last long, however.

Meeting in Munich on 29–30 September the leaders of Great Britain, France, Germany and Italy (the sponsor of the conference) resolved their differences and agreed that the Sudetenland should be handed over to Germany forthwith.

Neither Czechoslovakia nor the USSR were consulted about the conference and both were excluded from its proceedings. On the second day of the conference the Czechs were presented with a demand for their immediate withdrawal from the Sudetenland.[47] Before taking a decision Beneš asked Alexandrovsky to question Moscow about the USSR's attitude if Czechoslovakia decided to fight on alone, without French support. Alexandrovsky's telegram from Prague was received at 5.00 p.m. Moscow time. Forty-five minutes later, before the Soviets had time to reply to the first, a second telegram arrived stating that Beneš had withdrawn the question and would shortly announce Czechoslovakia's acceptance of the Munich agreement.[48]

One of the most tantalising, unanswered questions of the Munich crisis is what the Soviet Union would have done if Czechoslovakia had decided to stand and fight alone. In the former USSR regime historians always maintained that the USSR would have fought alongside Czechoslovakia and insisted that an offer of unilateral aid (i.e. one not dependent on French action) was communicated to Beneš. However, they were strangely vague and contradictory as to when and how this offer was made and never produced any hard evidence to confirm their assertions. Moreover, in December 1988 the Soviet journal *International Affairs* published a document which proved beyond reasonable doubt that the USSR did not offer to aid Czechoslovakia unilaterally. The document in question is an account of the last days of the Czechoslovak crisis by the Soviet ambassador in Prague, Sergei Alexandrovsky, written in October 1938. Alexandrovsky discusses quite explicitly the issue of Soviet unilateral aid in the context of an account of the Czechoslovak domestic debate about whether or not such aid would be forthcoming, but makes no mention of any such Soviet offer. He also clarifies the reason why: no clear request for such a commitment was forthcoming from Beneš and the Czechoslovak government, at least not before .30 September 1938 (when the question was withdrawn before it could be answered). Further, that from the Soviet point of view Beneš was playing a subtle diplomatic game with them – on the one hand, anxious for Soviet aid, but on the other hand fearful that Moscow would be 'scared off' by the prospect of war with Germany without the involvement of Britain and France. Throughout the crisis, therefore, Beneš attempted to give Alexandrovsky the impression that British and French aid would be forthcoming come what may and tried to entice the USSR into unsolicited commitments on its part.[49] It was a game that Moscow was evidently not willing to play, at least not according to Beneš' rules.

The fact that Moscow did not make an offer of unilateral aid does not prove that the USSR would not have supported Czechoslovakia on its own in the event of a German attack. Judging by Alexandrovsky's report, not to say Soviet actions throughout the crisis, it would, in the end, have done so. But what could the Soviet Union have done to aid Czechoslovakia on its own? One who has addressed this issue is Telford Taylor. He points to three limitations on the USSR's ability to assist Czechoslovakia in the event of war with Germany:

1. The lack of a common frontier which would have meant Soviet forces travelling 300 miles across Romania and Slovakia to make contact with the invading Germans in Bohemia and Moravia – an operation that might have taken three months.
2. The absence of a common frontier with Germany meant that in order to apply direct military pressure on the Germans the Red Army would have had to cross Poland or the Baltic States.
3. The distances separating Czechoslovakia from the USSR would have made air support and supply difficult and hazardous.

Taylor concludes that the most likely forms of Soviet military assistance would have been the deployment of forces along the Polish border in order to restrain Warsaw's designs on Teschen, pressure on East Prussia via the threat of a lunge along the Baltic coast, efforts to gain Romanian co-operation in the passage of Soviet forces to Czechoslovakia, and material aid to the Czechs similar to that provided to the Spanish republicans. Even in the event of France coming to Czechoslovakia's aid, it is doubtful that the USSR would have been able to do much more than this – unless France invaded Germany and Poland agreed to the transit of Soviet forces across its territory.[50]

The intriguing question of whether the USSR would have fought alongside Czechoslovakia and what it could have done to aid the Czechs should not be allowed to obscure a much more important facet of the Munich crisis from the Soviet point of view. In Soviet eyes Munich was the last opportunity, short of all-out war, to halt Hitler's advance. The accretion of German power resulting from the annexation of Austria and the subjugation of Czechoslovakia signified to Moscow that the threat of war would no longer be enough to deter Hitler. To that extent Munich marked the final failure of collective security's original objective of checking German expansionism and postponing the outbreak of war for the foreseeable future.

The USSR did not abandon the collective security strategy after Munich; indeed, the spring of 1939 was to witness the revival of the Soviet collective security programme in the wake of Hitler's march on Prague. In April 1939 Moscow proposed a Soviet-French-British triple alliance that would guarantee the security and integrity of virtually the whole of Eastern Europe. But by that time the Soviet objective was not deterrence. It was a war-fighting alliance. Collective security had been superseded by a strategy of collective defence.[51]

Paradoxically, as Moscow reformulated its collective security project in new terms, the British and French began to embrace the pre-Munich Soviet formula of deterring Hitler by a strong stand and a show of force. Moscow, however, was convinced that war was inevitable and wanted a war-fighting alliance with the British and French, or nothing. This difference of aim – political deterrence versus military confrontation – lay at the root of the collapse of the Anglo-French-Soviet triple alliance negotiations of May–August 1939. By mid-August 1939 Moscow had come to the conclusion that an acceptable military alliance with Britain and France was not possible and that the time had come to stand alone, to secure the Soviet position by independent action rather than collective security and defence. At that moment began a decisive turn in Soviet foreign policy that resulted in a pact of non-aggression with Nazi Germany. That pact did not come out of the blue. Its seeds were sown during the course of Soviet-German relations following the Munich débâcle – a subject to which we now turn.

5 From Confrontation to Conciliation: Origins of the Nazi-Soviet Pact, 1938–1939

For nearly 50 years the course of Moscow's policy towards Germany during the months before the signature of the Nazi-Soviet pact in August 1939 remained something of a mystery. There were available a number of German diplomatic documents on relations between the two states in 1938–9 which shed some light on the origins of the Nazi-Soviet pact. But their reliability as a source of Soviet attitudes and policy was questionable. German reports and memoranda inevitably reflected German assessments of Soviet policy and German objectives in relation to the USSR. These essentially second-hand accounts were balanced on the Soviet side by only a scattering of documents and fragments from Moscow's archives.

Given this problem of sources, historians had no recourse other than speculation based on the evidence that was available and on what could be inferred from the course of events. The problem with the speculation was that it easily became embroiled in the contemporary cold war ideological debate about the nature of Soviet foreign policy. Did the USSR sincerely seek an anti-fascist alliance with the democratic west on the eve of the Second World War, or did Stalin really want a deal with his fellow-dictator Hitler all along? This was the political issue that dominated historical disputes about the Nazi-Soviet pact, and the gaps in the evidence provided plenty of space for speculation leading to either conclusion.

The problem with inferring the nature of Soviet policy towards Nazi Germany from the course of events was of an altogether different order. Quite simply: there was not much to infer from since from the middle of 1937 until the eve of the pact very little happened in Soviet-German relations. There was the pact itself and the events that followed it, but with respect to the task of tracing the diplomatic and political origins of these outcomes deductions based on hindsight were no substitute for actual evidence of the perceptions, calculations, decisions and actions of those responsible for them. The historiography of the Nazi-Soviet pact bore eloquent testimony to the fact that it was possible to draw radically different inferences about Soviet policies and motivations from exactly the same set of events.

Historical interpretation of the Soviet pact with Nazi Germany seemed destined to remain where it had been throughout the post-war period: locked in the realm of speculative interpretation and political polemic. In 1989–90, however, Moscow's archives finally began to disgorge some of their secrets. Diplomatic documents published from the Soviet foreign policy archives have furnished a near comprehensive record of Soviet relations with the Nazi regime in 1939 – reports of meetings with the Germans, instructions to Soviet diplomats, and the correspondence between Moscow and its Berlin embassy. Missing still is evidence from political sources on the internal deliberations of the Soviet leadership, but the new documents do make it possible to trace in some detail the evolution of Soviet policy towards Germany through Moscow's eyes.[1]

What does this new evidence reveal about Soviet policies and decision-making in the runup to the pact with Nazi Germany? Firstly, the long historical dispute about the timing and circumstances of the Soviet turn to a pact with Nazi Germany can now be settled. The turn in Soviet policy did not take place until the end of July 1939 at the very earliest and only began to gather real momentum in the middle of August. Before this time the operational objective of Soviet policy was to secure a suitable agreement with the western powers. Until mid-August 1939 Moscow's calculation remained that Soviet security would be best served by a combination against Nazi Germany rather than by an accommodation with Hitler. That calculation presupposed a successful conclusion of the triple alliance negotiations with Britain and France. It was when the triple alliance negotiations finally collapsed that Stalin turned to a deal with Hitler.

The assertion that Moscow did not change its policy towards Berlin before August 1939 is not meant to imply that the idea of an agreement with Germany had not been mooted much earlier. The prospect of such an agreement had been the subject of intense public speculation since the end of the Rapallo era and it would be surprising if there was no discussion in Stalin's circle about it too.

Secondly, there are the indications in the new evidence of the need to shift the parameters of the historical debate. The overarching interpretation of the Soviet decision for a pact with the Nazis has been in terms of a cool and calculated foreign policy manoeuvre with definite objectives – a mirror-image, in fact, of the typical interpretation of the German decision for a pact with the USSR. In this interpretation, Nazi Germany began its quest for a pact with the USSR in spring 1939 and from the outset pursued two clear goals: the prevention of an Anglo-Soviet-French alliance and Soviet neutrality in the event of a Polish-German war. In the case of the Soviet Union the assumption has been that there was a commensurate process of policy shift and goal-adoption. The historical argument has centred on when and why the change in Soviet policy occurred.

In this chapter I will challenge that perception and emphasise the contingent and makeshift nature of the process that led to the pact. On the Soviet side the pact emerged from a process of short-term crisis management in which the Soviet leadership (primarily Stalin and Molotov) responded to the initiatives and actions of others. The picture that emerges from the new evidence is that the pact was more a product of accident than design, a result of policy drift rather than goal-oriented policy direction, the consequence not of strategic calculation but of a series of tactical shifts and adjustments.

Two questions have dominated the historical debate about the genesis of the Nazi-Soviet pact:

1. When did the USSR decide to embark on political negotiations with Nazi Germany with a view to securing a German-Soviet détente?
2. How, from Moscow's point of view, did these negotiations progress from their general inception to the Nazi-Soviet non-aggression treaty and spheres of influence agreement of 23 August 1939?

There are a number of views as to when the USSR decided to initiate the negotiations which ultimately culminated in the Nazi-Soviet pact: the period of Kandelaki's mission in Berlin in the mid-1930s (dealt with in chapter 3); in the aftermath of Munich; when Stalin made his speech to the 18th Party Congress in March 1939; around the time of Litvinov's dismissal as People's

Commissar for Foreign Affairs in May 1939. Each of these hypotheses has its advocates.[2]

The argument that the USSR began its search for rapprochement with Germany as a result of Munich rests mainly on the rationalisation that this was the obvious course of action following the west's betrayal of Czechoslovakia and the defeat of Soviet collective security policy. An examination of Soviet policy, however, reveals that that was not how Moscow saw things. Munich was indeed a shattering blow to the collective security strategy but the Soviets neither renounced the policy of a grand alliance against Hitler nor did they make any moves to mend their fences with the Germans. As Litvinov told Payart in November 1938:

> We consider the Munich agreement to be an international misfortune. England and France will now hardly succeed in retreating from the policy they have charted which amounts to the unilateral satisfaction of the demands of all three aggressors, Germany, Italy and Japan. They will present their claims in turn, and England and France will offer them one concession after another. I believe, however, that they will reach the point where the peoples of England and France would have to stop them. Then they will probably have to return to the old path of collective security, for there is no other way to organise the peace.[3]

The period after Munich constitutes an isolationist hiatus in Soviet foreign policy in which Moscow awaited developments which would enable the USSR to once again take the initiative in international relations. The opportunity came with Germany's occupation of the rest of Czechoslovakia in March 1939. This event set in motion a chain of events which led to Britain's unilateral declaration guaranteeing the security of Poland on 31 March 1939 and Soviet proposals on 17 April for an Anglo-Soviet-French triple alliance which would guarantee small states against German aggression – a project that was to dominate the diplomatic scene in Europe for the next four months. Munich represented the nadir of the Soviet drive for collective security in the 1930s but it turned out to be merely a prelude to its climax in the triple alliance negotiations of summer 1939.[4]

What has been called the 'Stalin speech' hypothesis is probably the best-known interpretation of the genesis of the Nazi-Soviet pact. Numerous writers have argued that Stalin's attack on western appeasement policies in his speech to the 18th Party Congress in March 1939 constituted a signal to Berlin that Moscow was ready to do business with it. Often cited in support of this hypothesis is Molotov's toast to Stalin on the occasion of the signature of the Nazi-Soviet pact in which he said it was the Soviet leader's speech the previous March that had brought about a reversal in political relations.

It is not unknown for political leaders to use public speeches to send diplomatic signals but no credibility whatsoever should be attached to this particular interpretation. For a start there is no point in sending signals if you make no effort to find out whether or not they have been received, and there were no private Soviet approaches to the Germans either before or after Stalin's speech. Then there is the fact that early March 1939 was a most unpropitious moment for any political approach to the Germans. This was a time when Soviet-German relations were at a very low ebb. Indeed, the Soviets were still smarting from the snub that the Germans had just delivered in very publicly cancelling a trip to Moscow by their trade negotiator Dr Karl Schnurre.[5] Finally, as D. C. Watt has pointed out, if the speech was intended to foreshadow a Soviet-German agreement then most diplomats in Moscow missed the message.[6] As Seeds, the British ambassador in Moscow, reported to London: 'Stalin's speech ... contained little that was new or unexpected.'[7]

Seeds' judgement is supported by an examination of the content of the speech. Stalin began his report by expounding the fundamental perspectives on international relations developed during the collective security period. International affairs were characterised by a struggle for the redivision of the world between two blocs of imperialist states: a 'bloc of three aggressor states' consisting of Germany, Japan and Italy, and a group of 'non-aggressive states, primarily England, France and the United States'. Further, 'a new imperialist war is already in its second year ... The map of Europe, Africa and Asia is being forcibly redrawn. The entire post-war system, the so-called regime of peace, has been shaken to its foundations.'

Stalin continued that 'combined, the non-aggressive, democratic states are unquestionably stronger than the fascist states, both economically and in a military sense'. Why, then, had fascist expansionism hitherto proceeded unchecked? Because, he said:

> England and France, have rejected the policy of collective security, the policy of collective resistance to the aggressors, and have taken up a position of non-intervention, a position of 'neutrality' ... the policy of non-intervention means conniving at aggression, giving free rein to war, and, consequently, transforming the war into a world war. The policy of non-intervention reveals an eagerness, a desire, not to hinder the aggressors in their nefarious work: not to hinder Japan, say, from embroiling herself in a war with China, or, better still, with the Soviet Union; not to hinder Germany, say, from enmeshing herself in European affairs, from embroiling herself in a war with the Soviet Union ...

But, Stalin warned, the actual direction of fascist expansion may not be what Britain and France thought. Germany 'instead of marching farther east, against the Soviet Union ... [has] ... turned, you see, to the west and [is] demanding colonies.' Stalin reaffirmed the traditional principles of Soviet foreign policy and remarked that 'the big and dangerous political game started by the supporters of the policy of non-intervention may end in a serious fiasco for them' and warned that the USSR would not be 'drawn into conflicts by warmongers who are accustomed to have others pull their chestnuts out of the fire for them'.[8]

The substance of Stalin's speech was no different from that delivered by Molotov to the Supreme Soviet in November 1938.[9] Its critique of the 'policy of non-intervention' was one that Litvinov had made many, many times in the past and its analysis of the diplomatic state of play reflected no more than the conclusions reached by Soviet diplomats in their private correspondence to and from Moscow during the previous few months.[10] One should note also that Stalin, like Litvinov, retained a distinction between aggressive fascist and non-aggressive democratic states and that despite the acuity of its critique of Anglo-French foreign policy the speech fell short of proclaiming a plague on all capitalist houses: the main threat to Soviet security was still seen as emanating from Germany. As to the meaning of his famous reference to pulling chestnuts out of the fire, there is no real mystery. All

Stalin was saying was that the USSR was not prepared to fight British and French wars for them – a sentiment which is perhaps more apparent from a literal translation of his chestnuts phrase – 'to rake the fire with somebody else's hands'('zagrebat zhar chuzhimi rukami').

The important message in Stalin's speech was a declaration of non-involvement in inter-capitalist quarrels and plots that threatened to drag the USSR into a war that was not in its interests – hardly surprising in view of recent events and of the perpetual Soviet suspicion that the west was encouraging a German *Drang nach Osten*. But perhaps the most significant feature of Stalin's speech was not this, but its wholly negative tone and content which reflected the uncertainty and stagnation of Soviet foreign policy following the Munich crisis and the lack of any new programme for action. Although Stalin could condemn western appeasement policies and warn Britain and France about the possible consequences, the USSR had little option – given the continuing threat from Hitler – but adherence to the collective security aim of creating some kind of anti-fascist alliance. Moscow could only hope that circumstances would change and the possibility of realising such an aim would come back onto the diplomatic and political agenda.

The theory of the origins of the Nazi-Soviet pact most widely accepted by historians is that Moscow began its pursuit of a rapprochement with Germany – or at least decided to open up the possibility of a Soviet-German détente – in April 1939. The occasion, it is said, was a meeting in Berlin on 17 April 1939 between the Soviet ambassador, Alexei Merekalov, and Ernst Weizsäcker, State Secretary in the German foreign ministry. According to Weizsäcker, Merekalov's visit to him was the first since the Soviet ambassador had taken up his post in Berlin. The ostensible purpose of the visit was to discuss the fulfilment of Soviet orders with the Skoda arms factory in German-occupied Czechoslovakia. But, wrote Weizsäcker, Merekalov seized the opportunity to raise political matters and led the conversation to the following concluding statement:

> Russian policy had always moved in a straight line. Ideological differences of opinion had hardly influenced the Russian-Italian relationship and they did not have to prove a stumbling

block with regard to Germany either. Soviet Russia had not exploited the present friction between Germany and the Western democracies against us, nor did she wish to do so. There exists for Russia no reason why she should not live with us on a normal footing. And from normal, the relations might become better and better.[11]

Merekalov's reported remarks have been cited time and again as dramatic evidence that in April 1939 Moscow was interested in a rapprochement with Berlin.[12] In fact, the Merekalov–Weizsäcker meeting was of no political significance whatsoever as far as Soviet policy towards Germany was concerned.

Merekalov's visit to the Wilhelmstrasse to complain about German violation of Soviet contracts with Skoda was prompted by a telegram from Litvinov on 5 April 1939. It contained no mention of flying any kites about Soviet-German political relations.[13] In line with his instructions Merekalov gave a detailed statement of Soviet complaints to Weizsäcker.[14] Following the meeting Merekalov reported back to Moscow:

I was received by Weizsäcker. I presented him with the note and made a statement about the breaking of the 'Skoda' agreements ... The statement highlighted the abnormality in the position: the restriction, applying only in relation to orders made by Soviet organisations, was direct discrimination and contradicted the spirit of the Reichschancellor's declaration of 22 March which reaffirmed the validity of old agreements with Czechoslovakia. Parrying Weizsäcker's efforts to transfer the problem to the plane of business relations with the commercial representatives of Skoda, I cited the direct interference of the German military authorities and requested the speedy removal of these irregularities and the fulfilment of Skoda's accepted obligations. Saying he thought these measures temporary, Weizsäcker promised to study the matter and to reply, joking how is it possible to deal in arms when the question of an air pact [between Britain, France and the USSR] has arisen. Weizsäcker confirmed that three months of talks have been held with the Poles about the transfer of Danzig and the construction of an extraterritorial motorway across the Polish 'corridor', in return for a guarantee of Poland's western borders.

Germany did not want to attack anybody. Everyone was mobilizing, even Holland, Belgium and Sweden. Germany had not called anyone up beyond the normal, although in this regard it could do a lot. England had created a tense atmosphere, issuing guarantees to small countries which did not want them. Lately the Soviet press had conducted itself noticeably more correctly than the English. Germany has differences of political principle with the USSR. All the same it wants to develop economic relations with it.[15]

Merekalov was accompanied to the Wilhelmstrasse by his deputy in Berlin, Georgei Astakhov, the Soviet chargé d'affaires. According to Astakhov's record of the meeting, following an exchange of views on Skoda the conversation turned to general political issues during the course of which Merekalov asked a number of questions about the current situation – the state of Franco-German relations, German demands on Poland, the tense atmosphere in Europe, and so on. Weizsäcker, reported Astakhov, was very keen on this exchange of political views and answered Merekalov's questions with great interest. In the course of one of these exchanges Weizsäcker asked if the USSR felt threatened by Germany. Merekalov replied that the USSR was interested in removing the danger of war, and as to Germany he didn't feel especially threatened. This is virtually the only political comment of Merekalov's recorded by Astakhov. The meeting concluded with a question from Merekalov about Weizsäcker's perspectives on Soviet-German relations. 'Now they could not be better', Astakhov quotes Weizsäcker as lightheartedly saying, adding in a more serious tone: 'you know that between us there are contradictions of an ideological character. But, at the same time, we sincerely want to develop economic relations with you.'[16]

From both Merekalov's and Astakhov's reports it clear that the Soviet-German meeting of 17 April 1939 was not the occasion of a Moscow probe about the possibility of a rapprochement with the Nazi regime. If anything, the signals for détente were coming from the German, not the Soviet, side. Striking too is the complete absence in the Merekalov–Astakhov reports of any reference to the political remarks attributed to the Soviet ambassador by Weizsäcker.

Bearing in mind D. C. Watt's point that Weizsäcker's memorandum was directed at German Foreign Minister Ribbentrop and 'was strongly slanted towards convincing his much-despised boss that the Soviet Union was ready to slide into a neutralist stance',[17] it may be that Merekalov's reported statement about improving Soviet-German relations was either pure invention or a wild exaggeration on Weizsäcker's part. However, it is highly likely that Merekalov did make some encouraging remarks about Soviet-German relations for at a subsequent meeting with Astakhov on 30 May Weizsäcker repeated what he thought the Soviet ambassador had said about 'the possibility of a normalisation or even further improvement of German-Russian political relations'.[18] These remarks, however – whatever their precise content – originated with Merekalov not Moscow and were probably prompted by the Soviet ambassador's desire to encourage the resumption of intermittent economic negotiations with Germany about a new trade treaty between the two countries. Merekalov had been intimately involved in these discussions, had a personal interest in their success, and to this end he made some encouraging political noises about Soviet-German relations. These noises convinced some of the Germans that it might be possible to deflect the Soviets from their projected alliance with the British and French. Merekalov's purpose, however, was related to economics not politics.[19]

The Merekalov–Weizsäcker meeting illustrates the pitfalls of interpreting Soviet policy through the prism of German diplomatic documents – essentially second-hand accounts tainted by German preoccupations, perceptions and policy objectives. Another example concerns the dismissal of Litvinov as Soviet Foreign Minister and his replacement by Molotov on 4 May 1939. This too was interpreted by the Germans as a sign that Moscow was preparing to change its foreign policy line. It was a theme that was subsequently taken up by many historians. For example, Richard Overy and Andrew Wheatcroft write:

> On 4 May Litvinov was sacked ... In his place Stalin appointed Vyacheslav Molotov, Chairman of the council of Commissars, a noted Soviet nationalist, whose sympathies had long been with a pro-German rather than pro-western foreign policy ... One of Stalin's intimates, his appointment as

Commissar for Foreign Affairs was a signal that the era of collective security was past. During May there were regular contacts between the two sides as they explored what each had to offer.[20]

The problem with this interpretation is that Litvinov's replacement by Molotov was followed not by a change in Soviet foreign policy, not by a turn to Germany, but by the continued pursuit of a triple alliance with Great Britain and France. Indeed, there is good reason to believe that Litvinov may have been sacked because he was sceptical about the Soviet triple alliance initiative. It may be, even, that Litvinov's fall led to a strengthening of the Soviet campaign for a trilateral security pact. There is also clear evidence that Litvinov's sacking was at least as much a result of internal politics as a question of foreign policy. The internal politics of Molotov's succession was the assertion by Stalin of direct control of foreign policy on the eve of the Second World War.[21] And herein lies perhaps the true significance of the end of the Litvinov era in Soviet foreign relations. It marked the beginning of Stalin's active and visible involvement in foreign policy matters. Hitherto the Soviet dictator's attention had been concentrated on domestic affairs and politics, with Stalin content to set the terms of reference for foreign relations without overly dominating it – a stance which had facilitated internal discussion and debate about policy and action. With Litvinov gone and Stalin and Molotov directing foreign policy themselves that wider collective discussion began to grind to a halt, and at a time of critical decisions when it was needed more than ever.[22]

But what was Stalin's foreign policy purpose in ousting Litvinov and taking control? Perhaps it was the case that the spring and summer of 1939 were witness to a Soviet double-game: the dual pursuit of a triple alliance with the west alongside political contacts with Germany aimed at keeping open the option of a deal with Hitler. This is a view to which many historians have subscribed and it is certainly a possible scenario based on a reading of the German documents alone. German accounts of relations with the USSR consistently paint a picture of Soviet wooing of Berlin. However, reading the Soviet documents – surely the best guide to Soviet thinking, policy and tactics – it is clear that completely the opposite was the case. From Moscow's point of view the story of Soviet-German relations between May and August 1939 is one of persistent wooing by Berlin. Not until the end of July 1939 did the Soviets even begin to respond to these German overtures. Until then Moscow remained both sceptical and impassive in the face of numerous attempts by the Germans to initiate discussions about improving political relations between the two countries – and thereby drive a wedge between the USSR and the western powers, who they knew were engaged in negotiations about an anti-Hitler coalition.

German efforts to woo the USSR away from its projected alliance with Britain and France began on 5 May 1939 when Schnurre informed Astakhov that Soviet contracts with Skoda would be honoured.[23] Four days later Astakhov met with Baron von Stumm, deputy head of the German foreign ministry's press department. The occasion was the introduction of the new Tass representative in Berlin but, according to Astakhov's report of the meeting, Stumm took the opportunity to raise the question of improving German-Soviet relations, pointing out that the Germans had already made a number of efforts in this direction. Astakhov replied:

> To all [Stumm's] arguments I made corresponding objections, pointing out that the German side openly and on its own initiative had caused the deterioration of German-Soviet relations, and that their improvement depended mainly on them. The Soviet side has never shunned an improvement in relations provided there was a basis for it. As regards the symptoms of improvement that [Stumm] spoke about, dismissing or at least doubting the majority of them, I noted that ... we had not yet any grounds for taking them seriously, beyond the limits of a short-term tactical manoeuvre.[24]

Astakhov's stated scepticism about German policy – a diplomatic stance he maintained for the next three months – was the public face of an attitude that in private verged on the scornful. In a letter to Potemkin on 12 May Astakhov offered the following assessment of the position in the wake of Litvinov's dismissal:

> From my telegraph reports and diary notes you may have noticed that the Germans are striving to create the impression

of an impending or even already achieved improvement in German-Soviet relations. Throwing aside all the absurd rumours fabricated by the Germans or by idle foreign correspondents, only one thing can be stated as certain fact – this is a noticeable change in the tone of the German press in relation to us. ... But while noting these instances, we cannot, of course, close our eyes to its exceptional superficiality, and to their non-committal nature ... It is only too obvious what the motives behind this change in the German attitude towards us are, and for the present time does not warrant any serious consideration.

I think, therefore, that you will not object that in response to advances by the Germans and those close to them I replied that for the present we have no grounds for trusting the seriousness of this 'change', although we are always prepared to meet halfway when it comes to improving relations.[25]

On 17 May Astakhov met Schnurre to discuss changes in the legal status of the Soviet trade mission in Prague. In accordance with the sentiments he had expressed in his letter to Potemkin a few days earlier, Astakhov's response to Schnurre's enquiry about the prospects for improving Soviet-German relations was both re-strained and low-key. Apart from a change in the tone of the German press towards the USSR there was no evidence of German desire for such an improvement, Astakhov told Schnurre. On the other hand, the Soviet Union had never excluded the pos-sibility of an improvement in relations with Germany, provided Berlin could demonstrate that was what it wanted. The above summary of the 17 May meeting is based on Astakhov's report to Moscow on his conversation with Schnurre. Turning to Schnurre's report of the very same meeting, however, we get a completely different picture of what transpired. There is no mention of the fact that (according to Astakhov) it was Schnurre who raised the question of improving Soviet-German relations, emphasising, too, the desirability of such a development. Moreover, according to Schnurre, Astakhov 'referred in great detail to the development of Soviet-German relations' and 'stated in detail that there were no conflicts in foreign policy between Germany and Soviet Russia, and that therefore there was no reason for any enmity between the two countries ... To substanti-ate his opinion concerning the possibility of a change in German-

Soviet relations, Astakhov repeatedly referred to Italy.' None of this figures in Astakhov's report.[26]

Which account of the meeting is more accurate is less important than the fact that if Astakhov did say the things attributed to him by Schnurre he could not be bothered to report them to Moscow. If Astakhov was expressing anything more than diplomatic niceties he was certainly not acting under instructions from Moscow. But whatever the provenance and significance of Astakhov's reported remarks to Schnurre (at this and other meetings), he certainly impressed Berlin, which shortly launched a major diplomatic initiative to improve German-Soviet relations.

On 20 May Schulenburg, the German ambassador, approached Molotov with a proposal that the negotiations for a new credit treaty should be resumed and that Schnurre should come to Moscow for that purpose. Molotov's reply was an unequivocal rejection of the proposal:

> I told the ambassador that this was not the first time we had heard about Schnurre's trip to Moscow. Schnurre was to leave for Moscow, but his train had been cancelled. Economic negotiations with Germany during the recent period had begun more than once without result. I further stated that we had gained the impression that the German government was playing some sort of game instead of conducting business-like economic negotiations; and that for such a game it should have looked for its partner in another country and not the government of the USSR. The USSR was not going to participate in such a game.

'Throughout the whole discussion', Molotov further noted in his report, 'it was evident that for the Ambassador my statement was most unexpected.'[27]

Berlin was dismayed by this response, but not for long. The Germans took heart from Schulenburg's report that Molotov had said that 'the Soviet Government could only agree to a resumption of the [economic] negotiations if the necessary "political bases" for them had been constructed'.[28] Molotov's own version of this remark makes it clear that this was not, as the Germans hoped, an invitation to political discussions but a harking back to the earlier experience of the cancelled Schnurre visit:

We had come to the conclusion that for the success of the economic negotiations it was necessary to create a corresponding political basis. Without such a basis, as shown by the experience of negotiations with Germany, it is not possible to settle economic questions.[29]

Berlin, nevertheless, resumed its approaches on 30 May when Weizsäcker invited Astakhov to his office for further discussions about improving Soviet-German economic and political relations. In the German shop there were many 'goods' for the Soviet Union to choose from, Weizsäcker told Astakhov. If the USSR wanted to talk along these lines, all well and good; if the USSR was going to join Britain and France in a policy of encirclement then Germany was prepared for that too. Weizsäcker's aim, Astakhov reported to Moscow, was to explore 'the possibility of negotiations with us about improving relations and to restrain our rapprochement with England. It is typical, however, that they refrain from committing themselves to any statement, avoiding even the term "the improvement of relations".'[30]

The day after the Weizsäcker–Astakhov meeting Molotov made a keynote report on the international situation to the Supreme Soviet. In his speech Molotov continued Stalin's theme in March 1939 of a dual attack on Anglo-French appeasement and German aggressiveness. However, in noting the shift away from appeasement in British and French policy and welcoming the prospect of an alliance with the western powers – providing suitable terms could be arrived at – Molotov delivered a very public rebuff to recent German approaches. 'How do we define our tasks in the present-day international situation? We believe that they accord with the interests of other non-aggressive countries. They consist in stopping further aggression and creating for this purpose a reliable and effective front of non-aggressive powers.'[31]

The only glimmer of hope for the Germans in this speech was Molotov's announcement that the triple alliance negotiations with Britain and France did not preclude commercial relations with Germany and that credit negotiations with Germany might soon be resumed. In fact more than six weeks were to pass before Moscow formally agreed to negotiate a new trade and credit agreement. In the interim economic discussions between the two states were confined to 'talks about talks'.[32]

On the political front the Soviets continued to drag their feet in relation to the possibility of an improvement of relations with Germany. The only hint that Moscow might be deflected from its course of a triple alliance with the western powers came at a meeting between Astakhov and Draganov, the Bulgarian ambassador in Berlin, on 14 June. The next day the Bulgarian spoke to Ernst Woermann, head of the political division of the German Foreign Office. According to Woermann's memorandum of his conversation with Draganov, Astakhov had told the Bulgarian that Russia was wavering between a pact with Britain and France, spinning out the triple alliance negotiations, or an agreement with Germany. Not only that but 'rapprochement with Germany ... was closest to the desires of the Soviet Union'. Astakhov had further stated, according to Draganov, that 'if Germany would declare that she would not attack the Soviet Union or that she would conclude a non-aggression pact with her, the Soviet Union would probably refrain from concluding a treaty with England ... Several circumstances also spoke for [continuing] to conduct the pact negotiations with England in a dilatory manner. In this case the Soviet Union would continue to have a free hand in any conflict which might break out.' [33]

Woermann's account of his conversation with Draganov appears to have been pretty accurate, for on the same day the Bulgarian reported home to Sofia in similar terms: Russia was prepared to enter into an agreement with Germany provided Berlin could satisfy Moscow about its intentions and make a suitable offer. [34]

Many historians have seized on the Astakhov–Draganov conversation as evidence for the view that Moscow was interested in a deal with Berlin all along – notwithstanding the triple alliance negotiations with Britain and France being conducted at this time. However, when we turn to Astakhov's version of the meeting with Draganov a somewhat different picture emerges. On the surface, it appears from Astakhov's diary entry on the meeting that the views imputed to him were in fact Draganov's opinions. It is also possible, however, that Draganov's account is accurate and that Astakhov was expressing views which he wished to hide from Moscow by imputing them to Draganov. Be that as it may, according to Astakhov's diary, Draganov expressed the view that Germany would only start a war if a pact between the USSR and Britain was concluded, but if there was no pact then the problem of Danzig and the Polish corridor would be resolved without war. Further, that if there was an Anglo-Soviet-French pact then the Poles would provoke a conflict. 'You would do better to spin out the negotiations', Astakhov quotes Draganov as saying, 'if you are worried about the appearance of Germans in the Baltic, Bessarabia, etc., you can make an agreement with the Germans who would readily enter into the broadest exchange of views on these questions.'[35]

It may be that Astakhov's account is inaccurate – that he did say many of the things attributed to him by Draganov (although it is difficult to imagine such crude and blatant indiscretion on the part of the Soviet Counsellor). But in that case the episode is no more than an instance of personal kite-flying by Astakhov. If Astakhov had been under instructions from Moscow to test the waters in Berlin via Draganov then those instructions would have been reflected in the Soviet diplomat's report home on the meeting. That no such instructions existed, that indeed Astakhov was being left largely to his own devices in Berlin, we know from his other communications to Moscow in this same period. On 14 June 1939 he wrote to Molotov:

> If our conversations with the Germans were not limited to trade and credit questions and touched upon political factors, it would be useful, it seems to me, to bring them to the attention of the German government as well. This would not be superfluous even if wasn't the case that Schulenburg didn't have the personal confidence of Ribbentrop and that it is possible the latter interprets his reports differently. It would give us the possibility of obtaining some positive statements from local leaders, or at least clear up some issues of interest to us directly from primary sources ... if we want to talk to the Germans about anything without particularly committing ourselves, in these cases it would be more expedient to do it here.[36]

On 19 June 1939 Astakhov pointed out to Molotov that it would be 'desirable to have from you rough guidelines on our negotiations with England, and also about our attitude to conversations with Weizsäcker and Schulenburg'.[37]

As we shall see, Astakhov's plea to Moscow for more latitude in his dealings with the Germans in Berlin fell on deaf ears until the end of July 1939. In the meantime, Astakhov continued in his role as a passive conduit of German approaches about the possibility of some kind of rapprochement. On 17 June Astakhov met Schulenburg, who was on leave in Berlin, and was told that the Germans were still awaiting a reply to Weizsäcker's approach of 30 May. The conditions for an improvement in relations were ripening, urged Schulenburg, but, in the absence of a definite brief from Moscow, Astakhov was in a position only to repeat general noises to the effect that the USSR was not against an improvement of relations with Germany.[38]

On 28 June Schulenburg, back in Moscow, met Molotov to convey both Hitler's and Ribbentrop's desire for improved relations with the USSR. Schulenburg pointed to the recent non-aggression treaties with Latvia and Estonia as proof of Germany's intentions towards the USSR. In reply, Molotov argued that these non-aggression treaties were concluded on Germany's own account and not out of friendship towards the Soviet Union. He also drew attention to Germany's recent abrogation of its non-aggression pact with Poland, and to the Anti-Comintern Pact and to the Pact of Steel with Italy.

The best that could be said of Molotov's response was that he was ready to hear what Schulenburg had to say. But since the German ambassador had no definite proposals to make the meeting ended on a generally negative note.[39]

Molotov's rebuff of Schulenburg was followed by a month-long lull in German advances to the Soviets. As Astakhov noted in a letter to Molotov on 19 July, while the Germans continued to drop indirect hints of a willingness to change their policy towards the USSR they were afraid to continue their direct approaches of a few weeks earlier.[40] On 24 July, however, these approaches did resume. At a meeting with Astakhov, Schnurre proposed a three-stage programme for the normalisation of Soviet-German relations: completion of the trade and credit talks; improvements in cultural relations; and political discussions.

On 26 July Astakhov met with Schnurre again. Insisting that he spoke for Ribbentrop and Hitler, Schnurre stated that Germany was serious about the normalisation and improvement of relations with the USSR. When Astakhov queried whether this was the case, Schnurre replied: 'Tell me what proof you want? We are ready to demonstrate the possibility of reaching agreement on any question, to give any guarantees.' Later in the conversation, Schnurre said that Germany had renounced any aspirations in the Ukraine and was prepared to treat the Baltic countries in the same way. At this point Astakhov began to feel the conversation was going too far and he decided to divert the discussion to more general themes – the current status of Hitler's plans for eastern expansion outlined in *Mein Kampf* and issues connected to Polish-German, Anglo-German and German-Japanese relations. The meeting concluded with Astakhov promising to report home, but stating also that he was not sure that Moscow would take such novel ideas seriously.[41]

Astakhov's first report to Moscow on the two meetings with Schnurre was a telegram home on 27 July:

Germany is prepared to discuss and come to an understanding with us on all the questions that both sides are interested in, and to give all the security guarantees which we would require from them. Even in relation to the Baltic countries and Poland it would be easy to come to an agreement, as it would in relation to the Ukraine (which Germany would leave alone). To my question about how confident he was that his words reflected the mood and intention of higher circles, Schnurre said that he spoke on the direct instructions of Ribbentrop ... Germany was prepared to give us a choice of everything from friendship to enmity. Naturally, we didn't give Schnurre any hopes, limiting ourselves to general noises and promising to bring the talks to your attention.[42]

Moscow replied to this telegram on 28 July: 'in restricting yourself to hearing out Schnurre's statements and promising to pass them on to Moscow you did the right thing', cabled Molotov.[43] Astakhov's detailed reports on his conversations with Schnurre reached Moscow on 29 July. On the same day Molotov telegraphed to Astakhov a full statement of Moscow's response to the German overtures:

Political relations between the USSR and Germany may improve, of course, with an improvement in economic relations. In this regard Schnurre is, generally speaking, right. But only the Germans can say concretely how political relations should improve. Until recently the Germans did nothing but curse the USSR, did not want any improvement in political relations with it and refused to participate in any conferences where the USSR was represented. If the Germans are now sincerely changing course and really want to improve political relations with the USSR, they are obliged to state what this improvement represents in concrete terms. Not long ago I was with Schulenburg who also spoke about improving relations, but did not want to propose anything concrete or intelligible. Here the matter depends entirely on the Germans. We would, of course, welcome any improvement in political relations between the two countries.[44]

With this grudging response Moscow had finally opened the door to political détente with Berlin. It was not so much a decision to negotiate as the first real sign of a readiness to listen to and consider what the Germans had to say. But why now, at the end of July rather than in May, or June? The answer to this question remains unclear but it may have been connected to the triple alliance negotiations with the British and French.

It seems likely that all along Moscow had suspected that Berlin's approaches were part of some kind of *petit jeu* aimed at disrupting the Anglo-Soviet-French triple alliance negotiations. By the end of July, however, the negotiations on the political part of the security pact the Soviets wanted were more or less complete and the western powers had also agreed to begin military talks. With these commitments in the bag the danger of German mischief-making was minimal and Moscow could feel more confident about playing the German card as part of its own pressure-tactics in relation to London and Paris. Furthermore, the experience of negotiating with the British and French had not exactly been encouraging. From Moscow's point of view London and Paris had dragged their feet throughout the triple alliance negotiations. A classic summation of the course of these negotiations may be found in A. J. P. Taylor's *The Origins of the Second World War:*

The diplomatic exchange shows that the delays came from the West and that the Soviet government answered with almost breathtaking speed. The British made their first tentative suggestion on 15 April; the Soviet counter-proposal [for a triple alliance] came two days later, on 17 April. The British took three weeks before designing an answer on 9 May; the Soviet delay was then five days. The British took thirteen days; the Soviets again took five. Once more the British took thirteen days; the Soviet government answered within twenty-four hours. The British next needed nine days; the Soviets two. Five more days for the British; one day for the Russians. Eight days on the British side; Soviet answer on the same day. British delay of six days; Soviet answer the same day ... *If dates mean anything, the British were spinning things out, the Russians were anxious to conclude.* (emphasis added)[45]

Taylor was writing before the release of the Soviet documents on the triple alliance talks. These, however, amply bear out his judgement. On 17 July, for example, Molotov in a letter to his London and Paris ambassadors described the Anglo-French negotiators as 'crooks and cheats' and bemoaned that 'it seems nothing will come of the endless negotiations', warning that then the British and French 'will have no one but themselves to blame'.[46] In this light the German offers of détente undoubtedly warranted more attention than previously, particularly when the evidence was accumulating that the crisis in German-Polish relations over Danzig – brewing since Hitler's renunciation at the end of April of the German-Polish non-aggression pact – was about to break.[47] With war on their doorstep perhaps only days away the Soviet leadership clearly felt the need to keep all their options open.

While calculations such as these may have been behind the adjustment in Soviet policy towards Germany at the end of July, their importance should not be exaggerated. Molotov's statement of Soviet policy on Germany on 29 July indicates that Moscow did not really know what to do about Berlin's offer of political discussions.

The statement was a curiously low-key and passive response to Schnurre's hints of a Soviet-German condominium in Eastern Europe. Behind it lay uncertainty about Hitler's intentions and about the final outcome of the Polish crisis. Was Hitler's aim the total subjugation of Poland or a new 'Munich'? Would the British and French honour their guarantees and stand and fight alongside Poland? For how long and how successfully could Poland resist a German invasion? Above all, what would be the length and nature of the 'breathing space' that the Nazis seemed to be offering the Soviet state?[48] Such questions continued to be a source of indecisiveness in Moscow's policy right up until the very eve of the Nazi-Soviet pact. Indeed, the lingering doubts that they generated persisted for some time after the pact.

There is also a rather more mundane factor to be taken into account when considering Soviet policy towards Germany in summer 1939. Molotov was a new Foreign Minister and for the first three months of his tenure in office he had his hands full negotiating a complex and contentious treaty of alliance with the British and French. He headed, too, an organisation that had been wracked by years of successive purges including, most recently, a major assault on the personnel of its central apparatus in May 1939. In addition, Molotov retained his responsibilities as Chairman of the Council of People's Commissars. Quite simply, it is likely that Molotov had little spare time and energy to devote to tactics in relation to Berlin and, given the commitment to a triple alliance with Britain and France, not much inclination. This may help to explain why it was that between May and July 1939 Moscow pursued (or rather didn't pursue) a 'non-policy' towards Germany. This contention is borne out by the evidence that until the end of July 1939 Astakhov, Moscow's main point of contact with Berlin, was left largely to his own devices – with no instructions on how to respond to numerous attempts by the Germans to involve the USSR in discussions about political détente.

As a result of this non-policy Russia's conduct of its relations with Germany during the crucial weeks leading to the Nazi-Soviet pact was characterised by passivity and indecisiveness. As we shall see, the pact on the Soviet side derived not so much from a process of conscious political bargaining as a process of policy drift, which was in turn an effect of a stream of events, perceptions and pressures that buffeted Moscow along to the final outcome.

Moscow was dithering but Astakhov in Berlin was arguing for the adoption of a more definite game-plan. In a letter to Potemkin at the end of July he argued that German efforts at improving relations with the USSR had taken on a persistent character and that:

I have no doubt that if we wanted to we could involve the Germans in far-reaching negotiations and get from them assurances about the questions that interest us. Of course, what the value of these assurances would be is another question.

In any case this readiness of the Germans to talk to us about improving relations should be taken into account and, perhaps, we ought to give them some encouragement, in order to retain in our hands a trump card which we could use in the event of necessity. From this point of view it would, perhaps, be useful to say something, to pose them some questions, in order not to let go of the thread that they have placed in our hands and which, handled carefully, can hardly do us any harm.[49]

It is worth pausing briefly to consider the significance of this letter to Moscow from Astakhov – in charge of the Soviet embassy during the period and the man who has gone down in history as the go-between of the Nazi-Soviet negotiations of 1939. Two points emerge from the passage quoted above. Firstly, as late as the end of July 1939 Astakhov was evidently not authorised even to encourage Berlin's soundings of him, let alone to enter into negotiations with the Germans. Secondly, Astakhov was obviously keen to explore what the Germans had to offer. Over the next two weeks this inclination was to develop into a barely disguised enthusiasm for a deal with Berlin. As we shall see, Moscow was much more hesitant in its response to Berlin's overtures than Astakhov, but his increasingly positive reports about his discussions with the Germans must have had a considerable impact back home.

Astakhov's immediate game-plan was to give the Germans some encouragement in order to keep going the thread of his discussions in Berlin. Before Moscow could respond to his proposal, however, the Germans once again took the initiative. On 2 August Ribbentrop himself told Astakhov that 'we consider that there are no contradictions between our countries from the Black Sea to the Baltic. On all problems it is possible to reach agreement; if the Soviet government shares these premises we can exchange views in more concrete terms.'[50]

The next day Schulenburg, in a meeting with Molotov, followed up this overture, proposing an improvement in relations in three stages: (a) the conclusion of an economic agreement; (b) better press relations; and (c) the development of cultural and scientific co-operation. These would lay the basis for an improvement in political relations. Schulenburg stressed the new course in German foreign policy, in particular that there were no political contradictions between Germany and the USSR in the Baltic and that Berlin had no plans that ran counter to Soviet interests in Poland.

Molotov's response was more positive than on previous occasions, but still guarded. On the one hand he stated that 'the Soviet government has a favourable view of the German government's desire for an improvement in relations'. But on the other hand he continued to cast doubt on German policy towards the USSR, rehashing old arguments about the Anti-Comintern Pact, Germany's attitude to the USSR in international affairs, and so on.[51] For his part Schulenburg concluded from the meeting:

> My overall impression is that the Soviet Government is at present determined to sign with England and France if they fulfil all Soviet wishes ... it will ... take considerable effort on our part to cause the Soviet Government to swing about.[52]

That German effort to swing the Russians away from the triple alliance was about to be mounted. However, on 4 August Molotov telegraphed Astakhov instructions to the effect that Soviet policy was to continue with the exchange of views in general terms but that more concrete discussions depended on the outcome of the trade-credit talks.[53] This non-committal position was one that Moscow maintained for the next two weeks – despite mounting diplomatic pressure by the Germans and a stream of reports from Astakhov that left no doubt about what Berlin had in mind.

Significantly, this period of continued Soviet reticence and wavering coincided with the arrival in Moscow (on the 10th) of an Anglo-French military delegation to negotiate a military counterpart of the political trisecurity pact; the beginning of the military negotiations (on the 12th); and the effective breakdown of the talks (14th–17th) over the issue of Polish and Romanian consent to the passage of Soviet forces across their territory.

The more evidence from Soviet archives on these military talks that becomes available, the more certain it becomes that Moscow embarked on them intent on reaching an agreement on a military convention to fight the Germans.[54] However, that agreement had to be watertight, leaving no room for manoeuvres by appeasers in London and Paris, and securing for Russia practical and worthwhile military support in the event of war with Germany. Moscow, however, had serious doubts about the likelihood of success. The experience of the political negotiations with London and Paris did not augur well nor did the dilatory behaviour of the Anglo-French military delegation which – at the height of the German-Polish crisis over Danzig – did not fly to Russia but travelled by a slow merchant ship. Then there was the relatively low rank and status of the Anglo-French military negotiators and the fact that the British had no written powers to negotiate, and that although the French did have the power to negotiate they were not authorised to sign any agreement. During the talks themselves it became clear that Britain and France had no strategic and operational plans for a joint war against Germany. The Soviets were not impressed by the small forces the British and French proposed to mobilise and detected more than a hint of the defensive 'Maginot' mentality about how they proposed to respond to enemy attacks in the early days of hostilities. Finally, there was the question of the right of passage of Soviet forces across Poland and Romania – vital to Soviet operational plans for war against Germany. The British and French could not answer this question and seemed reluctant to concede the USSR right of passage without Polish and Romanian consent.

As the military negotiations progressed so Moscow's doubts about the triple alliance project as a whole grew, and so the door to an agreement with Germany was opened wider. But not until the moment of the final breakdown of the military negotiations with Britain and France were the Germans invited across the threshold.

While all this was going on in Moscow the German diplomatic offensive to secure their own agreement with the Russians, started by Ribbentrop on 2 August, was proceeding. On 5 August Astakhov telegraphed Moscow that Schnurre had suggested the idea of a 'secret protocol' attached to any credit agreement that might be signed.[55] Molotov replied on 7 August, stating that it was not appropriate to sign such a protocol under a trade treaty.[56] This was the first mention of some kind of secret Soviet-German deal.

In a letter to Molotov on 8 August Astakhov summed up the stage reached in the 'negotiations' between the two states. What the Germans were proposing, wrote Astakhov, was the updating of Rapallo and other German-Soviet political treaties by a new treaty or 'some protocol'. Discussions around this and related topics

were not excluded even in the event of a successful conclusion of
the Anglo-Soviet-French negotiations. However, the real interest of
the Germans was in the settlement of a number of territorial-
political issues in Eastern Europe. In return for Soviet disinterestedness in the fate of Danzig and former 'German Poland' Berlin
would renounce any aspirations in the Ukraine and, in effect,
would give the USSR a free hand in 'Russian Poland', Bessarabia
and the Baltic States (except for Lithuania). In conclusion
Astakhov wrote:

> It goes without saying that I am not in any way claiming that ...
> the Germans would maintain a serious and long-term observa-
> tion of the eventual commitments. I think only that in the im-
> mediate future they consider it conceivable to come to a certain
> understanding ... in order to neutralise us in the event of war
> with Poland. As regards the future then the matter would, of
> course, depend not on these obligations but on the new situ-
> ation which would result and that I cannot foresee at the
> moment.[57]

Molotov replied to Astakhov on 11 August. Moscow was interested
in the points made in his letter but such discussions required
preparation and a period of transition from the trade and credit
agreement to other problems, and it would be preferable for such
discussions to be held in Moscow.[58] This was the first sign that
Moscow was seriously considering a wide-ranging deal with Berlin.
But a further week was to elapse before Moscow was ready to fully
grasp the nettle of a pact with the Nazis. That week was the same
one in which the triple alliance negotiations finally collapsed with
the failure (from Moscow's point of view) of the Anglo-Soviet-
French military talks. But in the meantime Moscow continued to
hedge its bets.

From Berlin Astakhov continued to nudge Moscow towards a
decisive move. On 12 August he reported to Molotov that he
had met with Schnurre and carried out the instructions
telegraphed the day before. However, events were moving
quickly and in view of the coming conflict with Poland the
Germans did not want to dwell on secondary issues; they wanted
to discuss political-territorial problems. The Germans, he reported, are:

obviously worried by our negotiations with the British and French military and they have become unsparing in their arguments and promises in order to prevent a military agreement. For the sake of this they are now ready, I believe, to make the kind of declarations and gestures that would have been inconceivable six months ago. The Baltic, Bessarabia, Eastern Poland (not to speak of the Ukraine) – at the present time this is the minimum they would give up without a long discussion in order to secure a promise from us not to intervene in their conflict with Poland.[59]

On 13 August there was another Schnurre–Astakhov meeting. Events were moving quickly, said Schnurre, and there was no time to waste in opening negotiations about the improvement of Soviet-German relations. The German government would prefer discussions to be held in Berlin – close to the Führer – but appreciated the Soviet desire for them to be held in Moscow. To this end Schnurre raised the possibility of a Nazi emissary to Moscow, someone trusted by Hitler and with the authority to speak on behalf of the government.[60]

Schnurre's suggestion of a special emissary came to nothing, however, and Berlin chose to move through official channels. On 15 August Schulenburg met Molotov and proposed that Ribbentrop should visit Moscow for face-to-face negotiations. Molotov welcomed Schulenburg's reaffirmation of previous German statements of political good will, but insisted that prior to a visit by Ribbentrop there would have to be clarification of a number of matters.

One would have thought that the Germans could hardly have made their intentions clearer. Yet at this meeting Molotov chose a curiously indirect way to probe for the details of the kind of deal on offer. He referred to a dispatch from the Soviet embassy in Rome at the end of June which reported the existence of a 'Schulenburg Plan' for improving Soviet-German relations. The plan proposed German intercession in Soviet-Japanese conflicts in the Far East; a non-aggression pact between Germany and the USSR and a joint guarantee of the Baltic States; and the conclusion of a wide-ranging economic agreement between the two countries. Molotov wanted to know whether the Schulenburg Plan represented the basis for further negotiations and, in particular, the German government's attitude to the idea of a non-aggression treaty. Schulenburg was embarrassed, for the 'Plan' that bore his name was a myth, the result, he said, of rumours emanating from conversations between himself and Rosso, the Italian ambassador in Moscow. Schulenburg nevertheless promised to convey to Berlin Molotov's interest in the points of the so-called plan.[61]

Molotov's roundabout probing of German intentions can be interpreted purely and simply as a negotiating tactic: Moscow wanted Berlin to make its offer before revealing its own hand. But there was also a deeper motive underlying Russian reluctance to embark on explicit negotiations about a Soviet-German condominium in Eastern Europe. Moscow still lacked a new strategic agenda for action. Hitherto the operational objectives of Soviet foreign policy had revolved around the project of a triple alliance with Britain and France. By 15 August that project was in the latter stages of its disintegration. But Moscow had yet to formulate a new strategic-political agenda to take its place; and was not to finally do so until the eve of the Red Army's invasion of Eastern Poland on 17 September. The only clear goal of Soviet foreign policy from mid-August to mid-September 1939 was that of avoiding a war with Nazi Germany in Eastern Europe while Britain and France stood on the sidelines. A new policy of security through strategic-political expansion and co-operation with Hitler was foreshadowed in the Nazi-Soviet pact, but its actualisation was slow and hesitant, an effect of a series of ad hoc responses and reactions to the dynamic of events rather than the result of prior decision or planned policy.

Moscow's lack of a new strategy was certainly evident at Molotov's next meeting with Schulenburg on 17 August. At this meeting Molotov handed Schulenburg a formal written statement proposing a non-aggression pact between the two states (or a reaffirmation of the Soviet-German neutrality treaty of 1926), together with a 'special protocol' which would form an 'integral' part of that pact.

The moment of Stalin's decision to deal with Hitler rather than the British or French had finally arrived. But what kind of deal? Here the position remained unclear. Schulenburg had a formal statement to make too. Picking up on Molotov's earlier enquiries about the 'Schulenburg Plan', Berlin proposed a non-aggression treaty, a joint guarantee of the Baltic States, and German help in improving Soviet-Japanese relations. In response all Molotov would say was that the new German proposals would have to be studied. Schulenburg attempted to draw Molotov on what Moscow envisaged would be the content of this 'special protocol' they proposed. But all Molotov would say was that both sides had to think about what the content of the protocol should be. He resisted, too, all Schulenburg's representations that Ribbentrop should fly to Moscow immediately for direct negotiations.[62]

Molotov's reticence about the content of the proposed 'special protocol' and his refusal to set a date for Ribbentrop's arrival in Moscow were linked. At a further meeting with Schulenburg on 19 August Molotov made it clear that before Ribbentrop came to Moscow it had to be certain that an agreement would be reached and this meant that the matter of the special protocol had to be clarified first. The matter of the protocol was a serious one, he told Schulenburg, and it was up to Berlin to think about its content.

Schulenburg's meeting with Molotov ended at about 3.00 p.m. However, the German ambassador was summoned back to the Kremlin for a further meeting at 4.30 p.m. when he was told that the Soviet government agreed that Ribbentrop could come to Moscow on 26–27 August. No reasons were given for this change of policy and Schulenburg assumed, probably correctly, that Stalin had intervened.[63]

Presumably, the Soviet calculation was that during the coming week the matter of the 'special protocol' could be clarified. It is also possible that Stalin had not entirely given up on the British and French and agreed to Ribbentrop's visit with a view to strengthening his hand in those negotiations which had not yet formally ended. In any event this sudden change in tactics was illustrative of how in these critical days Soviet foreign policy was being made on the hoof. A further example of the reactive and makeshift nature of Soviet diplomacy on the eve of the pact with Nazi Germany was to occur two days later.

On 21 August Schulenburg presented Molotov with an urgent personal message from Hitler to Stalin. The substance of the message was an urgent plea that in view of the international situation (i.e. the Polish-German crisis over Danzig) Ribbentrop should visit Moscow in the next couple of days to sign a non-aggression pact and to negotiate the 'supplementary protocol'. Two hours later Stalin replied personally in a letter to Hitler, agreeing that Ribbentrop arrive in Moscow on 23 August.[64]

Ribbentrop's trip to Moscow was announced on 21 August and on 23 August he flew into the Soviet capital. Negotiations between Ribbentrop, Stalin and Molotov were conducted during two conversations – one in the afternoon and another in the evening, stretching into the early hours of the morning. Agreement was reached on the conclusion of a treaty of non-aggression and a 'secret additional protocol' which delineated Soviet and German spheres of influence in Eastern Europe. The signature of the two agreements was sealed by a toast to the new era in German-Soviet relations.[65]

As Ribbentrop was leaving Stalin told him that:

> The Soviet Government takes the pact very seriously. He could guarantee on his word of honour that the Soviet Union would not betray its partner.[66]

It was a promise that Stalin kept. The era of collective security had finally come to a close.

6 The Nazi-Soviet Pact and the Partition of Poland

The conclusion of the German-Soviet Non-Aggression Treaty of 23 August 1939 constituted the most stunning volte-face in diplomatic history. On the very eve of war the state of enmity that had bedevilled Soviet-German relations for over six years was declared dissolved as the two states signed a treaty pledging non-aggression, neutrality, and mutual consultation over matters of foreign policy. Attached to this published treaty was a secret protocol, which must surely be one of the most famous documents in the history of international relations:

1. In the event of a territorial and political rearrangement in the areas belonging to the Baltic States (Finland, Estonia, Latvia, Lithuania), the northern boundary of Lithuania shall represent the boundary of the spheres of influence of Germany and the USSR ...
2. In the event of a territorial and political rearrangement of the areas belonging to the Polish state the spheres of influence of Germany and the USSR shall be bounded approximately by the line of the rivers Narew, Vistula and San.[1]

Despite the dramatic flavour of these much-quoted words the deal embodied in this pact was a limited one: a promise of Soviet neutrality in the coming conflict between Hitler and the western powers over Poland in return for a German pledge to keep their hands off Finland, Estonia, Latvia and Eastern Poland. As A. J. P. Taylor argued: 'the pact was neither an alliance nor an agreement for a partition of Poland ... the agreement was in the last resort anti-German: it limited the German advance eastwards in case of war.'[2]

This is not the generally accepted view of the Nazi-Soviet pact which posits that on 23 August 1939 Moscow gave the green light to Hitler's attack on Poland and that there was a definite agreement between Germany and the USSR to partition Poland and to allow Soviet subjugation of the Baltic States. Germany did attack Poland on 1 September; Poland was partitioned between Russia and Germany; and the Baltic States did come under Soviet sway. But none of these things is evidence of prior knowledge, intention and commitment to those outcomes. The pact, the Polish partition, and the Soviet takeover of the Baltic States do not form a single package concocted on 23 August 1939. Each constituted distinctive sets of events in an evolving political and military situation. There was no grand plan, or even inclination, for Soviet expansion into Eastern Europe in 1939.

In signing the pact with Nazi Germany Stalin finally abandoned the policy of collective security and opted for safeguarding Soviet interests via neutrality and independent manoeuvring. Beyond that the new foreign policy embodied in the pact remained fluid. A strategy of territorial expansion into Eastern Europe was only one of the possibilities present at the moment of the signing of the pact, and whether or not it would be the chosen course of action would depend on the circumstances. After all, on 23 August 1939 nothing was certain. Would Hitler really attack Poland? Would the Poles fight back and how successful would they be? What would Britain and France do? What were the chances of another 'Munich'? What would be the consequences of any forward Soviet strategy in Eastern Europe? Until these and many other quandaries were resolved there could be no question of any precipitate action. In the meantime Soviet foreign strategy was kept in a state of abeyance. Only an analysis along these lines can explain the surprising ambiguity, hesitancy and uncertainty that characterised Soviet foreign policy in the days and weeks immediately following the conclusion of the pact with Nazi Germany.

'The sinister news broke upon the world like an explosion', Churchill wrote of the Nazi-Soviet pact.[3] Yet the immediate diplomatic fall-out from the pact, as far as Soviet foreign policy was concerned, was curiously muted. True, the pact had wrecked the Anglo-Soviet-French military negotiations and the USSR had nailed its colours to the mast of neutrality in the event of war, but apart from these (admittedly, very large) matters it was business as usual.

When the Chinese ambassador met Lozovsky, Soviet Deputy People's Commissar for Foreign Affairs, on 26 August he was told that the pact, like other non-aggression treaties signed by the USSR in the past, was a contribution to the struggle for peace.

Moreover, that although the negotiations with Britain and France had been broken off they could be resumed and there was still a possibility of reaching agreement.[4]

Lozovsky, of course, was not privy to the Soviet-German discussions of 23 August nor to the content of the secret protocol. The same was true of Sharonov, the Soviet ambassador in Warsaw, but presumably he was not acting against instructions when he told Beck on 26 August that the non-aggression treaty with Germany did not affect Polish-Soviet relations.[5] Certainly, Marshal Voroshilov's hint in a newspaper interview the next day that the Soviet Union might be prepared to supply Poland with raw materials and military equipment in the event of a German attack must have had official sanction.[6] The day after Poland was attacked Sharonov is reported to have asked Beck why no Polish request for such aid had been forthcoming.[7] These indications of goodwill continued at a friendly meeting between Molotov and Grzybowski, the Polish ambassador, on 3 September.[8] However, at a meeting with Grzybowski on 5 September Molotov turned down a Polish request for the supply of war materials.[9]

Moscow's initially benign attitude toward Poland during this period was not dissimulation but a sign of the indecision that gripped Soviet foreign policy while Stalin waited to see how the international situation developed.

A new, neutralist course for Soviet foreign policy had been charted by the pact with Nazi Germany, and this was publicly spelt out by Molotov in a speech to the Supreme Soviet on 31 August:

> The chief importance of the Soviet-German Non-Aggression Pact lies in the fact that the two largest states of Europe have agreed to put an end to the enmity between them, to eliminate the menace of war and to live at peace with each other, making narrower thereby the zone of possible military conflicts in Europe.

Molotov also made it clear that should war break out the USSR was 'not obliged to involve itself in war either on the side of Great Britain against Germany or on the side of Germany against Great Britain'. The Soviet Union would not involve itself in any European war and would pursue, as Molotov put it, 'new possibilities of increasing our strength, further consolidation of our positions, and the further growth of the influence of the Soviet Union on international developments'.[10]

However, a neutralist stance was one thing, an active foreign policy strategy to secure Soviet interests was quite another. That would depend on the outcome of the coming German-Polish war.

Further light on Stalin's wait and see policy is shed by the decisions and discussions of the Communist International during this period.[11] For the first two weeks after the pact the Comintern leadership in Moscow was left to its own devices in formulating policy for the communist movement in the new situation. The position they adopted was broadly similar to that spontaneously arrived at by the communist parties abroad, i.e. support for the Soviet diplomatic manoeuvre in signing the pact with Nazi Germany but a continuation of the anti-fascist struggle at home and abroad. Nazi Germany continued to be identified as the main enemy of the working class, no more so than after the invasion of Poland on 1 September.

This line was maintained until 7 September when Dimitrov, the Comintern leader, had a meeting with Stalin, Molotov and Zhdanov. At this meeting Stalin reportedly told Dimitrov that 'we would have preferred an agreement with the so-called democratic countries, hence we entered negotiations with them, but Britain and France wanted us to be their hired hand ... and without pay'.[12] More importantly, Stalin set out a new line for the Comintern based on the idea that the war was an inter-imperialist one and there was no reason why the working class should side with Britain, France and Poland against Germany. In effect Stalin decreed the end of the anti-fascist policy the Comintern had followed since its 7th World Congress in 1935. The new line was accepted by the Comintern's leaders and adopted by the rest of the communist movement in the course of the next month.[13]

Stalin's intervention in Comintern affairs in early September signalled a second, decisive turn in Soviet foreign policy. The essence of this shift in policy, which was at least on a par with that represented by the Nazi-Soviet pact, was firstly, a decision to invade Eastern Poland and to occupy militarily the sphere of influence allocated to it on 23 August and, secondly, a diplomatic and political realignment of the USSR alongside Germany.

Contrary to historical orthodoxy, this turn in Soviet policy was not a planned or automatic consequence of the pact with Nazi Germany. There was no specific agreement or intention on 23 August to partition Poland. There are a number of documentary clues which support this assertion.

Firstly, there is the fact that the first clause of the secret additional protocol to the pact concerned not Poland but Soviet-German spheres of influence in the Baltic. This was a curious textual order of priorities for two states that had supposedly just decided to carve up between them another major state. What it reflected was the fact that the Soviet priority in August 1939 was to exclude German influence from the Baltic. The fate of Poland was important too. Hence the eastern limit of German military expansion into Poland agreed in the secret protocol. But how Moscow would deal with the rump Polish state that would be left was a matter for the future.

Secondly, there is a whole series of messages from Berlin to its Moscow embassy during the last week in August concerning press reports that Red Army units had been withdrawn from the Soviet-Polish border. Schulenburg was urgently instructed to approach Molotov with a view to securing a public denial that this was the case.[14] On the eve of the planned attack on Poland Berlin was concerned to keep up the pressure on the Poles. In none of this correspondence was there any hint of a Soviet-German partition agreement concluded on 23 August. Had there been such an agreement then surely Berlin's response to these press reports and its representations in Moscow would have been much stronger?

The foregoing evidence can also be read as demonstrating German anxiety about the Soviets keeping to their side of the partition bargain. However, and this is the third documentary clue, on 3 September Ribbentrop telegraphed Schulenburg the following instruction:

> We definitely expect to have beaten the Polish army decisively in a few weeks. We would then keep the territory that was fixed at Moscow as a German sphere of interest under military occupation. We would naturally, however, for military reasons, also have to proceed further against such Polish military forces as are at that time located in the Polish area belonging to the Russian sphere of interest.

Please discuss this at once with Molotov and see if the Soviet Union does not consider it desirable for Russian forces to move at the proper time against Polish forces in the Russian sphere of interest and, for their part, to occupy this territory. In our estimation this would not only be a relief for us, but also, in the sense of the Moscow agreements, in the Soviet interest as well.[15]

Clearer evidence that there was no explicit prior agreement to partition Poland militarily would be difficult to find. What other explanation can there be for Ribbentrop's evident need to interpret the 'sense' of the Moscow agreements of 23 August?

That there was indeed a need to interpret the secret protocol is confirmed in a comment by Ribbentrop at a meeting in Moscow with Stalin and Molotov on 27 September 1939: 'One question that remained unresolved during the Moscow negotiations of August 23, 1939 was that of creating an independent Poland. Since then the idea of a clear partition of Poland seemed to have become nearer to the Soviet government's understanding as well. The German government had appreciated this point of view and decided on a clear delimitation.'[16]

The partition of Poland in September 1939 was the direct result not of the Nazi-Soviet pact but of the unforeseen rapidity of the Polish military collapse. This was the circumstance in which Berlin offered and Moscow opportunistically accepted a share of the spoils of war. Still it was only after some more hesitation that Moscow finally threw in its lot with the Germans. On 5 September Molotov replied evasively to Ribbentrop's request for military action against Poland, agreeing that Soviet action was necessary but arguing that premature intervention 'might injure our cause and promote unity among our opponents'.[17] It was only on 9 September that Molotov gave way to German badgering for action and announced to Schulenburg that Soviet forces would move into Poland in the next few days.[18] But even after the decision had been taken a number of contradictory pressures continued to bear down on the Soviet leadership.

Obviously the occupation of Eastern Poland was militarily a strategically desirable objective and, in view of German successes, perhaps a necessary one. There was a real possibility that if the USSR did not move into Eastern Poland, Germany would; most certainly the spheres of influence agreement would favour the

Germans if they controlled their part of Poland while the Russians did not directly control theirs. Failure to meet Ribbentrop's request could also seriously endanger the future of Soviet-German relations and upset Soviet calculations of avoiding conflict with Germany while a war of attrition raged in the west.

Entangled with these political-strategic factors was a 'national' question. The proposed Soviet zone of occupation corresponded roughly to the territories east of the so-called 'Curzon line' – the frontier between Russia and Poland recommended by a commission of the Paris Peace Conference in 1919. A majority of the people in these territories were of Ukrainian or White Russian stock. An invasion of Poland, therefore, embodied a certain 'nationalistic' dynamic.

On the other hand, the Russians had to consider what stance Britain and France would adopt should the Soviet Union join the attack on Poland. Would it occasion an Anglo-French declaration of war against the USSR? Another possibility was that the Soviet Union would march straight into the trap of a new 'Munich'. Britain and France had declared war on Germany but as yet had not aided Poland directly or launched an attack in the west. Could it be that the appeasers were plotting some kind of deal with Hitler which would be at the Soviet Union's expense?

Such cross-currents continued to operate even after the Soviet announcement to Germany of a move against Poland. Consequently, Soviet preparations for the invasion were relatively slow. It was not until 17 September that the Red Army actually crossed the border into Poland.

Practical factors also influenced the delay in Soviet military action. Firstly, like everyone else the Soviet leadership must have been surprised by the speed of the German advance and the rapid collapse of the Polish state. Less time was available for mobilisation than had been anticipated. Secondly, there was a danger that Japan might take advantage of Soviet military involvement in Europe to escalate the fighting along the Russian-Chinese frontier that had broken out between the two states earlier in 1939. This problem was resolved on 15 September by an agreement between the USSR and Japan to end the conflict and to establish a joint commission to negotiate a settlement of the territorial disputes.[19] Thirdly, the USSR needed a pretext for invading Poland. To attack as early as the Germans wanted would have appeared as an act of naked aggression, completely lacking in legal, political and ideological credibility. At one point Molotov even suggested to Schulenburg that he would issue a statement declaring the Soviet Union had intervened to save the Ukrainians and White Russians from the Germans. The Germans protested strongly against any such proposal![20]

Molotov's 17 September radio broadcast on the Soviet invasion omitted any reference to the German threat. It concentrated instead on the collapse of the Polish state and the plight of Ukrainian and White Russian minorities in Eastern Poland:

> The Polish-German war has revealed the internal bankruptcy of the Polish State ... the Polish State and its Government have virtually ceased to exist. Treaties concluded between the USSR and Poland have thereby ceased to operate. Abandoned to its fate and left without leadership, Poland has become a fertile field for any accidental and unexpected contingency, which may create a menace to the USSR. Hence, while it was neutral hitherto, the Soviet Government can no longer maintain a neutral attitude towards these facts.
>
> Nor can the Soviet Government remain indifferent when its blood brothers, the Ukrainians and White Russians living on Polish territory, having been abandoned to their fate, are left without protection.[21]

Significantly, Molotov's broadcast had been preceded by articles in *Pravda* and *Izvestiya* attacking Polish repression of the non-Polish population in Eastern Poland and reporting growing resistance to Polish rule in that region.[22]

The Soviet invasion of Eastern Poland was completed in less than a week. As the Red Army mopped up what little resistance there was, the Soviet press carried glowing reports of the enthusiastic welcome the local populace had given to their 'liberators' from the East.[23]

Following the Soviet invasion, elections to people's assemblies were held in the occupied regions. In November these newly elected assemblies voted unanimously for incorporation into the USSR. The degree of actual support for the Soviet occupation and for the subsequent sovietisation is difficult to assess. Support appears to have been greatest in Western Byelorussia (White

Russia), where the local communists were well established. The Red Army was welcomed, too, in the Western Ukraine and in areas of Jewish settlement, at least initially. But this support was based more on resentment against the Poles, and in the case of the Ukrainians on nationalist aspirations, than on support for the Soviet regime. Whatever the real level of support it did not last long, for the Soviet occupation of Eastern Poland was no ordinary territorial annexation. The entry of Soviet forces into Western Byelorussia and Western Ukraine unleashed a revolution. A revolution from abroad utilising the instruments of military conquest, political terror and inter-ethnic communal violence, but a revolution nonetheless – one in which the existing social order was raised to the ground and then reconstructed Soviet-style.[24]

The Soviet decision to invade Eastern Poland was a fateful one. With this decision the faltering process of realigning the USSR alongside Germany, which had begun at the end of July 1939, was finally completed. It marked the beginning of a new Soviet foreign strategy under the aegis of the pact with Hitler. On 23 August the Russians had opted, via rapprochement with Germany, to remain aloof from any European war and to manoeuvre independently to secure their own interests. On 17 September they embarked on a course of territorial and political expansion into Eastern Europe designed to meet the long-term threat to Soviet security posed by Nazi Germany. The occupation of Eastern Poland constituted the first link in a chain of defence that was destined to stretch from the Baltic to the Black Sea.

Moscow's new strategy was sealed with the signature of a second Nazi-Soviet pact on 28 September 1939. Under the terms of the German-Soviet Boundary and Friendship Treaty the two sides agreed a new demarcation line in Poland which separated ethnic Poland from the predominantly non-Polish ethnic areas bordering the USSR. This required a transfer of Polish territory occupied by the USSR to Germany, in return for which Lithuania was (under the terms of a secret protocol) transferred to the Soviet sphere of influence.[25]

Following the talks in Moscow between Stalin, Molotov and Ribbentrop the Soviet Union and Germany issued a joint declaration calling for an end to the war now that Poland had collapsed and blaming the western powers for the continuation of hostilities.[26] The theme of Anglo-French culpability for the

continuation of the war was taken up by Molotov in his speech to
the Supreme Soviet on 31 October 1939:

> In the past few months such concepts as 'aggression' and
> 'aggressor' have acquired new concrete connotation, new
> meaning. It is not hard to understand that we can no longer
> employ these concepts in the sense we did, say, three or four
> months ago. Today, as far as the European great powers are
> concerned, Germany is in the position of a state which is striv-
> ing for the earliest termination of war and for peace, while
> Britain and France ... are in favour of continuing the war and
> are opposed to the conclusion of peace ... they do not want war
> stopped and peace restored but are seeking new excuses for
> continuing the war with Germany.

Molotov's chastisement of Britain and France was in sharp contrast to his remarks on Germany:

> Since the conclusion of the Soviet-German non-aggression pact
> on 23 August an end has been put to the abnormal relations that
> have existed between the Soviet Union and Germany for a
> number of years. Instead of the enmity which was fostered in
> every way by certain European powers, we now have a rapproche-
> ment and the establishment of friendly relations. ... This radical
> change in relations between the Soviet Union and Germany, the
> two biggest states in Europe, was bound to have its effect on the
> entire international situation. ... We have consistently striven to
> improve relations with Germany and have wholeheartedly wel-
> comed similar strivings in Germany herself. Today our relations
> with the German State are based on friendship, on our readiness
> to support Germany's efforts for peace, and at the same time the
> desire to contribute in every way to the development of Soviet-
> German economic relations to the mutual benefit of both States.

Another significant feature of Molotov's speech was its attack
on the Versailles peace treaty and his championing of Germany's
revisionist cause:

> Relations between Germany and other western European bour-
> geois States have in the past two decades been determined

primarily by Germany's efforts to break the fetters of the Versailles treaty ... This it was which in the long run led to the present war in Europe.

The relations between the Soviet Union and Germany were based on a different foundation which had nothing whatever in common with perpetuating the post-war Versailles system. We have always held that a strong Germany is an indispensable condition for a durable peace in Europe.[27]

These were precisely the terms in which Soviet Russia had justified the Rapallo relationship with Germany in the 1920s. Molotov's words heralded a partial return to that relationship – the recreation of the co-operation and partnership of the 1920s. Such indeed was to be the main tenor of Soviet-German relations over the next 12 months. However, in the midst of a European war Moscow's main concern was Soviet strength and security. Alongside coexistence with Germany ran Soviet expansion into Eastern Europe – the construction of a territorial, military and po-litical glacis against a Nazi attack. Russia was preparing for war with none other than its new partner. For all Molotov's public panegyrics about Germany there was no confidence in Moscow that the new Rapallo would prove to be more than a temporary respite.

7 Expansion and Coexistence, 1939–1940

The year following the Nazi-Soviet pact and the partition of Poland was a period of further Russian territorial, political and military expansion into Eastern Europe. In September–October 1939 mutual assistance treaties and Soviet military bases were forced on the Baltic States of Estonia, Latvia and Lithuania. In summer 1940 the Baltic governments were deposed by Soviet fiat, the countries occupied by the Red Army, and their internal regimes subject to 'sovietisation'. In early August 1940 all three states were incorporated into the USSR. At the end of November 1939 Finland was attacked by the Soviet Union and following the Winter War of December 1939–March 1940 was forced to cede large tracts of territory to the USSR. In July 1940 the Romanian territories of Bessarabia and Northern Bukovina were summarily annexed by the Soviets. On a less dramatic note Moscow also during this period mounted a major diplomatic offensive to extend Soviet influence and enhance Soviet security in the Balkans.

All these actions were conducted within the framework of the Nazi-Soviet pact and the new Rapallo relationship that Germany and Russia began to construct following the outbreak of the Second World War. The Germans allowed the Russians a free hand in the Baltic, did not intervene in the Soviet conflict with Finland, and supported Moscow's diplomatic initiatives in the Balkans. The quid pro quo was Soviet neutrality in the European war,[1] the political and diplomatic realignment of the USSR alongside Germany, a degree of covert military co-operation, and the conclusion of a series of mutually lucrative trade deals which increased commerce between the two states to a level comparable with the heyday of the Rapallo era.[2]

Under the auspices of the Nazi-Soviet pact the USSR gained time, space and resources in which to shore up Soviet security, build up the country's defences, and prepare for war. The irony was that the Soviet neutralist stance in the European war and its expansionist policy in Eastern Europe were directed against the very same state that made both of them possible. As Stalin put it in October 1939:

> The Germans might attack. For six years German fascists and the communists cursed each other. Now in spite of history there has been an unexpected turn, but one cannot rely upon it. We must be prepared in time. Others, who were not prepared, paid for it.[3]

In retrospect it is possible to discern a controlled pattern of the gradual expansion and progressive consolidation of a Soviet buffer zone in Eastern Europe. In fact, the Soviet movement into Eastern Europe was more like a series of improvised and often clumsy reactions to a changing German threat. There was no grand plan of Soviet expansion in 1939–40. The move into the Baltic States in autumn 1939 was a limited incursion that developed into a full-scale operation only in response to Hitler's conquest of Western Europe in summer 1940. The action in relation to Romania was prompted by the fear of an Axis carve-up of the Balkans. The ill-judged onslaught on Finland in the Winter War was the result of a combination of genuine security concerns, military arrogance and fleeting fantasies of a Finnish socialist revolution.

The main site of Russian expansionism was the Baltic – an area long identified by Moscow as the conduit for any German invasion of the USSR. Throughout the 1930s Moscow strove for a great-power agreement that would alleviate its security concerns there. An insistence on Soviet-western security guarantees of the Baltic States was at the centre of Moscow's bargaining stance during the ill-fated triple alliance negotiations with Britain and France in summer 1939. Particularly worrying for Moscow was the signature in June 1939 of non-aggression treaties between Germany and Estonia and Latvia, which indicated that the two Baltic countries might be sliding into the German sphere of influence.[4] Not surprisingly, therefore, at the heart of the Nazi-Soviet pact was an agreement excluding German influence from Baltic countries. The very first clause of the secret protocol attached to the pact dealt with the Baltic States:

> In the event of a territorial and political rearrangement in the areas belonging to the Baltic States (Finland, Estonia, Latvia

and Lithuania), the northern boundary of Lithuania shall represent the boundary of the spheres of influence of Germany and the USSR.[5]

Thus, as a result of the pact Moscow had secured German agreement to a Soviet sphere of influence in Estonia, Latvia and Finland (with Lithuania, for the time being, remaining in the German orbit). But what did that mean? According to many historical accounts what it meant was what happened later, i.e. the Soviet takeover of the Baltic States, the Winter War, and the attempted communist subversion of Finland (see below). However, the evidence indicates that when the pact was signed Moscow had no idea what course of action it was going to pursue in the Baltic. During the first month after the pact Moscow made no moves whatsoever in this area.[6] It was only at the end of September 1939 that Moscow began to take action in the Baltic – and the policy that it devised was an improvised one, primarily structured by the results of Germany's unexpectedly rapid and crushing victory over Poland.

The successful German attack on Poland and the Soviet invasion of Eastern Poland on 17 September brought into being a military border between the USSR and Germany. With a victorious German military machine now standing poised on its frontiers it was imperative for the USSR to strengthen its strategic-political defence line in the Baltic. Moscow's chosen tactic, which emerged towards the end of September 1939, was to draw the Baltic States into its sphere of influence by forcing the conclusion of mutual assistance pacts and the establishment of military bases. Included in the Soviet prospectus was Lithuania, as well as Estonia, Latvia and Finland. Lithuania, adjacent to East Prussia and German-occupied Poland, was seen as of crucial strategic importance by Moscow. As Molotov later told the Lithuanians: 'Lithuania has a long frontier with Germany' and 'Lithuania is much more important to the Soviet Union than Latvia and Estonia'.[7] As far as the Russians were concerned, if Lithuania was not included in the Soviet sphere of influence it would inevitably become a German protectorate. This was the tenor of reports from the Soviet embassy in Kaunus and it certainly seems to be what Stalin believed. 'If Lithuania had fallen under German rule', he said, 'she would without doubt have become a German protectorate.'[8]

To forestall this eventuality Moscow moved to prise Lithuania from Hitler's hands. In discussions with Ribbentrop in Moscow on 27–28 September a new division of interest in Eastern Europe was negotiated with Germany and agreement was reached on the transfer of Lithuania to the Soviet sphere of influence in return for Russian withdrawal from parts of Eastern Poland. The new deal with Nazi Germany done, Moscow could now turn its full attention to drawing the Baltic States into the Soviet orbit.

Soviet moves in the Baltic began with the arrival in Moscow on 24 September of Selter, the Estonian Foreign Minister. Selter was in Moscow to sign a trade agreement with the USSR. His presence in the Soviet capital was, it seems, largely the result of his own desire to sign the trade treaty personally and there had been no hint before his arrival that the Soviets had anything else in mind.[9] Moscow seized the opportunity, however, and Selter was immediately confronted with a proposal from Molotov for a Soviet-Estonian mutual assistance pact which would provide for Soviet air and naval bases on Estonian territory.[10] Molotov backed up his proposal with the threat that:

> You can be sure that the Soviet Union one way or another will safeguard its security. If you do not agree to our proposal, the Soviet Union would take security measures of another kind, according to its own wishes and without the agreement of Estonia.[11]

Speaking softly as well as wielding a big stick, Molotov added:

> Don't worry, the assistance agreement with the Soviet Union does not represent any threat. We do not intend to infringe your sovereignty or system of government. We do not intend to impose communism upon Estonia. We do not want to infringe the economic system of Estonia. Estonia will retain its independence, its government, parliament, foreign and internal policy, army and economic system. We won't infringe any of these.[12]

Molotov repeated these reassurances at a second meeting with the Estonian delegation on 24 September and drew attention to further Soviet concessions to Estonian sensibilities: the land upon which Soviet bases would be located would remain Estonian territory; the mutual military assistance in the proposed pact would not be automatic, but on request; and only aggression in the Baltic region would call for the assistance provided for in the pact. Molotov also agreed, albeit reluctantly, that Selter could return to Tallinn for instructions.[13]

The Estonians arrived back in Moscow on 27 September, armed with instructions to accept a mutual assistance treaty but to try to alleviate its terms. They found themselves faced, however, with an escalation of Soviet demands: Moscow's military bases were to be protected by 35,000 Soviet troops. At this point Stalin became involved in the negotiations and in response to Estonian protests he agreed to reduce the number of troops to 25,000 and also to the proviso that they would remain in the country only for the duration of the European war. Stalin also agreed to locate the proposed Soviet naval base at Paldiski rather than Tallinn and accepted that mutual assistance in the pact would apply only in cases of aggression by a great power.[14] Stalin added his own reassuring words to those of Molotov:

> Do not be afraid of these garrisons. We have assured you that the Soviet Union does not want in any way to affect Estonian sovereignty, her government, or her economic system, nor her internal life or foreign policy. We do not want to act the way Germany has in Czechoslovakia. Consequently, the Soviet troops will refrain in everything that is not in harmony with these promises.[15]

The Soviet-Estonian Pact of Mutual Assistance was signed on 28 September 1939. The text contained all the concessions extended by the Soviets to the Estonians and included the highly unusual article that it would not 'to any extent whatsoever, affect the sovereign rights of the Contracting Parties, notably, their economic system and state system'.[16]

It was the Latvians' turn next. A delegation headed by Latvia's Foreign Minister, Vilhelms Munters, arrived in Moscow on 2 October. The Latvians were presented with the same demands as the Estonians had been, and treated to a similar display of brutal frankness on the part of the Soviets. At the first meeting, on 2 October, Molotov told Munters: 'We cannot permit small states to be used against the USSR. Neutral Baltic States – that is too insecure.' Stalin said: 'I tell you frankly a division into spheres of influence has taken place ... As far as the Germans are concerned we could occupy you. But we want no abuse.'[17] The negotiations themselves followed the same pattern as those with the Estonians. Soviet insistence and threats regarding compliance with demands for a mutual assistance pact and military bases combined with reassurances about Latvian sovereignty and internal independence. As with the Estonians, Moscow was prepared to make some concessions, for example reducing the number of troops to be stationed in Latvia from 50,000 to 25,000.[18]

The Soviet-Latvian Pact of Mutual Assistance and confidential protocol was signed on 5 October. Its terms were to all intents and purposes identical with those agreed with the Estonians.[19]

The Soviet negotiations with Lithuania took a somewhat different course from those with Estonia and Latvia. There were a number of differentiating and complicating factors. Firstly, there was the question of the 'return' of Vilna (Vilnius) to Lithuania. Vilna, the ancient capital of Lithuania and part of the Tsarist empire for 120 years, had been seized in 1920 by Poland. The Poles had historic, ethnic and legal claims to the city and their occupation of it was accepted as legitimate by most of the international community. The Lithuanians, however, had never relinquished their claims and dreamt of securing the return of the city from Poland. Indeed, during the inter-war period they were supported in these claims by the Soviet Union.[20] When, therefore, the Nazi-Soviet pact was signed the Russians must have had no difficulty in agreeing with the Germans a clause in the secret protocol that recognised 'the interest of Lithuania in the Vilna area'. Nor did Moscow have any problem with the idea of transferring Vilna to Lithuania – it fell within its sphere of influence in Poland and had been occupied by Soviet troops on 18 September 1939. Vilna was a useful carrot to entice the Lithuanians into co-operation with Soviet plans for the Baltic, and its transfer to Lithuania would lend legitimacy to the Soviets' own incorporation of Western Byelorussia and Western Ukraine – which had also been 'stolen' by the Poles in 1920.

Soviet manipulation of the Vilna issue was complicated, however, by another agreement with Germany. In the secret protocol to the German-Soviet Boundary and Friendship Treaty of 28 September 1939 which placed Lithuania in the Soviet sphere of influence, Moscow had also agreed to the transfer of a strip of Lithuanian territory to Germany.[21] This commitment tended to cut across Moscow's claim that it was Lithuania's friend and benefactor. When the proposal for a ceding of territory to Germany was raised in the Soviet-Lithuanian negotiations it was furiously opposed by the Lithuanians. In the end the Soviets managed to fudge the issue and avoid meeting the German demand for Lithuanian territory, but only at the cost of antagonising the Lithuanians at the very beginning of the negotiations.[22]

A Lithuanian delegation headed by Foreign Minister Urbsys arrived in Moscow on 3 October.[23] At a meeting that evening the Soviets presented their demands: a treaty on the return of Vilna to Lithuania; a mutual assistance pact and the placing of 50,000 Soviet troops in Lithuania; and a treaty on the transfer to Germany of a strip of Lithuania.

Urbsys reacted strongly against the proposed transfer of territory to Germany and rejected the stationing of Soviet troops in Lithuania on the grounds that the country would in effect be occupied. Stalin replied that the USSR was not threatening Lithuania's independence and argued that the stationing of Soviet troops would guarantee the country. He also said that the number of troops could be reduced to 35,000.

Urbsys returned to Kaunus for consultations on 4 October. On 7 October he returned to Moscow and presented a set of counterproposals to the Soviets. There would be a mutual assistance pact but no Soviet garrisons in Lithuania. Soviet forces would enter Lithuania only in the event of an attack on the country; in the meantime various forms of military consultation and co-operation could be developed between the two states. Molotov rejected the Lithuanian proposals and told Urbsys that 'Lithuania should not forget under what conditions Europe is now living. The present war has not unfolded entirely; it is difficult to forecast its repercussions and, therefore, the Soviet Union considers its security. We do not know what can happen in the West. The Germans can turn against us, if they would win the war. The aims of England are not clear either, if Germany should lose.'[24]

The next day, 8 October, Stalin joined in the fray, insisting strongly on the establishment of Soviet military bases in Lithuania. They were 'the most precious element in the service of Lithuanian security', he told Urbsys.[25] Just as Molotov had done the day before, Stalin emphasised that there would be no Soviet interference in Lithuania's internal affairs. He even offered to curb the activities of Lithuania's communists and said that the number of Soviet troops could be reduced to 20,000.

On 10 October the two sides convened for the last time. At this meeting the Soviets presented their final, take-it-or-leave-it draft. Among its most notable points were: the combining of the Vilna transfer and mutual assistance treaties into one; joint defence of Lithuania's borders, including the stationing of 25,000 Soviet troops; and a strengthening of the provision concerning non-interference in each other's internal affairs. The Lithuanians made one final protest and then caved in. The treaty was signed at 10.00 p.m. that same evening.[26]

Thus ended the Soviet-Baltic negotiations of autumn 1939. The rapid and determined imposition by Moscow of mutual assistance treaties and Soviet military bases on the Baltic States is often presented as being the result of careful planning and orchestration. However, as we have seen, intermingled with Moscow's single-minded thrust to secure its military requirement in the region – if necessary by force – were elements of improvisation, a propensity to bargain and compromise, and a genuine concern to allay Baltic fears about the future of the countries' independence. In relation to this last point we have seen that throughout the negotiations Stalin and Molotov made plain the limit of their ambitions in the Baltic, even incorporating formal commitments to this effect in the treaty documents. There was, indeed, no limit to the commitments the Soviets were willing to give about the continuation of capitalism and the internal regimes of the Baltic States. Stalin swore on his Bolshevik word of honour that there would be no Soviet subversion of the Baltic States. He even joked to Urbsys that 'our troops will help you put down a communist insurrection should one occur in Lithuania'.[27]

A more formal commitment to non-interference in internal Baltic affairs was stated by Molotov in his speech to the Supreme Soviet on 31 October 1939:

These mutual assistance pacts in no way imply any interference by the Soviet Union in the affairs of Estonia, Latvia, or Lithuania ... On the contrary, all these pacts strictly stipulate the inviolability of the sovereignty of the signatory states and the principle of non-interference in each other's affairs. They are based on mutual respect for the political, social and economic structure of the contracting parties and are designed to strengthen the foundations for peaceful neighbourly co-operation between our peoples.[28]

Moscow's public commitment to the continued independence of the Baltic States, albeit with circumscribed foreign policies, was mirrored in the private thinking of the Soviet leadership. In a series of telegrams to Soviet legations in the Baltic States in autumn 1939 Molotov gave strict instructions that there was to be no interference in the internal affairs of the Baltic States and made it clear that there was no perspective of eventual sovietisation.[29]

On 25 October Stalin told Dimitrov, the leader of the Communist International:

> We think that in the mutual assistance pacts we have found the form which will enable us to draw a number of countries within the orbit of Soviet influence. But to accomplish this, we must show restraint: we must strictly comply with the requirements of their internal regime and sovereignty. We will not pursue their sovietization. The time will come when they'll do it for themselves.[30]

Of course, Stalin did not always speak truthfully to foreign communists, but on the face of it Soviet policy in the Baltic in autumn 1939 was to incorporate the Baltic States not into the Soviet system but into the Soviet sphere of influence. Mutual assistance pacts, military bases and the co-operation of Baltic governments was sought – and that was all. Revolution and socialism in the Baltic States achieved by indigenous political action remained a desirable ideological goal, but for the present Moscow had no interest in anything other than its stated policy of co-operation with the existing Baltic regimes on the terms laid down in the mutual assistance pacts. All this was consistent with the USSR's Baltic policy in 1939–40.[31] There was, it is true, to be a sharp turn in Soviet policy in May–June 1940 when Moscow adopted a much more radical set of aims in relation to the Baltic States. But, as we shall see, that policy shift was very much related to the circumstances of the time. It was not inscribed in Soviet strategy in the Baltic in autumn 1939, which was definitely limited in scope.

The limited, security-oriented nature of Soviet aims in the Baltic area was also apparent in Moscow's policy toward Finland. The USSR had long been concerned to secure the defence of Leningrad – less than 20 miles from the Finnish border, vulnerable to attack from that direction or through the Gulf of Finland.[32]

On 5 October 1939 Moscow invited Helsinki to send a delegation to the Soviet Union to discuss Finnish-Soviet relations and the conclusion of a mutual assistance treaty along the lines of those recently completed between the USSR and the Baltic States.[33] The Finnish delegation arrived in Moscow on the 11th and their first meeting with Stalin and Molotov was held the next day. The Soviets proposed that Finland should lease the Port of Hango to the USSR as a naval base, that the frontier with Leningrad should be adjusted to the north, and that several small islands in the Gulf of Finland should be ceded to the Soviet Union. In exchange the Russians offered territorial compensation in the Karelia region and to withdraw their objections to Finnish fortification of the Aaland Islands – an issue of longstanding dispute between the two states.[34] In the ensuing negotiations Moscow never varied from this position, although it was prepared to compromise over the details, and nothing more was heard of its initial suggestion of a mutual assistance treaty. For their part the Finns were prepared to make some adjustments in their frontier near Leningrad and to concede some islands in the Gulf of Finland, but on no account were they prepared to lease Hango to the Soviet Union – a demand which they considered an affront to their national sovereignty.[35]

Negotiations continued intermittently throughout October but the impasse was not broken. By early November negotiations had broken down completely. As the tension in Soviet-Finnish relations rose Moscow's impatience grew and the USSR prepared for war. On 29 October Voroshilov ordered the drawing up of operational plans for war with Finland.[36] In early November Molotov gave his ambassador in Sweden, Alexandra Kollantai, short shrift when she pleaded for a moderate approach in the Finnish negotiations.[37] In mid-November 1939 Stalin reportedly told the Military Council that 'we shall have to fight Finland'.[38] Around the same time Voroshilov ordered that the concentration of Soviet forces be completed by 21 November and commanders prepared to put into effect military plans regarding Finland.[39] By the end of November the tension along the Finnish-Soviet frontier had escalated into a full-scale border clash near the village of Mainila on the Karelian Isthmus. On 28 November Molotov renounced the 1932 non-aggression pact between the USSR and Finland. On 29 November Deputy Commissar for Foreign Affairs Potemkin announced diplomatic relations with Finland were at an end. On 30 November the war began.[40]

According to the Soviets war broke out as a result of 'armed provocations' by the Finns. According to the Finns the Red Army started the war by an unprovoked invasion. All the evidence points to the Finnish version of events being true.[41] More importantly, if Khrushchev's memoirs are to be believed, the Soviet leadership did not anticipate war with Finland over its demands concerning the security of Leningrad. They appear to have believed that the Finns would back down in the face of a threat of military action or, at worst, surrender when the first shots were fired.[42] If this is what they believed, they blundered badly. The Finnish-Soviet war lasted more than three months. Soviet expectations of a quick and easy victory were confounded by difficult terrain, military incompetence and a spirited and popular Finnish defence. The Red Army emerged from the war with its reputation badly battered and tens of thousands of dead and wounded.[43]

The diplomatic cost of the war was high too – the humiliation of expulsion from the League of Nations for aggression; a 'moral embargo' by the United States on the shipment of war-related goods to the Soviet Union; the withdrawal of the Soviet ambassador from Italy following popular anti-Soviet manifestations; almost universal condemnation of the Soviet action; and the dispatch from a number of countries of volunteers to fight on the side of the Finns. But most important was the impact of the war on Anglo-Soviet and Franco-Soviet relations. As the Winter War progressed, Soviet relations with the western powers were heading for a gigantic crisis. In London and Paris plans were being drawn up to dispatch an allied expeditionary force to help the Finns and bomb the Baku oil fields. The former action would almost certainly have led to the spread of the war to the whole of Scandinavia as the Germans would have intervened to protect their strategic interests (primarily connected to Sweden's iron ore deposits) from Anglo-French encroachments. What had begun as almost a 'policing' operation to improve the defence of Leningrad increasingly threatened to drag the Soviet Union into full-scale involvement in the European war.

It is against this background of military miscalculation and diplomatic crisis that Moscow's reception of peace overtures from Finland has to be viewed.

The first Finnish peace overture was made on 4 December 1939 via the Swedish envoy in Moscow. Molotov rebuffed this approach on the curious grounds that the USSR no longer recognised the Helsinki government and would only deal with the 'People's Government of Finland'.[44] The 'People's Government of Finland' was headed by Otto Kuusinen, a leading Finnish communist and Comintern leader. It was purely of Soviet creation and its only effective acts were to conclude a mutual assistance treaty with the USSR and to accept Moscow's demands concerning the safety of Leningrad in exchange for 70,000 square kilometres of Soviet Karelia.[45]

It is tempting to pass over the Kuusinen government as a mere propaganda ploy. However, this episode is much more interesting than that, for the Kuusinen government is a fascinating and instructive example of the complex role of ideology in Soviet foreign policy.

Any ideology – any system of political belief – only impacts on policy and action in so far as it figures in the process of reasoning leading to decision. Sometimes ideology has a presence in reasoning/decision-making, sometimes it does not. Hence in much of this book the ideology of communism/Marxism-Leninism has not featured very prominently except in its role of providing a backdrop for a series of subjective and experiential attitudes – fears, suspicions, hostilities – concerning the outside world. In the case of the war with Finland the formal system of belief was much more important. The Kuusinen government embodied a series of beliefs about the spreading of socialism, the class nature of Finnish society and the expected response of the Finnish working class to a Soviet attack. Moscow believed, it seems, that the Red Army's invasion of Finland would be hailed by a popular uprising against the Helsinki government. Moscow believed its own propaganda.[46] Moreover, to an extent Moscow could do no other. For ideologies are not only beliefs that exist in people's heads, but public discourses – political languages through which individuals communicate with each other and discuss and decide on action. The ideology of Soviet communism was a discourse structured around concepts that, among other things, denoted the USSR as an international agent of class liberation. Foreign policy action was publicly debated and decided upon in these terms. The invasion of Finland, we may surmise, was an act decided upon in a discourse which had the effect of transforming a limited security action into an act of socialist liberation. As we shall see, a similar process came to operate in the case of the Baltic States in summer 1940 – and was to result in their sovietisation and incorporation into the USSR.

Another way of viewing the role of ideology in Soviet policy towards Finland is in terms of the difference between the intention behind an action and the intentions that become embodied in the implementation of the action. The USSR initiated the attack on Finland with the aim of securing a better defensive position around Leningrad. In deciding upon and implementing that policy, however, the Soviets carried with them a set of ideological baggage – beliefs and discourse – which signified that their invasion of Finland would be supported by the Finnish people and would lead to the overthrow of the 'bourgeois' government in Helsinki and its replacement by the People's Government. Such illusions quickly ran up against the reality of military and political failure. The Finnish people rallied to Helsinki not Moscow and waged an effective defence against Soviet attack. Moscow quickly ditched its ideological baggage and reverted to the original, limited security-based intentions and action. Ideology is a set of beliefs and a resource of communicative action that coexists with others, including ideas and discourses of expediency and realpolitik.[47]

With the return to more straightforward calculations of possible gains and losses, the 'People's Government' quickly disappeared from view and, with the diplomatic and political pressure growing, by early 1940 Moscow was prepared to enter into serious peace negotiations with the Finns. Throughout January and February 1940 unofficial negotiations under the auspices of the Swedish government were conducted in Stockholm with Alexandra Kollontai.[48] The breakthrough came when the Finns, faced with a deteriorating military situation and fearful, too, of being dragged into the European war, conceded the essential Soviet demands of a naval base on Hango and a substantial adjustment of the Finnish-Leningrad border. Finnish negotiators arrived in Moscow in early March. The peace treaty was signed on 12 March 1940.[49]

Given that Moscow was by this time in a position to occupy the whole of their country, the Finns didn't get a bad deal. They retained their sovereignty and independence and the territorial changes forced by the Soviets were not much greater than those Moscow had originally demanded in October 1939. The calculation behind Moscow's relative generosity is summed up by a dispatch from Maisky on 13 March 1940:

> Today I listened to Chamberlain informing Parliament about the peace treaty signed by the USSR and Finland and got further evidence of how great the danger had been of Britain and France intervening on the side of Finland ... More than ever before it became clear that the peace was signed opportunely.[50]

Although the main thrust of the Soviet security drive of 1939–40 was in the Baltic area, Moscow also undertook some important diplomatic initiatives in the Balkans. These efforts focused on relations with two states: Turkey and Bulgaria. Moscow's strategy here was to prevent either state aligning itself in the European war and, ideally, to forge political alliances of its own with Sofia and Ankara. Such a strategy represented a complete break with the policy Moscow had pursued before the pact with Nazi Germany. In the pre-pact period the aim had been to integrate Bulgaria and Turkey into an anti-German collective security bloc led by Great Britain, France and the USSR. With the abandonment of the collective security project in August 1939 Soviet policy toward Turkey and Bulgaria changed dramatically. Before the Nazi-Soviet pact Moscow's policy was some kind of Black Sea pact directed against Germany.[51] After the pact the aim was a Moscow-led, neutral Balkan bloc directed as much against Britain and France as Germany.

The Soviet about turn in policy is particularly striking in the case of Turkey. In early August 1939 Moscow had revived the idea of a Soviet-Turkish mutual assistance pact linked to a Soviet-western triple alliance and to security alliances between Turkey and Britain and France. The Turks responded positively and over the next few weeks there were numerous contacts between Moscow and Ankara over this issue.[52] In early September 1939, however, signals of a change in Soviet policy began emanating from Moscow.[53] The nature of this change in policy is evident from Soviet contacts with the Germans during this period. On 2 September 1939 Molotov told Schulenburg that, in line with German expectations, the USSR would work for the permanent neutrality of Turkey in the war. On 5 September Schulenburg saw Molotov again and urged him to secure closure of the Dardanelles. At a further meeting, on 17 September, Stalin informed Schulenburg that any Soviet-Turkish mutual assistance pact would include a clause debarring Soviet involvement in a war with Germany and that the overall objective of such a pact would be Turkish neutrality, including the closure of the Straits to foreign warships.[54]

Saracoglu, the Turkish Foreign Minister, arrived in Moscow on 25 September.[55] During his three-week stay he had only two meetings with Stalin and Molotov, on 1 and 16 October – a sign that the Soviet-Turkish mutual assistance pact that he had come to negotiate was not at the top of Moscow's list of priorities. Sure enough, at the first meeting with Saracoglu, Stalin and Molotov made it quite clear that they were not so much interested in a Soviet-Turkish mutual assistance agreement as in averting Turkish security pacts with Britain and France. Saracoglu was willing to conclude a mutual assistance treaty with the USSR but would not concede Moscow's demand that the proposed Turkish pact with Britain and France should be dropped.[56] Nor was Ankara prepared to close the Straits, despite Molotov's insistence at the 16 October meeting that a protocol on closing the Dardanelles 'was an essential pre-condition of the conclusion of a mutual assistance pact' and that 'without this protocol the pact was impossible, it loses meaning if we are unable to agree on this question.'[57] In the face of such differences the negotiations broke down. As Molotov told Schulenburg on 17 October the negotiations had achieved no 'definite results'.[58] For his part Saracoglu returned home to sign, in the face of further Russian protests, a mutual assistance pact with Britain and France on 19 October, although the agreement did preclude Turkey's involvement in war against the Soviet Union.[59]

Any prospect of a Moscow-led, neutral Balkan bloc died with the collapse of the Soviet-Turkish negotiations, but Moscow retained hopes of drawing Bulgaria into the Soviet orbit.

Indispensable to any Soviet-Bulgarian rapprochement was Moscow's recognition of Bulgarian territorial claims on Romania. Before the Nazi-Soviet pact Moscow had, in the interests of the wider collective security front, opposed Bulgarian revisionism. As early as 25 August, however, Moscow was expressing support for the return of South Dobroudja (which Bulgaria had been forced to cede to Romania under the 1919 Neuilly Treaty).[60] This conciliatory gesture was followed, in September, by a favourable response to Bulgaria's declaration of neutrality.[61]

On 20 September Molotov proposed to the Bulgarian ambassador a mutual assistance pact between the two states. This was raised again by Moscow at the end of September during the course of a visit by the chief of the Bulgarian Air Force.[62] Sofia rejected these approaches on 16 October,[63] but Moscow continued to pursue the matter. A. I. Lavrentiev, head of the Narkomindel's East European section, together with a large staff, was dispatched to Bulgaria as ambassador.[64] In a meeting with the Bulgarian Prime Minister on 3 November Lavrentiev quizzed him about the rejection of the Soviet offer. In reply, Kyoseivanov stressed that it was not clear just what support the Soviet Union could offer Bulgaria in the event of war.[65] In response, on 12 November Molotov instructed Lavrentiev to secretly tell Sofia that 'if the Bulgarians find themselves in any trouble they can count on the Soviet Union not abandoning them and rendering Bulgaria effective assistance, if they so desired'.[66] Molotov's message was delivered to Kyoseivanov on 14 November, who responded that Bulgaria would like to sign a political agreement with the USSR but in the present tense atmosphere such a move would arouse suspicion in the Balkans. However, if the situation changed Bulgaria would quickly move to strengthen political ties with the Soviet Union.[67] Thus encouraged, Moscow's courtship of Bulgaria was to continue into 1940 and beyond.

The failure of Soviet diplomacy to materially strengthen the security of the USSR's south-western borders contrasts sharply with the successes achieved by military threats and force of arms in

Poland, Finland and the Baltic States. Still, the overall balance sheet six months after the great turn in Soviet foreign policy inaugurated by the pact with Nazi Germany was undoubtedly positive. As Molotov stated in his report to the Supreme Soviet on 31 March 1940 'as regards safeguarding the security of our country we have achieved no mean success'.

Molotov made two other statements of interest in this speech. In relation to the mutual assistance pacts with the Baltic States he said: 'Our experience during the six months that have elapsed since these pacts were concluded has enabled us to reach very definite positive conclusions concerning these treaties. ... The pacts with Estonia, Latvia and Lithuania are being carried out in a satisfactory manner and this creates premises for a further improvement in relations between the Soviet and these countries.' In relation to Romania, Molotov noted the continuing dispute about Bessarabia (a disputed Tsarist province reoccupied by the Romanians in 1918) but stated that 'we have never raised the question of recovering Bessarabia by military means. Hence there are no grounds for any deterioration in Soviet-Romanian relations.'[68]

Within a few weeks of these statements Moscow had executed a turn in policy which completely contradicted both of them. In mid-June 1940 Molotov delivered ultimatums to each of the Baltic States demanding the formation of new, pro-Soviet governments and acquiescence in Soviet military occupation. This was followed in rapid succession by socio-economic socialisation, the establishment of Soviet-style political systems and, finally, formal incorporation into the USSR. Contrary to all previous Soviet statements and promises the USSR in summer 1940 annexed the Baltic States.

At the end of June 1940 the USSR also delivered an ultimatum to Romania, demanding – under threat of force – the return of Bessarabia and, for good measure, North Bukovina as well – a territory with a Ukrainian population, but one to which the Soviets had never laid claim before.

The key to this series of Soviet annexations was not hard to find. In April 1940 the Germans launched their invasion of Western Europe. By June 1940 the Germans had conquered Norway, Denmark, Holland and Belgium, and France was on the verge of defeat. These stunning military successes spurred the

Russians to take action to shore up their military-political position in Eastern Europe.

In the case of Estonia, Latvia and Lithuania Soviet moves to bolt the door to German expansionism had an additional spur: Moscow's suspicion that there was a conspiracy to transform the 'Baltic Entente' of the three countries into an anti-Soviet military alliance. Moscow was determined to quash this perceived conspiracy. Hence the ultimatums to the three countries on 14–16 June 1940 demanding the installation of pro-Soviet governments and the occupation of major population centres by the Red Army. Within hours of the ultimatums the Soviet occupation forces had moved in and shortly after that Moscow dispatched special emissaries to each of the Baltic States with a brief to supervise the setting up of new, pro-Soviet regimes. New governments, composed mainly of left-wing democrats – were selected, sanctioned and installed in the three countries in the period 18–22 June.

Within a few days of its ultimatums Moscow had achieved its foreign policy objectives in the Baltic States. At this point, however, a new dynamic began to envelop the region. The Soviet overthrow of the unpopular authoritarian regimes of the Baltic States and Moscow's imposition of leftist governments sparked off internal political upheavals in all three countries. These political upheavals convinced Moscow's special emissaries and other Soviet representatives on the ground that a socialist revolution was sweeping the Baltic States. In their reports home they painted a picture of mass demonstrations against the old regimes, of enthusiastic welcomes to the 'liberators' of the Red Army, of paeans of praise for Stalin and other Soviet leaders, of popular agitation for sovietisation, and of working-class demands for Estonia, Latvia and Lithuania to become republics of the USSR.[69] Unlike the People's Government of Finland those installed by Soviet military action in the Baltic States matched the revolutionary dreams of the old Bolsheviks in Moscow.

Moscow embraced what was seen to be the pro-Soviet radical mood and movement in the Baltic States and by early July 1940 had decided on their incorporation into the USSR. Elections to new people's assemblies were called. These took place on 14–15 July – the only candidates allowed being those who supported the new Baltic governments and who stood under the auspices of communist-led popular alliances of the left. The people's assemblies, packed with communists and their allies, met a week later, passed resolutions on wholesale social and economic socialisation, and requested admission to the USSR. In early August the Supreme Soviet voted to admit Estonia, Latvia and Lithuania to the Union.[70]

This turn of events in the Baltic was, to say the least, extraordinary. It illustrates dramatically the role of external circumstances, forces and influences in the making of Soviet foreign policy. The annexation of Estonia, Latvia and Lithuania that summer was the combined result of Hitler's military successes, Moscow's perception that there was an inter-Baltic conspiracy directed against its interests, the activities of a militant alliance of workers, peasants and intellectuals, and leftist fantasies that a pro-Soviet revolution was sweeping the region. It was certainly not the simple case of planned and controlled Soviet expansionism depicted by many historians.

The annexation of Bessarabia and North Bukovina, on the other hand, was a much simpler affair. On 23 June Molotov told Schulenburg that the Soviet Union intended to demand the return of Bessarabia and to use force if the Romanians refused. He also announced to the Germans that the Soviet claim now included Bukovina too. Berlin urged a peaceful negotiation of the issue, which Moscow refused. But in deference to German pressure the Soviets did agree to restrict their claim to the northern part of Bukovina. The Soviet ultimatum to Romania was delivered on 26 June and, on German advice, was accepted by Bucharest two days later.[71]

The occupation of Bessarabia and North Bukovina effected a westward shift in the Soviet defensive line in south-eastern Europe. To that extent it was a straightforward security move in response to the German conquest of Western Europe, one probably inspired by the opportunity provided by the military defeat of the Anglo-French military coalition that in April 1939 had issued a guarantee of Romania's independence. But there was also a more complex dimension of this Soviet expansionist move. The Soviet rush into Romania was intimately bound up with Moscow's calculation that the war was about to end and that the moment was ripe for a new spheres of influence agreement with Germany, this time in the Balkans. Contrary to expectations, however, Moscow's pursuit of this objective resulted not in the further development of the Nazi-Soviet alliance but the beginning of a fateful crisis in Soviet-German relations which was to end in war.

8 Crisis and Conflict, 1940–1941

Under the aegis of the Nazi-Soviet pact the USSR gained time, space and resources in which to prepare for war. But there were two problems with this strategy. The first was that Russia was not the sole beneficiary of the pact. Nazi Germany also gained time, space and resources in which to prepare for war – against Russia. Moscow hoped that the phoney war in the west would not last and that eventually Germany would be drawn into a costly war of attrition with Britain and France. That hope was destroyed by the German blitzkrieg in Western Europe. When France fell in June 1940 Soviet Russia found itself in a position more vulnerable to attack than it had been in 1939. The Russians now faced a Germany with its military might unimpaired and with the combined resources of much of continental Europe at its disposal. Britain, led now by Churchill, seemed determined to fight on but its capacity to resist either Hitler or the siren voices of appeasement at home calling for peace seemed doubtful.

The second problem was that Russia's freedom to manoeuvre and expand in Eastern Europe whilst at the same time maintaining the Nazi-Soviet détente depended in the last resort on German gratuity. The Russo-German spheres of influence agreements were indispensable to Moscow's ability to pursue a policy of expansion whilst at the same time avoiding a clash with Germany over Eastern Europe. A breakdown of the spheres of influence relationship threatened both détente with Germany and the USSR's freedom to manoeuvre freely along its western borders.

The Soviets attempted to resolve the dilemmas thrown up by these two problems by a number of measures. First, by stepping up the tempo of domestic preparations for war. In mid-1940 Moscow took a number of decisions designed to increase Soviet military capacity and to counter the new power and position of Germany in Europe.[1] Second, by enhancing the Soviet defensive position along the USSR's western borderlands. Hence the takeover of the Baltic States and the move into Romania.[2] Thirdly, and this was the critical manoeuvre on which the future of Soviet-German relations rested, Moscow attempted to extend its spheres of influence agreements with Berlin to the Balkans.

Far from resolving Moscow's difficulties, however, the various Soviet manoeuvres actually deepened them. The problem was that the Germans viewed the Soviet moves in the Baltic States, into Romania and the build-up of the Red Army in its new forward positions as a threat. In response they acted to protect their position from what they saw as the growing Soviet menace in the east. In particular, they refused to countenance any further extension of Soviet power and influence in Eastern Europe, offering the Russians instead a junior partnership in their project of a German Europe and an Axis-dominated world.[3] Moscow, however, was only interested in an alliance with Germany on its own terms. The result of all this was the onset of a crisis in Soviet-German relations as Moscow and Berlin struggled for position in the Balkans.

The first sign that Moscow was interested in a new spheres of influence agreement with Germany came on 4 June when Molotov asked Schulenburg about reports from Rome that Italian entry into the war would pave the way for a tripartite agreement on the Balkans. The reply from Berlin ten days later coldly rebuffed the Soviet overture.[4] Moscow did not give up its design for a deal in the Balkans – an inclination that may have been reinforced by intelligence reports that Germany and Italy were intent on excluding Soviet influence from the area.[5] Instead, Moscow turned its attentions to Italy, which had entered the war on 10 June.

On 13 June Molotov had a friendly conversation with the new Italian ambassador, Rosso. In this, and during a further discussion on 20 June, Molotov probed Italian policy toward south-eastern Europe, particularly the content of any exchanges or agreement with Germany.[6] Rosso summarised his discussions with Molotov as follows:

> Molotov made it very clear that the USSR is very much interested in and wants to become involved in the Balkans. However, he also let me know that she had no pretensions of exercising a predominant influence, least of all an exclusive one. Moreover, it is my feeling that he wants to reach agreement with Italy and Germany on the problems of the Danubian-Balkan Basin, or, at the very least, participate in eventual Italo-German consultations involving that part of Europe.[7]

On 22 June the Italians and Soviets had a further positive discussion, this time in Rome between Foreign Minister Ciano and the Soviet ambassador.[8] What the Russians concluded from these talks became evident three days later when Molotov made a formal declaration to Rosso which, in effect, proposed a division of the Balkans into Soviet and Italo-German spheres of influence:

> The USSR has no claims with regard to Hungary. Our relations with Hungary are normal. The USSR considers that there is a basis for Hungary's claims against Romania.
>
> With Bulgaria the USSR's relations are those of good neighbourliness. The basis exists for them to become closer. There is a basis for Bulgaria's claims against Romania, and also against Greece.
>
> The fundamental claims of the USSR with respect to Romania are known. The USSR would like to obtain from Romania what belongs by right to the Soviet Union, without the application of force, but that will become necessary if Romania proves intransigent.
>
> Regarding other territories of Romania, the USSR is mindful of the interests of Italy and Germany and is prepared to come to an understanding with them on this question.
>
> Turkey arouses mistrust, given the unfriendly attitude she has displayed towards the USSR (and not the USSR alone) by the conclusion of a pact with Britain and France.
>
> This mistrust is strengthened because of Turkey's tendency to dictate her own terms to the USSR about the Black Sea, claiming that she is the sole mistress of the Straits, and also because of the habit she has made of threatening the Soviet Union in the areas south-east of Batum.
>
> As to the other regions of Turkey, the USSR takes account of the interests of Italy, and hence too of those of Germany, and is ready to come to an agreement with them on this question.
>
> As to the Mediterranean, the USSR considers it entirely just that Italy should hold a position of pre-eminence in that sea. And here the USSR hopes that Italy will take account of the interests of the USSR as the principal Power in the Black Sea.[9]

Having been spurned by the Germans, the Soviets had evidently decided to initiate negotiations for a tripartite accord through the more amenable Italians. Perhaps they also perceived some tactical advantage from dealing with Rome – such as the possibility of separate accord or of a joint approach to Berlin, or the sowing of dissension in the Axis camp. But they could have been under no illusion that a major division of the Balkans could take place without the agreement of Berlin.[10]

A territorial and political squeeze on Romania was at the heart of the Soviet prospectus for the Balkans. Hence the rush into Bessarabia at the end of June 1940 – in advance of any general deal that might be concocted between Moscow, Berlin and Rome or, in the worst case scenario, of any agreement that might already have been arrived at by Rome and Berlin alone. This was also why the Soviets supported Hungary's claims on Transylvania and Bulgaria's on Dobroudja – both parts of Romania.[11]

Moscow's next move was a proposal to Italy to re-establish trade relations on a 'new basis'. At a meeting with Rosso on 27 July Mikoyan made it clear that this new basis consisted of a 'clarification of political relations' together with a 'political accord' similar to the Soviet-German treaties of 1939.[12]

Despite Rosso's enthusiasm for such a deal, Rome was not so keen. Neither, more importantly, were the Germans. They too supported Hungarian and Bulgarian territorial claims, but with the aim of subordinating Romania to their strategic purpose. In Vienna on 31 August Germany and Italy arbitrated the Hungarian-Romanian dispute, awarding Transylvania to Hungary. Simultaneously the two states guaranteed the territorial integrity of what would be left of Romania after the settlement of pending Bulgarian claims to Dobroudja.[13] In a single move Hitler had crushed Soviet hopes of a spheres of influence agreement in the Balkans. Moreover:

> This guarantee put the key positions in South-East Europe into Hitler's hands; for even within her new frontiers, Romania still extended in an unbroken belt from the eastern frontier of Hungary to the west coast of the Black Sea in Northern [Dobroudja]; and the establishment of Germany's hegemony over Romania within these frontiers far more than cancelled the advantage that Russia had gained by acquiring a narrow glacis in Bessarabia and Northern Bukovina. It was in vain that Russia had recovered her frontage along the north bank of the

northernmost Danube Delta. She was still insulated from Bulgaria by a strip of Romanian territory in Northern [Dobroudja] that was now covered by a German guarantee, and this meant that the whole of South-East Europe, south-west of the line of the Carpathian range and the River Pruth could now be dominated by Germany and Italy without the Soviet Union being able to interfere.[14]

When informed by the Germans of the details of the Vienna Award, the Russians claimed it was in violation of article 3 of the non-aggression pact which provided for consultation on problems affecting their common interests. A long wrangle followed about the interpretation of the relevant article and alleged violations of it by both sides. In the course of this exchange the Soviet side made clear that its main objection to the Vienna Award concerned the guarantee of Romania's territorial integrity which was 'primarily directed against the USSR'.[15]

The Vienna Award presaged a sharp deterioration in Soviet-German relations which finally came to a head at a conference between Molotov, Hitler and Ribbentrop in November 1940. This encounter in Berlin was prefaced by a number of worrying developments from Moscow's point of view. In September 1940 a German military mission arrived in Romania. The Soviet embassy in Bucharest reported to Moscow:

The arrival of German troops in Romania signifies Romania's final political and economic subordination to Germany and further German penetration of the Balkans. The gaining of the foothold by the Germans on the Black Sea and the building of air bases are a direct threat to the interests of the Soviet Union.[16]

To add to the Soviets' problems, German military units appeared on Finnish soil on 22 September. Five days later Germany, Italy and Japan signed the Tripartite Pact under which they pledged to assist one another should they be attacked by a power then not involved in the war. Romanian and Hungarian affiliation to the pact was a predictable sequel. Then, on 28 October, Italy invaded Greece.

Against this background of rising tension, Ribbentrop invited Molotov to Berlin:

I should like to state that in the opinion of the Führer ... it appears to be the historic mission of the four powers – the Soviet Union, Italy, Japan and Germany – to adopt a long-range policy and to direct the future development of their peoples in the right channels by delimitation of their interests for the ages.[17]

After what seems to have been much discussion the Soviet leadership accepted the invitation.[18] Stalin, however, struck a more cautious note than Ribbentrop in his reply:

I agree with you that a further improvement in relations between our countries is entirely possible on the permanent basis of a long-range delimitation of mutual interests ... As to joint deliberation on some issues with Japanese and Italian participation, I am of the opinion that this question would have to be submitted to a previous examination.[19]

Stalin's cautious response set a pattern for the Soviet stance throughout the forthcoming negotiations. General A. M. Vasilevsky, a member of the Soviet delegation, recalled that on the way to Germany 'it became clear that the Berlin talks would be of a purely political nature and that the trip's basic purpose was connected with the Soviet Government's desire to define Hitler's intentions further and help hold off German aggression for as long as possible.'[20]

Some confirmation of Vasilevsky's account of Soviet aims can be found in one of Molotov's telegrams to Stalin from Berlin:

Our preliminary discussion in Moscow saw in a correct light the questions which I would run into here. For the time being I am trying to obtain information and to feel out the partners. Their responses in the talks were not always clear and demand further clarification. Hitler's biggest interest is in negotiating and having a stronger friendship with the USSR in regard to spheres of influence.[21]

This report by Molotov also indicates, however, that there was more to the Soviet purpose in Berlin than just sounding out Hitler's intentions. Molotov went to Berlin in order to begin negotiations about a new Soviet-German agreement. This agreement would have to be on Soviet terms, and it is doubtful that Moscow had more than a slim hope that this would be the outcome of the talks. Nevertheless, the negotiation of an agreement was what Moscow was interested in. As Molotov made clear in his speech to the Supreme Soviet on 1 August 1940 the continuation of the détente with Germany remained central to Soviet foreign strategy:

> The first year of the European war is drawing to a close but the end is not yet in sight. It is more probable that we are now approaching a new stage in which the war ... will become more intense ... Far from reducing the significance of the Soviet-German non-aggression pact, events in Europe have, on the contrary, emphasised the importance of its existence and further development.[22]

Molotov arrived in Berlin on 12 November. Talks with Hitler and Ribbentrop began on the same day and continued until 14 November when Molotov departed for Moscow. Reading both the German record of these discussions and the telegrams exchanged between Molotov and Stalin while they were in progress it is evident that the Soviet aim was a new spheres of influence agreement with Germany.[23] The most important terms of this new Nazi-Soviet pact would be:

1. The withdrawal of the German military presence from Finland, i.e. confirmation that Finland still fell within the Soviet sphere of influence (as agreed on 23 August 1939).
2. The placing of Bulgaria in a Soviet sphere of influence in the Balkans – in the form of a Soviet guarantee to Bulgaria and the establishment of Soviet military bases in that country.
3. An understanding regarding Turkey that would guarantee Soviet security in the Black Sea and control of the Straits.

This is the kind of agreement the Soviets wanted. Hitler and Ribbentrop, however, refused to enter into any negotiations along these lines. They refused, in fact, to make any concessions on the points that interested Moscow. What they offered was (a) Soviet participation in the tripartite pact; (b) Soviet acceptance (in effect) of German hegemony in Europe, including Eastern Europe; and (c) Russian expansion in a direction that would precipitate a Soviet clash with Britain (i.e. towards India). As Ribbentrop put it to Molotov: 'the decisive question was whether the Soviet Union was prepared ... to co-operate ... in the great liquidation of the British Empire'.[24] Molotov was having none of this, however, and his exchanges with Hitler and Ribbentrop degenerated into the diplomatic equivalent of blazing rows.

According to the Soviet diplomat Valentin Berezhkov, who acted as an interpreter at the talks, after the first day Moscow sent a message to Berlin with instructions for the rest of the negotiations:

> The Soviet Government categorically declined Hitler's attempt to involve us in discussions about the 'division of British property'. The instructions again stressed that we should press the German Government for explanations connected with matters of European security and questions which touched directly on the interests of the Soviet Union.[25]

Such a clearcut message has yet to be published,[26] but Berezhkov's recollection is an accurate reflection of the Soviet stance in the negotiations once it became clear that it would not be possible to arrive at an acceptable spheres of influence agreement with the Germans. As a result, Molotov left Berlin with the talks at a complete impasse.

Back in Moscow, Molotov and Stalin had to consider their response to the German draft of a four-power pact between Germany, Italy, Japan and the USSR. In essence the German draft pledged the four powers to mutual non-aggression and political and economic co-operation and delineated their respective spheres of influence and the direction of their territorial aspirations.[27] Moscow's response to this proposal came on 25 November when Molotov told Schulenburg that he was prepared to accept the German draft of a four-power pact on the following conditions:

1. The withdrawal of German troops from Finland.
2. A Soviet-Bulgarian mutual assistance pact (including the establishment of Soviet military bases) which would guarantee the security of the Straits.

3. Recognition that the area south of Batum and Baku in the general direction of the Persian Gulf was the centre of Soviet aspirations (as opposed to India and the Indian Ocean, proposed in the German draft).
4. An agreement with Turkey that would provide for Soviet army and navy bases on the Bosporus and the Dardanelles (as opposed to just a revision of the Montreux Treaty which would close the Straits to all foreign warships apart from those of the Black Sea powers).
5. Japanese renunciation of rights to coal and oil concessions in North Sakhalin.[28]

Assessing this Soviet counter-proposal, John Erickson has commented:

> Stalin's response ... was in every sense a test of Hitler's intentions: the Soviet terms for joining a four power pact amounted to giving Hitler full freedom in the west only at the price of foreclosing his option to wage a successful war against the Soviet Union.[29]

One should also note the significance of two specific differences between the German and Soviet drafts. The first concerned the German draft's designation of India as the direction of the USSR's territorial aspirations. The Soviets changed this to the Persian Gulf. The German proposal set up a collision course between British and Soviet interests. Moscow's amendment designated an area (particularly Iran) where the Germans were seeking to extend their influence.[30]

The second difference of note between the Soviet and German drafts concerned Turkey. In a circular to Soviet embassies on his Berlin trip Molotov commented:

> The discussions revealed that the Germans want to appropriate Turkey under the guise of guaranteeing her security in the manner of Romania and cajole us with the promise of revising the Montreux Convention in our favour and the offer of helping us in this matter. We did not consent to this because we think that, firstly, Turkey must remain independent and, secondly, the Straits regime can be improved through negotiations with Turkey and not behind her back.[31]

Moscow's stand on these two issues indicated a willingness to resist German expansionism in areas considered vital to Soviet security – at least at the negotiating table. Whether or not Moscow's strong words would translate into action remained to be seen.

Given the unlikelihood of a positive German response to Soviet proposals,[32] Moscow decided to take unilateral action to defend its interests. The most important decision was to resist the German march in the Balkans by reviving the project of drawing Bulgaria into the Soviet orbit. A delegation headed by A. A. Sobolev, General Secretary of the Narkomindel, was despatched to Sofia. On 25 November Sobolev, in a meeting with King Boris, renewed the proposal of a Soviet-Bulgarian mutual assistance pact.[33] Sobolev emphasised the importance of a mutual assistance pact as opposed to a unilateral Soviet guarantee and proposed that the USSR be granted naval and air bases in Bulgaria. Hand in hand with this diplomatic initiative went a Comintern-inspired campaign in Bulgaria in support of an alliance with Soviet Russia.[34]

This combined offensive produced no results. On 30 November the Bulgarians told the Soviet ambassador of the decision to decline the offer of a mutual assistance pact. Moscow did not give up hope, however, and the Comintern campaign inside Bulgaria continued.[35]

Soviet resistance to the Germans in the Balkans extended to Yugoslavia as well. Yugoslavia entered the picture for the first time in April 1940 with the commencement of a series of trade discussions. By May a number of bilateral economic agreements had been signed.[36] Significantly, the USSR initially stressed the purely economic content of discussions with Belgrade and on 10 May issued a denial that Soviet aid had been promised in the event of an attack on Yugoslavia.[37] Subsequently, however, Lavrentiev was sent to Belgrade on a special mission and by the end of June diplomatic relations had been established. It is reported that the Soviets gave Gavrilovic, the new Yugoslav ambassador in Moscow, the impression they would give Yugoslavia as much support as possible against Germany.[38]

In the autumn, Soviet political overtures to Yugoslavia shifted into a higher gear. On 17 October Moscow instructed its Belgrade embassy to inform the Yugoslav government that the Soviet Union 'shows understanding for Yugoslavia and for the struggle of the

Yugoslav people for their political and economic independence'. On 5 November Vyshinsky told Gavrilovic that 'the interests of the USSR coincide with the interests of all Balkan states, with the interest of Yugoslavia in particular'.[39] As in Bulgaria, Soviet diplomatic gestures were buttressed by an internal Yugoslav communist campaign for rapprochement with the USSR.[40]

Soviet overtures to Yugoslavia gained further momentum as the war in Greece developed. In November the first British military units arrived on the Greek mainland. Italian military setbacks made German intervention inevitable. Taking its cue from these events, the Soviet embassy in Belgrade counselled Moscow that it:

> can and should oppose the shift of the flames of war to this part of Europe. But the success of Soviet actions presupposes active Bulgarian and Yugoslav opposition to British and German intentions to move the war to the Balkans. Only sincere rapprochement by these countries can give the Soviet Government effective instruments for preserving peace in the Balkans.[41]

On 7 February 1941 the Soviet ambassador in Belgrade informed the Yugoslavs that the USSR 'stands for peace in the Balkans'.[42] But would the Bulgarians and Yugoslavs resist Germany? In the case of Bulgaria, the answer was soon apparent. In early January there were reports that Bulgaria had agreed in principle to adhere to the Tripartite Pact and that German troops would be allowed into the country.[43]

On 13 January 1914 Tass issued a statement denying Soviet consent to the passage of German troops through Bulgaria.[44] Four days later the Soviet ambassador in Berlin handed the Germans a note protesting against any occupation of Bulgaria by foreign powers:

> The Soviet Government has on several occasions stated to the German Government that it considers the region of Bulgaria … to be a security zone of the USSR and therefore it cannot remain indifferent to events which threaten the security interests of the USSR. In view of all this, the Soviet Government deems it its duty to give warning that it will consider the appearance of any foreign armed forces in the region of Bulgaria … to be a violation of the security interests of the USSR.[45]

On 28 February Bulgaria informed the Soviet government that it intended to adhere to the Tripartite Pact. The next day Lavrentiev was told that Bulgaria had agreed to allow German troops in.[46] Soviet protests at this action were extremely muted. 'The German Government must understand' stated the Soviet démarche, 'that it cannot count on support from the USSR for its acts in Bulgaria.' A similarly restrained protest was delivered to the Bulgarians on 3 March.[47] Moscow, it seemed, had given up in Bulgaria and decided it had no recourse except the niceties of formal diplomatic protest.

The fall of Bulgaria was the turning point in the Soviet-German contest in the Balkans. With its powerful domestic movement in favour of friendship with the Soviet Union, Bulgaria had represented Moscow's best hope of stemming the German tide in the Balkans. Yugoslavia, the last independent state in the whole of Eastern Europe, remained. But Moscow saw the anti-German forces in Yugoslavia as far weaker than those in Bulgaria. Moscow must have been surprised, therefore, when Yugoslavia's 25 March decision to join the Axis was overturned two days later by a popular-backed coup. But Moscow did respond quickly. On 30 March the Soviet chargé d'affaires in Belgrade reported that the Yugoslavs were asking for war materials and suggesting a military and political alliance with the USSR.[48] Moscow responded with urgent telegrams arranging for the immediate flight of a Yugoslav delegation to the Soviet capital for face-to-face negotiations. Moscow also indicated strong support for the Yugoslav stand against Germany.[49]

In the event, Moscow would countenance only a friendship and non-aggression treaty with Yugoslavia – not a military alliance, which would 'disturb' its relations with the Germans.[50] The importance of the latter factor in Soviet calculations is indicated by the fact that on 4 April Molotov took the trouble to inform Schulenburg about the forthcoming treaty, reassuring the ambassador that the agreement was aimed only at ensuring peace in the Balkans.[51] The Soviet-Yugoslav Treaty was signed in Moscow on 5 April. Clause 2 specified that the two countries would undertake 'to observe a policy of friendship' toward each other, if attacked by a third power.[52] The meaning of this declaration was put to the test on 6 April when Germany invaded Yugoslavia. No Soviet support for Yugoslavia was forthcoming.

According to Gavrilovic, Stalin indicated that had Yugoslavia held out against the Germans, Soviet aid would have been forthcoming, although not to the extent of direct military assistance.[53] Even within those limitations, a breach with the Germans would have developed very rapidly, perhaps leading to an early declaration of war. In the event Soviet determination to support Yugoslavia, short of all-out military aid, was never really tested. Within a fortnight of the German attack, Belgrade sued for peace.

The Soviet-Yugoslav treaty was Moscow's last gesture of defiance to Berlin. It was succeeded by a series of conciliatory moves designed to revitalise the Germans' flagging commitment to the German-Soviet non-aggression and friendship treaties. Hitler's stunning campaign in Yugoslavia and the equally effective intervention on behalf of the Italians in Greece had, it appears, convinced Stalin that the time for resistance was over.

9 Stalin and the Road to War, April–June 1941

By the spring of 1941 Germany and Russia were well set on a course to war. In December 1940 Hitler had given the final go ahead to Operation Barbarossa. The early months of 1941 witnessed the beginning of a massive build-up of German military forces along the Soviet border. By April 1941 practically the whole of Eastern Europe was under Hitler's thumb. For their part the Soviets continued their domestic preparations for war with Germany and took what diplomatic action they could to strengthen their position. Moscow's efforts to bolster Yugoslavia's resistance have already been dealt with; in addition the Soviets took steps to secure their southern and eastern flanks. In March 1941 the USSR concluded a neutrality agreement with Turkey.[1] This was followed in April by the signature of a neutrality pact with Japan.[2] With a German attack in the near future a very definite possibility it was imperative for the Soviet Union to alleviate the danger of a two- or three-front war.

There was one obvious course of action for Moscow: a move closer to Britain. It was a move that Moscow abjured, however, because of its view that the British were manoeuvring to direct further German expansion eastwards and to this end were attempting to involve the USSR in the war.[3]

Soviet policy remained one of avoiding conflict with Germany and prolonging peace for as long as possible – an inclination that must have been reinforced by the Nazi state's string of stunning military successes. In line with this objective the period April–June 1941 is peppered with Soviet gestures designed to convince the Germans that the USSR had no intention of breaking the peace between the two states.

The character of these gestures is personified in Stalin's ostentatious display on the occasion of the Japanese Foreign Minister's departure from Moscow on 13 April 1941. After the Japanese party's train had left the station, Stalin sought out Schulenburg, threw his arms around him and said 'we must remain friends and you must now do everything to that end'. A similar scene was enacted with Colonel Krebs, the German military attaché.[4]

135

What Stalin hoped to achieve by this display was, presumably, to make a good impression on Schulenburg – a known Russophile. This explanation fits in with Stalin's next public gesture of goodwill towards Germany. On 7 May he took over the premiership from Molotov. Moscow had long cultivated Stalin's image as a peacemaker and a conciliator. Sure enough, Schulenburg cabled home that he was 'convinced that Stalin will use his new position in order to take part personally in the maintenance and development of good relations between the Soviets and Germany'.[5]

Stalin's appointment as premier presaged a series of conciliatory moves towards Germany. On 8 May Tass issued a denial of rumours of troop concentrations along the Soviet border. The next day the Soviet government withdrew diplomatic recognition from the legations of the governments-in-exile of German-occupied Belgium, Norway and Yugoslavia. On 12 May the Soviet Union recognised an anti-British regime in Iraq. The fall of Crete in early June was followed by a rapid withdrawal of Soviet recognition of Greek sovereignty. All the while Soviet goods and materials continued to flow into Germany and Soviet anti-aircraft batteries refrained from firing on the ever more numerous German reconnaissance flights.[6] Schulenburg's impression of all this on 24 May was that Soviet policy was 'above all directed at the avoidance of a conflict with Germany'.[7]

These and similar gestures were designed to postpone war with Germany, but there could be no question of avoiding it altogether. A German attack was coming. Moscow knew it, believed it, and prepared for it. As John Erickson has pointed out, Stalin 'possessed continuous and accurate intelligence of German intentions' regarding an attack on the USSR.[8] During the months before the invasion there were numerous intelligence reports and summaries on German military preparations for war in the East.[9] There was also a stream of reports from Soviet embassies containing information on a forthcoming German attack.[10] These included a number of messages from the Soviet embassy in Berlin warning of an attack. On 15 June, for example, Ambassador Dekanozov telegraphed that it was no longer possible 'to speak about this concentration [of German forces on the Soviet border] as a demonstration by Germany with the aim of extracting concessions from the Soviet Union. It is clear now that things are leading to the immediate preparation for war with the Soviet Union.'[11]

Despite all this intelligence, when the Germans attacked on 22 June 1941 they achieved complete surprise – an advantage which contributed greatly to their success in thrusting hundreds of miles into Soviet territory during the first few weeks of the war.[12] The Germans were able to launch a successful surprise attack because to the very last Stalin refused to accept and act on the knowledge that the German attack was imminent.

Why did Stalin allow himself to be caught off guard in this way? The answer given to this question is usually couched in terms of some kind of psychological explanation. Alexander Dallin, for example, attributes Stalin's refusal to heed the warnings of a coming German attack to his inability to accept that the Nazi-Soviet pact had been a mistake: 'it was characteristic of Stalin that he never wanted to admit that he made an error, seeking instead to structure reality so as to justify his policy choices'.[13] Similarly, Jonathan Haslam links Stalin's dismissal of western warnings of a German onslaught to his 'deep-seated suspicion of others, bordering on paranoia'.[14] However, the more information from Soviet sources there is the more apparent it becomes that there was a rational basis for Stalin's failure to anticipate the timing of the German attack. Stalin's failure was not psychological but a *political failure* of perception, belief and calculation. As we shall see, everything Stalin believed was reasonable and understandable and his actions had a recognisably rational basis. The only problem was that he was wrong.

On the basis of the available evidence, Stalin's perceptions and beliefs as 22 June approached can be summarised as follows:

1. Stalin thought that there were good reasons to believe that a German attack would not come until 1942.
2. Stalin believed that even if he was wrong about the timing of the German attack that the USSR was militarily prepared for any contingency.
3. Stalin thought that any German attack would be preceded by an ultimatum and demands from Hitler for political and economic concessions.
4. Stalin believed that the warnings of an attack coming into Moscow were the result of a combination of German bluff tactics and a British plot to precipitate an immediate crisis in Soviet-German relations.

5. Stalin drew comfort from the fact that his perceptions were reinforced by many of his associates and subordinates.
6. Stalin desperately wanted to believe that his assessment was right because that opened up possibilities for Soviet pre-emptive action when the time was ripe.

It is generally accepted that although Stalin believed that a German attack was coming he did not believe that war was imminent and inevitable in summer 1941. In January 1941 Stalin told General Meretskov 'we shall of course be unable to stay out of the war until 1943. We can't help being involved. But it is quite possible that we shall manage to stay out until 1942.'[15] And Stalin later told Churchill: 'I thought I might gain another six months or so.'[16]

The strategic basis of Stalin's view that war would not come in 1941 was his belief that Hitler would not dare risk a two-front war. German military operations against Great Britain would be completed first and an invasion of the Middle East would be the prelude to an attack on the USSR – in order to seize the oil Hitler needed for his 'big war' against Bolshevism.[17] This calculation fitted in with Stalin's conviction that modern warfare was a 'war of engines'[18] and his expectation that the main thrust of the coming German attack would be in the south-west – in the direction of the Ukrainian wheat fields, the Donets coal basin and the oil of the Caucasus. 'Nazi Germany will not be able to wage a major lengthy war without these vital resources', he reportedly said to General Zhukov.[19]

So, Stalin did not believe that war was inevitable in 1941. But why did he maintain this conviction in the face of a mountain of evidence to the contrary? The first part of the answer to this intriguing question is that Stalin also believed that it did not matter if he was wrong.

One of the great myths about 22 June is that the Soviets were not prepared for the German attack. They were well prepared, or at least they thought they were. The problem was that they were prepared for the wrong war.

As early as April 1940 Germany was identified in Soviet military plans as the future enemy. During the same period the tempo of Soviet military preparations for war with Germany – which had begun in the 1930s – picked up and gradually accelerated.

Between 1939 and 1941 Soviet military manpower grew from under 2 million to over 5 million, from under 100 divisions to over 300. More than 7000 tanks and 17,000 planes were delivered to the Red Army during this period, along with 30,000 field guns, 50,000 mortars and 100,000 machine guns.[20] By June 1941 there had been a 280 per cent increase in Soviet combat strength since 1939 and the bulk of this massive force was deployed along or near the USSR's western borders.[21] The German military build-up on the 'Eastern Front' in 1940–1 was more than matched by the Soviets' own. Indeed, just before the eve of 22 June the Soviet estimate was that their forces were militarily superior to those the Germans had amassed.[22] Hence the confidence Molotov expressed to Admiral Kuznetsov in mid-June: 'Only a fool would attack us.'[23]

This confidence was reinforced by Soviet military doctrine and planning which failed to anticipate the massive and rapid surprise attack that the Germans actually launched on 22 June. It was assumed that the Germans would not be able to conceal the deployment of their main force for a surprise attack of massive weight. The expectation was that war would begin with classic frontier battles in which the attacking side would attempt to gain the tactical initiative. This would be followed by a time interval of several days during which each side would mobilise and then commit its main force. Within this conception a strategic surprise attack of the kind actually launched by the Germans in June 1941 was militarily inconceivable. Consequently, Soviet strategy was based on offensive operations rather than defence and on the assumption that there would be time to mobilise reserves for this purpose. In the meantime the not inconsiderable Soviet forces and fortifications on the western border would be able to hold up any German advance.[24]

The political effect of this doctrine was a reinforcement of Stalin's determination to gamble everything on putting off war for as long as possible. Stalin must have felt he had every reason to believe that whatever the Germans did the USSR was ready to cope with it. Hitler could well launch a sudden attack but the price of getting caught by surprise would not be very high.

Of course, had Stalin known before 22 June what happened after it then he would presumably have reinforced Soviet defences and brought his forces up to the highest level of alert. But he didn't know what was going to happen. Moreover: he thought that he did know what was going to happen.

There is good reason to believe that Stalin thought that the prelude to war with Germany would be an ultimatum from Hitler demanding Soviet political, economic and territorial concessions. As Molotov later told Cripps: 'though the Soviet military authorities had anticipated the possibility of war, they had never expected that it would come without any discussion or ultimatum.'[25]

Why did Stalin accept what has come to be called 'the ultimatum hypothesis' regarding German intentions? Firstly, because it meshed with the military doctrine that a surprise attack by the German main force was very unlikely, if not impossible, and there would be a time-lag between an initial attack and the deployment of strategic forces by both sides. Stalin may have reasoned that Hitler would not forego the possibility of major Soviet concessions for the sake of winning a few minor frontier battles, particularly if he could be convinced by Soviet forbearance in foreign policy that his demands would be met. The latter tactics might also persuade the German dictator to delay his ultimatum, perhaps for a few more months – by which time the USSR would be in a stronger military position.

The second reason Stalin accepted the ultimatum hypothesis was because of the success of the German deception operation. The disinformation campaign preceding Barbarossa was one of the largest in military history. German deception measures included 'false radio traffic, rumour-mongering, phoney army orders, fictitious preparations for state visits, and misleading press releases'.[26] All this generated a flood of disinformation that was intended to explain away the build-up of German forces along the border with the USSR: it was a precautionary measure to deter a Soviet attack on Germany; it was part of a war of nerves designed to extract political and economic concessions; it was intended to deceive the British, who were the real German target.[27] One should also note that it was not until few days before 22 June that the main German attack forces were deployed on the Eastern Front.[28]

The aim of deception is to create doubt and confusion but also to deceive the enemy into thinking that they have seen through the intelligence 'noise' and know what is actually going to happen. The Germans, it seems, succeeded in Stalin's case. They were able to do so not because Stalin was stupid but because, as Barton Whaley has pointed out, the ultimatum hypothesis fitted the intelligence available to him.

Whaley is the originator of the 'ultimatum hypothesis' idea and the author of the most thorough study of the warnings of a coming German attack. His argument is that not only did Stalin accept the ultimatum hypothesis but that 'it may well be that this particular hypothesis best fits the pot-pourri of then available data'.[29] Far from being an irrational quirk on Stalin's part the ultimatum interpretation was a rational one. The idea that the German military build-up along the Soviet border was designed to intimidate the USSR was, after all, the guiding light of most British intelligence estimates of Hitler's intentions until mid-June 1941.[30] And who would believe that even Hitler would be mad enough to launch an invasion of Soviet Russia? Moreover, as Whaley also points out, Stalin was not the only one to be surprised by the sudden German attack:

> the strategic surprise visited upon Stalin was not his alone. Aside from some of the Germans, only a handful of the world's many intelligence chiefs, national policy-makers, or press pundits unambiguously foresaw the denouement ... The great failure was ... a general failure.[31]

However, the available intelligence was also compatible, perhaps more so, with the surprise attack hypothesis. Why did Stalin accept one hypothesis and reject the other? The answer, as we have seen, is partly that Stalin believed he had the luxury of accepting the ultimatum hypothesis – even if it turned out to be wrong. But that is not the full explanation. Stalin, it may be conjectured, wanted to believe the ultimatum hypothesis. This belief was reinforced by the interpretation of intelligence information that was presented to him and by his conviction that there was an alternative explanation of the signs that pointed to a surprise German attack.

Stalin's prejudice in favour of the ultimatum hypothesis and his hope that war would not come in 1941 was very likely reinforced by the manner in which intelligence was presented to him. Golikov, the chief of Soviet military intelligence, is reported to have presented his information under two headings: 'from reliable sources' and 'from doubtful sources'. Under the former heading, it is reputed, was information reinforcing Stalin's belief that Germany was planning to invade Great Britain; under the second heading was transmitted the intelligence concerning Hitler's true intention to attack the USSR.[32]

In his memoirs, Zhukov, at the time Chief of the Soviet General Staff, recalled a specific instance of Golikov's presentational skills. On 20 March 1941, Golikov submitted a report on German military preparations for an attack on the USSR. The report, according to Zhukov, contained a very accurate summary of the Barbarossa Plan. Its conclusion, however, read as follows:

1. On the basis of all the aforesaid ... I consider that the most probable time operations will begin against the USSR is after the victory over England or the conclusion with her of an honourable peace treaty.
2. Rumours and documents to the effect that war against the USSR is inevitable this spring should be regarded as misinformation coming from the English or perhaps even the German intelligence service.[33]

A further example cited by Zhukov concerns Kuznetsov, the Naval Commissar, who on 6 May forwarded a report from his attaché in Berlin that the Germans were preparing to invade the USSR. But in a memorandum accompanying the report Kuznetsov stated: 'I consider this information is false and was specially sent through this channel so that the Germans could see how the USSR would react.'[34]

Of course, it is likely that Stalin's subordinates were telling him what they thought he wanted to hear. And the Soviet dictator was quite capable of making his own misestimates. There are many stories – both true and apocryphal – of Stalin's rejection of intelligence that contradicted his own beliefs. When told in May 1941 that Schulenburg had dropped hints about a forthcoming German attack, Stalin is reported to have said that 'now disinformation has reached ambassadorial level'.[35] When faced with reports from agents in Germany on preparations for war with the USSR Stalin dismissed them as disinformation because they came not from communists but from German officials.[36] On 17 June 1941 Stalin was presented with a report from an agent in the

German aviation ministry that 'all Germany's military measures in preparation for armed action against the USSR have been completed and an attack may be expected at any time'. In response Stalin wrote: 'This is not a "source", this is a disinformer.'[37]

It may be, too, that secret police chief Beria played an important role in shaping and reinforcing the Soviet leader's perceptions and prejudices. It is reported that on 21 June Beria wrote a memorandum to Stalin demanding the recall of Dekanozov from Berlin. The Soviet ambassador, alleged Beria, had been sending Moscow disinformation about German preparations for an attack on the USSR, including one that said the attack would start tomorrow. Beria, on the other hand, 'remembered your wise prophecy: in 1941 Hitler will not attack us!'[38]

Stalin's blindness in the face of what his own people were telling him was intimately connected to the conviction that the warnings of a coming surprise attack were part of a British plot to embroil the USSR in a war with Germany.

There was, of course, nothing novel about Stalin's fears of British plots and manoeuvres. Such apprehensions went back to the 1920s. The particular scenario that Stalin painted in his mind in summer 1941 is still not entirely clear, but Alexander Dallin has offered the following summary of the Soviet dictator's analysis of British policy towards the USSR:

> 1) at a minimum ... to stir up trouble between Moscow and Berlin that would terminate Soviet assistance to the Germans; 2) try to draw the Soviet Union into the war against Germany ...; 3) strike a bargain that would end the Anglo-German conflict so as to let either party (or both) turn against the Soviet Union.[39]

This kind of thinking probably began to take definite shape with the receipt in April 1941 of a memorandum from Stafford Cripps, the British ambassador in Moscow, that raised the possibility that, in the long run, Britain might opt for a peace settlement with Germany if the USSR did not enter the war on its side. This memo was coupled with the delivery around the same time of a message to Stalin from Churchill warning of a coming German attack on the USSR.[40] It seems likely that Stalin saw the two messages as indicative of British mischief-making of some kind, particularly when they coincided with an even more disturbing development. On the night of 10–11 May Rudolf Hess, Hitler's deputy, flew to Britain.

Stalin was well informed about Hess's flight to Britain. Intelligence reports from Kim Philby and other agents told him that Hess was on a peace mission with the aim of ending the war with Britain prior to an attack on the USSR.[41] London's official silence on the purpose of Hess's private mission served to strengthen Soviet suspicions that an Anglo-German deal was in the air.

The assessment of the Soviet embassy in London provided some comfort to Moscow. The general thrust of Ambassador Maisky's reports home seems to have been that the Hess mission had led to a renewal of the struggle between those who favoured a compromise peace with Germany and those who did not, with Churchill's anti-appeasement faction winning in the end. However, the possibility of an Anglo-German deal still remained.[42]

While Maisky's reports on the Hess affair may have assuaged Moscow's nightmare of an Anglo-German peace, his other communications served to reinforce the belief that rumours of an imminent German attack were being fostered by the British as part of a strategy to provoke conflict in Soviet-German relations. At meetings with Foreign Secretary Eden on 2, 10 and 13 June, Maisky displayed little concern about British information on German troop concentrations in the east, insisting that they were exaggerated and, at worst, were part of Hitler's war of nerves. At the first of those meetings, for example, he told Eden that he 'did believe in a German attack on the USSR'.[43] In responding and reporting in such a way Maisky was only toeing the line coming out of Moscow. He was instructed by Deputy Commissar for Foreign Affairs Vyshinsky to 'remember that various rumours about the probable German attack on the USSR are regarded by us as untrustworthy. But, in any case, you should also remember that the USSR is ready for any surprise and, if against expectations, anyone tries to attack, he will be repulsed in the proper manner.'[44] But Moscow's confidence in this respect must surely have been shaken by Maisky's telegram on a meeting with Cadogan (Permanent Under-Secretary in the Foreign Office) on 16 June. This time Maisky reported not general British warnings about the danger of a German attack but detailed intelligence on massive troop movements in the east.[45]

Indeed, by this time there were definite signs that Moscow was beginning to get worried. On 14 June the Tass agency issued a statement which denied British press rumours of an imminent Soviet-German war, stressing that there were no differences between the USSR and Germany and stating that there was no incipient crisis in relations between the two states.[46] The statement was, it appears, a diplomatic manoeuvre intended to open the way to negotiations with Germany. The hope was that if the talks could be dragged out for a few weeks then a German attack that summer could be avoided.[47]

Despite the fact that there was no response from the Germans to the Tass communiqué, Moscow did not give up hope that Berlin could be involved in talks. On 18 June Dekanozov asked to see Weizsäcker. From the German's report of the meeting nothing of any consequence was discussed and it is likely that the point of the meeting was to elicit some response to the Tass statement.[48] On 21 June Molotov summoned Schulenburg to the Kremlin and delivered what was effectively a plea for negotiations to ease the tension in German-Soviet relations.[49] Three hours later (about 12.30 p.m. Moscow time, 22 June 1941) Moscow telegraphed Dekanozov with instructions to arrange a meeting with Ribbentrop to relay a similar request.[50] These instructions were never carried out. By the time the meeting took place, the German invasion had begun and Dekanozov found himself listening to a declaration of war.[51] At about the same time (5.30 a.m. in Moscow) Schulenburg called on Molotov to deliver the same declaration.[52]

These frantic Soviet diplomatic moves right up until the very moment of the German attack demonstrate Moscow's desperation and determination to avoid war. Much of the background reasoning and thinking behind Soviet efforts to appease the Germans has already been discussed. But there is one final factor to be considered: the possibility that Stalin was contemplating taking the military initiative himself, at a time of his own choosing.

There has long been speculation and debate about whether or not Stalin was planning or thinking about some kind of pre-emptive strike against Nazi Germany in 1941. It was and still is a popular theme with Germans and Russians seeking to blame Stalin for Operation Barbarossa![53] But there was no hard evidence to support any such hypothesis. At best there were the various reports on Stalin's secret speech to the graduates of the military academies on 5 May 1941 which suggested that he said that it might be necessary to wage a preventive war against Germany.[54] However, Stalin's speech has now been published and he said no such thing, nor even hinted at it. Not surprisingly, given that his speech was delivered at a big, semi-public gathering.[55] A number of documents relating to Soviet military plans have also been published and neither do these contain any evidence of preventive war preparations. However, there is one piece of evidence which indicates that in May–June 1941 there might have been discussions in high Soviet military and political circles about preparations for a pre-emptive, offensive strike when the Germans began mobilising their forces for attack. The document in question is a draft by A. M. Vasilevsky, Deputy Chief of Operations, entitled 'Considerations on a Plan for the Strategic Deployment of the Armed Forces of the Soviet Union'. Dated 15 May 1941 and addressed to Stalin, the document begins by stating that Germany was in a position to launch a surprise attack against the USSR and goes on to make various proposals for cross-border Soviet offensive action designed to disrupt the mobilisation and development of a German attack.[56]

It seems likely, then, that the idea of a pre-emptive strike in response to the initiation of a German attack was in the air in senior Soviet circles in summer 1941. How might this have influenced Stalin's thinking and calculations? We don't know, but it may have planted the seed of thinking about the advantages of a Soviet military offensive against Germany. The best time for such a move would, of course, have been at the moment of the climax of the USSR's preparations for war with Germany. That moment had not arrived in June 1941. It is possible that the prospect of Soviet action against Germany later in 1941 or in 1942 reinforced Stalin's determination to do everything possible to delay the outbreak of war. This is only speculation, but it does fit in with the overall pattern of Soviet political, diplomatic and military activities in 1941. In the event, of course, any plans Stalin might have had were pre-empted by Hitler on 22 June 1941.

10 Conclusion

Writing on the 1917–18 period in Soviet foreign relations, Richard Debo concludes:

> Soviet foreign policy in the first years of the Bolshevik revolution was an amalgam of ideology and expediency, utopian expectation and realistic calculation, daring innovation and classical diplomacy.[1]

Much the same verdict applies to the USSR's role in the origins of the Second World War and Soviet relations with Nazi Germany. When Hitler came to power the Soviet preference was for a continuation of the Rapallo relationship with Germany. At one level this preference was just a matter of tradition and calculation. The Rapallo relationship had come into being because of a perceived need for a powerful ally in a world of hostile capitalist states. That need still existed in 1933 and Moscow saw no reason to disturb a lucrative political, military and economic relationship. This initial orientation to the Nazi regime also had an ideological dimension: the belief in the possibility and necessity of peaceful coexistence with all capitalist states. Peaceful coexistence was founded on the view that inter-imperialist economic contradictions provided a space for Soviet survival in a world of capitalism, as long as the USSR remained strong and exploited the differences between capitalist states. Peaceful coexistence was also seen as the guarantor of the final victory of socialism on a worldwide scale. Taking strength from its base in the world's first socialist state the international revolutionary movement would, in the long run of history, wage a successful struggle to replicate the Bolshevik victory of 1917.

As soon as it became clear that Hitler's foreign policies constituted a definite threat and that the Rapallo era was over, Moscow quickly abandoned hope of a continuing alliance with Germany and instead sought new partners in the capitalist world. Important changes in doctrinal outlook also occurred. Peaceful coexistence with all states remained the principle of Soviet foreign policy, but the doctrine was modified to incorporate a general distinction

147

between aggressive and non-aggressive states at a particular stage in the history of capitalism and imperialism, which in turn sanctioned the USSR's realignment alongside the Versailles powers against Hitler and German revisionism.

This shift in policy and outlook opened the way for one of the most creative and innovative periods in the history of Soviet foreign relations. During the collective security era the Soviet Union involved itself in all manner of projects – multilateral security arrangements, a more effective League of Nations, an alliance of states and peoples against fascism and militarism – which had they succeeded could have transformed international relations in the 1930s. And at the heart of the new collective security system would have stood a powerful Soviet state fully integrated into the international system.[2]

In 1939 the USSR abandoned the collective security project and returned to isolation, choosing to pursue its security interests in the context of a relationship with an old, but now feared and unreliable ally. This return to Rapallo was prompted too by a combination of calculation and ideology. The Nazi-Soviet pact and a deal with Hitler were seen as, on the one hand, providing the best shelter from the storm of war and, on the other, thwarting the anti-communist plans of the western powers who, as ever, were plotting to precipitate a Soviet-German war that would destroy the hated Bolshevik regime.

In adopting this course of action Soviet Russia had a decisive effect on the subsequent course of events. Hitler's decision to invade Poland was reinforced, the Polish state crumbled under a combined German and Soviet attack, and Britain and France – denied a great ally in the east – declared war on Germany but retreated into defensive and passive positions. Hitler's attack, Poland's rapid defeat, the phoney war on the Western Front might have happened anyway. But in abjuring the triple alliance in favour of the Nazi-Soviet pact the USSR precluded the historical possibility of deterring Hitler from war or, failing that, conducting in 1939 a two-front war against Germany that might have resulted in its early defeat.

Of course, the Soviets didn't know what the consequences of their action would be. More to the point, we have seen that Soviet leaders had no clear idea of either what they expected to happen or what they wanted to happen – apart from a general desire to safeguard Soviet security. The signature of the pact was not so much a matter of calculated expediency as a blind and desperate gamble.

After the outbreak of war Stalin and Molotov reasserted control and direction over Soviet foreign policy. They fashioned a dual strategy of building a Soviet sphere of influence in Eastern Europe and the maintenance of an economic and political détente with Germany. The aim was to gain time, space and resources with which to deal with an eventual contest with Hitler and the Nazis. But even in this period of supreme realpolitik and the crude deployment of Soviet power, ideological discourse continued to impact on foreign policy. Moscow felt impelled to offer an ideological rationalisation for the turn in Soviet policy – hence the forced abandonment of the Comintern's anti-fascist strategy and Molotov's return in autumn 1939 to the political and ideological themes of the Rapallo era. Eastern Poland was not only occupied but revolutionised. A limited war with Finland for security ends was temporarily transformed by ideology into a crusade for socialism. Moscow's belief that the day of revolution had arrived in the Baltic States in summer 1940 was crucial in determining their subsequent sovietisation and incorporation into the USSR.

In the final denouement of the 1939–41 period, however, ideology was far less important than a series of misperceptions and miscalculations regarding Soviet-German relations. The perspective of a gradual consolidation of the Soviet position while war raged in the west was upset by the German blitzkrieg defeat of France. Moscow responded to the new situation by first attempting to come to a new set of arrangements with Germany and then by opposition to Nazi expansion into Eastern Europe. When both these tactics failed the Soviets retreated into a sullen, appeasement-like stance in relation to Germany.

The calculation throughout was that the supreme goal of policy was to avoid war with Germany for as long as possible. The unswerving commitment to this course of action fed into and encouraged a series of mistaken beliefs about the timing, form and likely consequences of a German surprise attack. On the eve of Operation Barbarossa Stalin deserted the tradition of realism in Soviet foreign policy that stretched back to the signature of the Brest-Litovsk peace with Germany in 1918. The consequences of

Stalin's refusal to heed warnings of a coming German attack remain debated and debatable, but there can be little doubt that much of what was gained by the pact with Hitler in 1939 was effectively thrown away.

The German attack on the USSR in June 1941 brought to an end the most controversial period in the history of Soviet foreign relations. But the pact, the secret protocols, and the period of Russian expansionism that followed continued to haunt the Soviet leadership for the next 50 years. In political terms the issue was only finally laid to rest during the Gorbachev era when the secret protocols were published, openly discussed and, finally, in December 1989, pronounced upon by the Soviet Congress of People's Deputies.[3] By this time much more pressing issues than openness and truth in history had taken centre stage in Soviet politics: the crisis of the Soviet economy, the internal divisions in the communist party, inter-ethnic violence and the nationalist revolt, the dramatic end of Soviet rule in Eastern Europe, and the impending breakup of the USSR. The Nazi-Soviet pact was something that could be left to the historians.

Notes and References

1 INTRODUCTION: CONFLICTING VIEWS ON THE USSR AND THE ORIGINS
OF THE SECOND WORLD WAR

1. A. J. P. Taylor, *The Origins of the Second World War* (Harmondsworth, 1964; first published London, 1961).
2. For the debate on Taylor's *Origins* see W. Roger Louis (ed.), *The Origins of the Second World War: A. J. P. Taylor and His Critics* (New York, 1972); G. Martel (ed.), *The Origins of the Second World War Reconsidered: The A. J. P. Taylor Debate after Twenty-Five Years* (London, 1986); E. M. Robertson (ed.), *The Origins of the Second World War* (London, 1971); and articles in the *Journal of Modern History* (March, 1997).
3. To my knowledge the only major treatment of Taylor's views on Soviet foreign policy and the outbreak of the Second World War is T. J. Uldricks' 'A. J. P. Taylor and the Russians', in Martel (ed.), *Origins Reconsidered*.
4. This summary of Taylor's view is based on a reading of remarks scattered throughout the *Origins*, but see especially chs 9–10. The quote is from p. 319 of the Penguin edition of the book.
5. See G. Roberts, *The Unholy Alliance: Stalin's Pact with Hitler* (London, 1989), ch. 2.
6. Members of the collective security school of thought include the present author in *The Unholy Alliance*; T. J. Uldricks, 'Soviet Security Policy in the 1930s' in G. Gorodetsky (ed.), *Soviet Foreign Policy, 1917–1991* (London, 1994) and 'A. J. P. Taylor and the Russians'; G. Gorodetsky, 'The Impact of the Ribbentrop Pact on the Course of Soviet Foreign Policy', *Cahiers du Monde russe et soviétique* (January–March 1990) and 'The Origins of the Cold War: Stalin, Churchill and the Formation of the Grand Alliance', *The Russian Review*, 47 (1988); M. Jabara Carley, 'End of the "Low, Dishonest Decade": Failure of the Anglo-Franco-Soviet Alliance in 1939', *Europe–Asia Studies*, 45, no. 2 (1993) and 'Down a Blind Alley: Anglo-Franco-Soviet Relations, 1920–1939', *Canadian Journal of History* (April 1994); I. Fleischhauer, *Der Pact: Hitler, Stalin und die Initiative der deutschen Diplomatie, 1938–1939* ((Frankfurt, 1990); and B. Pietrow, *Stalinismus, Sicherheit und Offensive. Das Dritte Reich in der Konzeption der sowjetischen Ausenpolitik 1933 bis 1941* (Melsungen, 1983). An important but semi-detached member of this school is J. Haslam, *The Soviet Union and the Struggle for Collective Security in Europe, 1933–1939* (London, 1984), who writes: 'what is so striking from 1933–1939 is less the tentative soundings in Berlin – the echoes of Rapallo – than the merciless persistence with which the Russians so doggedly clung to the policy of collective security, a policy which so rarely showed any promise of

151

success' (p. 230). Exemplars of the old official Soviet line which argue the collective security case include I. K. Koblyakov, *USSR: For Peace, Against Aggression 1933–1941* (Moscow, 1976) and V. Sipols, *Diplomatic Battles Before World War II* (Moscow, 1982).

7. On the Rapallo period in Soviet-German relations see K. Rosenbaum, *Community of Fate: Soviet-German Diplomatic Relations 1922–1928* (Syracuse, NY, 1965); H. L. Dyck, *Weimar Germany and Soviet Russia 1926–1933* (London, 1966); R. H. Haigh et al., *German-Soviet Relations in the Weimar Era* (London, 1985); and the relevant volumes and sections of E. H. Carr's *A History of Soviet Russia* (London, 1950–78). Some new and interesting archival documents on Soviet-Germany military co-operation in the 1920s were published in *International Affairs* (Moscow), July 1990. A recent, interesting Russian/Soviet article on Rapallo is V. Sokolov and I. Fetisov, 'Rapallo and Prewar Poland', *International Affairs* (Moscow), March 1993. For a review of Soviet foreign policy as a whole in the 1920s see T. J. Uldricks, 'Russia and Europe: Diplomacy, Revolution and Economic Development in the 1920s', *International History Review*, no. 1 (1979).

8. Adherents of the 'German' school of thought include O. Pick, 'Who Pulled the Trigger? Soviet Historians and the Origins of World War II', *Problems of Communism* (January–February 1968); J. Hochman, *The Soviet Union and the Failure of Collective Security, 1934–1938* (Ithaca, NY, 1984); N. Tolstoy, *Stalin's Secret War* (London, 1981); R. Tucker, 'The Emergence of Stalin's Foreign Policy', *Slavic Review*, XXXVI (1977); and G. L. Weinberg, *The Foreign Policy of Hitler's Germany*, 2 vols (Chicago, 1970; 1980), *Germany and the Soviet Union 1939–1941* (Leiden, 1954). The 'German' interpretation has in recent years also found an echo among many Soviet/Russian historians. See e.g. M. I. Semiryaga, *Tainy Stalinskoi Diplomatii, 1939–1941* (Moscow, 1992).

9. See the two Uldricks articles cited above in Notes 3 and 6.

10. Doing business with the Nazis was, of course, the universal norm in the 1930s for all types of governments and states. See e.g. G. Dutter, 'Doing Business with the Nazis: French Economic Relations with Germany under the Popular Front', *Journal of Modern History* (June 1991).

11. The nature of Soviet collective security policy is explored further in Uldricks, 'Soviet Security Policy in the 1930s' and Roberts, *Unholy Alliance*, ch. 3. See also Haslam, *The Soviet Union, 1933–9* and R. Craig Nation, *Black Earth, Red Star: A History of Soviet Security Policy, 1917–1991* (Ithaca, NY, 1992), ch. 3.

12. The most important representatives of the 'internal politics' school are Haslam, *The Soviet Union, 1933–9* and, for the most sustained and explicit argument of this view, P. D. Raymond, *Conflict and Consensus in Soviet Foreign Policy, 1933–1939*, PhD thesis, Pennsylvania State University, 1979. See also Haslam's article in Gorodetsky (ed.), *Soviet Foreign Policy*.

13. On Soviet policy towards Japan see J. Haslam, *The Soviet Union and the Threat from the East, 1933–1941* (London, 1992).

14. Uldricks, 'Soviet Security Policy in the 1930s', p. 73.

15. The emphasis here on the ramshackle character of foreign policy in the 1930s is commensurate with the picture of crisis and chaos in Soviet domestic politics drawn by the so-called 'revisionist' historians. See, inter alia, J. Arch Getty, *Origins of the Great Purges: The Soviet Communist Party Reconsidered, 1933–1938* (Cambridge, 1985); G. T. Rittersporn, *Stalinist Simplifications and Soviet Complications: Social Tensions and Political Conflicts in the USSR, 1933–1953* (London, 1991); J. Arch Getty and R. T. Manning (eds), *Stalinist Terror: New Perspectives* (Cambridge, 1993); and, for a superb summary and commentary on the whole debate, C. Ward, *Stalin's Russia* (London, 1993). However, compared to internal politics, foreign policy and diplomacy was a relatively sane and controlled domain of decision-making. I also think that the divisions and conflicts over foreign policy were of a different character and order than those typical of domestic politics.

2 FROM CO-OPERATION TO CONFRONTATION: THE END OF RAPALLO AND THE TURN TO COLLECTIVE SECURITY, 1933–1935

1. J. Degras (ed.), *Soviet Documents on Foreign Policy*, vol. 3, 1933–1941 (Oxford, 1953), p. 56.

2. Soviet foreign policy archives. Cited by I. F. Maksimychev, *Diplomatiya Mira protiv Diplomatii Voiny: Ocherk Sovetsko-Germanskikh Diplomaticheskikh Otnoshenii v 1933–1939* (Moscow, 1981), p. 28. See also: *Documents on German Foreign Policy* (hereafter *DGFP*), series C, vol. 1, docs 6, 10 and 29.

3. E. H. Carr, *The Twilight of Comintern, 1930–1935* (London, 1982), p. 95 and Maksimychev, *Diplomatiya Mira*, p. 25.

4. See *Dokumenty Vneshnei Politiki SSSR* (hereafter *DVPS*), vol. 16, docs 51, 54 and 424 and *DGFP*, series C, vol. 1, docs 41, 43 and 73 and vol. 2, doc. 127.

5. *DVPS*, vol. 16, doc. 54. Cited by J. Haslam, *The Soviet Union and the Struggle for Collective Security in Europe, 1933–1939* (London, 1984), p. 7.

6. *DGFP*, series C, vol. 1, doc. 73.

7. Soviet foreign policy archives. Cited by Maksimychev, *Diplomatiya Mira*, p. 41.

8. Soviet foreign policy archives. Cited by ibid., pp. 41–2.

9. X. J. Eudin and R. M. Slusser (eds), *Soviet Foreign Policy 1928–1934: Documents and Materials*, vol. 2 (Pennsylvania, 1967), doc. 97.

10. For Soviet statements on the Hugenberg Memorandum see Degras, *Soviet Documents*, pp. 21–3. For Soviet protests: *DVPS*, vol. 16, doc. 189 and *DGFP*, series C, vol. 1, doc. 331. On Hugenberg's resignation: *DGFP*, series C, vol. 1, doc. 338.

11. Soviet foreign policy archives. Cited by Maksimychev, *Diplomatiya Mira*, p. 42. This was the first Soviet diplomatic document in which it was stated that Germany was preparing for war against the USSR, according to A. A. Akhtamzyan, 'Voenno Sotrudnichestvo SSSR i Germanii', *Novaya i Noveishaya Istoriya*, no. 5 (1990), 24.

12. Soviet–German military co-operation was ended by Moscow in June 1933, the ostensible reason being that the continuation of such co-operation was incompatible with Soviet participation in international discussions on disarmament. See *DGFP*, series C, vol. 1, docs 284, 339, 409, 439, 460 and 470 and series C, vol. 2, doc. 47.

13. Eudin and Slusser, *Soviet Foreign Policy 1928–34*, doc. 103.

14. See G. Roberts, *The Unholy Alliance: Stalin's Pact with Hitler* (London, 1989), pp. 40–3, 59–60.

15. Ibid., pp. 60–2.

16. *Istoriya Vtoroi Mirovoi Voiny 1939–1945*, vol. 1 (Moscow, 1973), p. 283; V. Ya. Sipols, *Vneshnyaya Politika Sovetskogo Souza 1933–1935* (Moscow, 1980), p. 150; and *DVPS*, vol. 16, n. 321, pp. 876–7, for the text of the politburo proposals. Appendix 1 of Roberts, *Unholy Alliance* contains an English translation.

17. On the USSR and the League see I. Plettenberg, 'The Soviet Union and the League of Nations', in *The League of Nations in Retrospect* (New York, 1983) and S. Dullin, 'Les diplomates soviétiques à la Société des Nations', *Relations Internationales*, no. 75 (autumn 1993).

18. Degras, *Soviet Documents*, pp. 48–61.

19. Ibid., p. 57

20. J. Stalin, *Works*, vol. 13 (Moscow, 1955), pp. 308–9.

21. Cited by V. Sipols, *Diplomatic Battles Before World War II* (Moscow, 1982), p. 44.

22. Ibid., pp. 44–5; Haslam, *The Soviet Union, 1933–9*, p. 36; and, for the text of the Polish-German agreement: *Official Documents Concerning Polish-German and Polish-Soviet Relations 1933–1939* (London, 1940), doc. 10.

23. Cited by Maksimychev, *Diplomatiya Mira*, p. 71.

24. *Dokumenty i Materialy po Istorii Sovetsko–Polskikh Otnoshenii*, vol. 6, doc. 106.

25. *DVPS*, vol. 17, docs 94 and 95; *DGFP*, series C, vol. 2, docs 362 and 364.

26. *DVPS*, vol. 17, docs 126 and 139.

27. On the negotiations for an Eastern Locarno see L. Radice, *Prelude to Appeasement: East Central European Diplomacy in the Early 1930s* (New York, 1981). The Soviet role in the negotiations is dealt with by Roberts, *Unholy Alliance* and Haslam, *The Soviet Union, 1933–9*.

28. A detailed documentary account of the Soviet view of the Eastern Pact and its stance in the negotiations is contained in 'Documents: The Struggle for Collective Security in Europe', *International Affairs* (Moscow), June, July, August and October 1963. On the proposed pact and its role in the Soviet conception of collective security, see Litvinov's interview with a French journalist in June 1934 in Degras, *Soviet Documents*, pp. 83–5 and R. Craig Nation, *Black Earth, Red Star: A History of Soviet Security Policy, 1917–1991* (Ithaca, NY, 1992), ch. 3.

29. On the German attitude to the Eastern Pact see Radice, *Prelude to Appeasement*.

30. *DVPS*, vol. 18, doc. 148.

31. See Roberts, *Unholy Alliance*, pp. 68–70.

32. Soviet foreign policy archives. Cited by Sipols, *Vneshnyaya Politika Sovetskogo Souza, 1933–1935*, p. 277. Litvinov's reference here to Poland and Japan is indicative that Moscow's fear of an attack on the USSR was not limited to Germany. Indeed, Rolf Ahmann has argued that one of the keys to understanding Soviet foreign policy in the 1930s is apprehension about the emergence of a German-Polish-Japanese combination directed against the USSR. See his 'Soviet Foreign Policy and the Molotov–Ribbentrop Pact of 1939: An Enigma Reassessed', *Storia delle relazioni Internazionali*, no. 2 (1989).

33. Stalin's retrospective assessment of the pact is also worth noting at this point. In December 1944 he reportedly told de Gaulle: 'When we concluded the Franco-Soviet agreement of 1935 not everything was clear. Later on we realised that Laval and his colleagues did not trust us as allies. In signing the agreement with us they wanted to tie us down and to prevent us from allying with Germany. For our part, we Russians did not completely trust the French and this mutual distrust destroyed the pact.' *Frantsuzskiye Otnosheniya vo vremya Velikoi Otechestvennoi Voiny, 1941–1945* (Moscow 1959), doc. 197. This reference was brought to my attention by N. Jordon, *The Popular Front and Central Europe* (Cambridge, 1992), pp. 259–60.

34. Degras, *Soviet Documents*, pp. 111–12.

35. Ibid., pp. 124–6. Tukhachevsky's article was personally edited by Stalin. See *Izvestiya Tsk KPSS*, no. 1 (1990), pp. 161–9.

36. On the Comintern see G. Roberts, 'Collective Security and the Origins of the People's Front' in J. Fyrth (ed.), *Britain, Fascism and the Popular Front* (London, 1985); J. Haslam, 'The Comintern and the Origins of the Popular Front', *Historical Journal*, no. 3 (1979); E. J. Hobsbawm, 'The Moscow Line and International Communist Policy' in C. Wrigley (ed.), *Warfare, Diplomacy and Politics* (London, 1986); and Carr, *History of Soviet Russia*. The main speeches at the 7th Congress are reproduced in *Report of the Seventh World Congress* (London, 1936).

37. *DGFP*, series C, vol. 4, docs 78 and 95.

3   CONFRONTATION VERSUS COMPROMISE: DILEMMAS OF COEXISTENCE
    WITH NAZI GERMANY, 1935–1937

1. *Dokumenty Vneshnei Politiky SSSR (DVPS)*, vol. 18, doc. 253.

2. E. Gnedin, *Iz Istorii Otnoshenii Mezhdu SSSR i Fashistskoi Germaniei* (New York, 1977) pp. 34–5. Gnedin's other recollections are in *Katastrofa i Vtoroye Rozhdeniye* (Amsterdam, 1977) and 'V Narkomindele, 1922–1939: Intervu s E. A. Gnedinym', *Pamyat: Istoricheskii Sbornik*, no. 5 (Moscow, 1981; Paris, 1982). These memoirs are critically examined by P. D. Raymond, 'Witness and Chronicler of Nazi-Soviet Relations: The Testimony of Evgeny Gnedin (Parvus)', *Russian Review*, 44 (1985). See also: T. J. Uldricks, 'A. J. P. Taylor and the Russians' in G. Martel (ed.), *The Origins of the Second World War Reconsidered* (London, 1986), pp. 178–9.

3. E.g. J. Hochman, *The Soviet Union and the Failure of Collective Security, 1934–1938* (Ithaca, NY, 1984), ch. 5. Also: G. Weinberg, who writes of this period: 'Stalin clearly wanted a new form of alignment with Germany and repeatedly attempted to obtain it.' See his 'German Diplomacy Towards the Soviet Union', *Soviet Union/Union Soviétique*, 18, nos 1–3 (1991), 320.

4. E.g. J. Haslam, *The Soviet Union and the Struggle for Collective Security in Europe, 1933–39* (London, 1984), pp. 80–2, 85–7, 89–93, 95–6, 100–1, 103, 106, 125–8. Also: P. D. Raymond, *Conflict and Consensus in Soviet Foreign Policy 1933–1939*, PhD thesis, Pennsylvania State University, 1976.

5. G. Roberts, *The Unholy Alliance: Stalin's Pact with Hitler* (London, 1989), ch. 5, espec. pp. 101–8.

6. 'Zapiska M. M. Litvinova I. V. Stalinu, 3 Dekabrya 1935g', *Izvestiya Tsk KPSS*, no. 2 (1990) and, most importantly, 'Osobaya Missiya Davida Kandelaki', *Voprosy Istorii*, nos 4–5 (1991) (hereafter 'Osobaya Missiya').

7. These themes in Soviet foreign policy are explored further in Roberts, *Unholy Alliance*, ch. 3.

8. On the status and role of the People's Commissariat of Foreign Trade and its representatives abroad see the piece on 'Soviet Foreign Trade' in M. Bornstein and D. R. Fusfeld (eds), *The Soviet Economy: A Book of Readings*, rev. edn (Homewood, Ill, 1966) and E. H. Carr, *Socialism in One Country, 1924–1926*, vol. 1 (Harmondsworth, 1970), ch. 8(b).

9. On the April 1935 credit agreement see Hochman, *Failure of Collective Security, 1934–8*, pp. 100–1.

10. Cited in 'Osobaya Missiya' pp. 146–7. Note: all citations given from this article refer to Soviet foreign policy archive documents quoted or referred to by its author.

11. The following citations in ibid. are relevant. On 14 January 1935 Suritz, the Soviet ambassador in Berlin, wrote to Litvinov: 'As you know your German friend has told us that there has been powerful pressure from influential Reichswehr circles and those close to Schacht insisting on a reconciliation and agreement with us. According to him the biggest impression on them has been our preparedness to develop economic relations'(p. 146). There is no information on this 'German friend', who was presumably a confidential contact of some kind. On 24 April 1935 a Soviet journalist wrote to Bukharin, at that time editor of *Izvestiya*, that 'recently the mood in German circles for an improvement in relations with the USSR has definitely grown stronger. At the same time Reichswehr circles often mention the names of Schacht and Goering in this connection'(p. 147). On 29 May 1935 Suritz wrote to Moscow that in a conversation with Schacht the German was 'very friendly and spoke about the necessity of an improvement in mutual relations' (p. 147).

12. *DVPS*, vol. 18 n. 157 and n. 160, pp. 646–7. The notes cited here, from which the information given in the text comes, refer to a telegram from Litvinov to the Soviet ambassador in Paris dated 26 June 1935 and a letter from Litvinov to Suritz dated 27 June 1935.

13. *Documents on German Foreign Policy (DGFP)*, series C, vol. 4, doc. 211.

14. The quote is from a letter to Litvinov from K. Urenev dated 31 July 1937 in *DVPS*, vol. 20, doc. 276. I am grateful to Haslam, *The Soviet Union, 1933–9*, p. 145 for this reference. Urenev, formerly ambassador to Japan, replaced Suritz as Soviet ambassador in Germany in summer 1937.

15. *DGFP*, series C, vol. 4, doc. 386.

16. *DVPS*, vol. 18, doc. 424.

17. *DVPS*, vol. 18, doc. 449.

18. *Izvestiya Tsk KPSS*, no. 2 (1990), pp. 211–12.

19. 'Osobaya Missiya', p. 147.

20. *DGFP*, series C, vol. 4, doc. 439.

21. Ibid., doc. 453.

22. See 'Moscow and the Nazis', *Survey* (October 1963), 129–31.

23. *DGFP*, series C, vol. 4, doc. 472.

24. 'Osobaya Missiya', pp. 147–8. Also: *DVPS*, vol. 18, n. 261, pp. 671–2.

25. *DVPS*, vol. 18, n. 261, p. 671.

26. Ibid., doc. 450.

27. Ibid., vol. 19, doc. 12.

28. See *DGFP*, series C, vol. 4, doc. 472; *DVPS*, vol. 18, n. 260, pp. 670–1; *DVPS*, vol. 19, docs 12 and 45. Also: Haslam, *The Soviet Union, 1933–9*, p. 96.

29. Haslam, *The Soviet Union, 1933–9*, p. 98.

30. The text of the April 1936 credit agreement is in *DVPS*, vol. 19, doc. 143. See also Hochman, *Failure of Collective Security, 1934–8*, p. 102 and G. L. Weinberg, *The Foreign Policy of Hitler's Germany* (Chicago, 1970), p. 222.

31. See I. F. Maksimychev, *Diplomatiya Mira protiv Diplomatii Voiny: Ocherk Sovetsko–Germanskikh Diplomaticheskikh Otnoshenii v 1933–1939 godakh* (Moscow, 1981), pp. 135–6, 140–1 and 'Osobaya Missiya', p. 149.

32. For Molotov's speech see J. Degras (ed.), *Soviet Documents on Foreign Policy*, vol. 3 (Oxford, 1953), pp. 151–8.

33. Ibid., p. 168.

34. Ibid., p. 84.

35. 'Osobaya Missiya', p. 149.

36. *DGFP*, series C, vol. 5, doc. 312.

37. *DGFP*, series C, vol. 5, doc. 341.

38. *DVPS*, vol. 19, doc. 239.

39. 'Osobaya Missiya', p. 149.

40. Ibid.

41. According to Hochman, *Failure of Collective Security, 1934–8*, p. 102, by the end of 1937 the Soviets had used only 183 million marks out of the 200 million credit allocated to them in April 1935.

42. *DVPS*, vol. 19, n. 160, p. 762.

43. See ibid., doc. 266 (Suritz to Krestinsky, 13/9/36) and doc. 305 (Suritz to Krestinsky, 12/10/36).

44. On Soviet policy towards Spain and its diplomatic consequences of Soviet aid to Spain see Roberts, *Unholy Alliance*, pp. 75–9 and Haslam, *The Soviet Union, 1933–9*, ch. 7.

45. The Soviet–German economic negotiations of autumn 1936 are hardly documented at all. But see *DGFP*, series C, vol. 5, doc. 549 and

Hochman, *Failure of Collective Security, 1934–8*, p. 113 and Weinberg, *Foreign Policy of Hitler's Germany*, pp. 310–11. On the Soviet side there is only an exchange of telegrams between Alexandrovky and Litvinov (*DVPS*, vol. 19, docs 328 and 331). From Prague on 23 October Alexandrovsky reported rumours about a forthcoming Soviet-German reapprochment and sought information about Kandelaki's activities in Berlin. Litvinov replied 2 days later that the rumours were untrue and that in this connection Kandelaki had been given no new directives.

46. 'Osobaya Missiya', p. 150.
47. *DGFP*, series C, vol. 6, doc. 183. The date of the meeting is taken from ibid.
48. 'Osobaya Missiya', p. 150.
49. Ibid.
50. Ibid., pp. 150–1.
51. 'Osobaya Missiya', p. 151.
52. This idea is derived from Haslam, *The Soviet Union, 1933–9*, pp. 120–8, who also deals with the background to Soviet fears and the political moves these inspired.
53. *DGFP*, series C, vol. 6, doc. 183.
54. 'Osobaya Missiya', p. 151–2.
55. *DGFP*, series C, vol. 6, doc. 195.
56. 'Osobaya Missiya', p. 152.
57. The fortunes of Soviet collective security policy in 1935–7 are dealt with in Roberts, *Unholy Alliance*, pp. 72–81 and Haslam, *The Soviet Union, 1933–9*.

4   TO THE BRINK OF WAR: THE CZECHOSLOVAKIAN CRISIS OF 1938

1. See Litvinov's speeches in *Against Aggression* (London, 1939).
2. *Dokumenty i Materialy po Istorii Sovetsko-Chekhoslovatskikh Otnoshenii*, vol. 3, docs 63 and 65. Jiri Hochman, *The Soviet Union and the Failure of Collective Security, 1934–1938* (Ithaca, NY, 1984), p. 53 says that the clause in the Soviet-Czechoslovak pact that tied its military implementation to French action was included at the behest of Moscow. His evidence is Czech archives but he neither quotes the evidence nor does he cite the archival reference. It is quite clear from the Soviet documents that this clause came from the Czechoslovak side. The Soviet version is confirmed by a British report on a meeting between Simon and Benes/ in Prague in May 1935 at which the negotiations with the USSR were discussed. See *British Documents on Foreign Affairs: Reports and Papers from the Foreign Office Confidential Print*, Part 11, series A: *The Soviet Union, 1917–1939*, vol. 12, doc. 302. Moreover, as cited in the present text, on 23 September 1938 at the League of Nations Litvinov stated publicly that the conditional clause was inserted at Czech request – a statement that was not questioned by anyone at the time.
3. Soviet policy during the Czech crisis is debated by M. L. Toepfer, 'The Soviet Role in the Munich Crisis', *Diplomatic History* (Fall 1977); B.

M. Cohen, 'Moscow at Munich: Did the Soviet Union Offer Unilateral Aid to Czechoslovakia?', *East European Quarterly*, 7, no. 3 (1978); J. Haslam, 'The Soviet Union and the Czechoslovakian Crisis of 1938', *Journal of Contemporary History* (July 1979); and I. Lukes, 'Did Stalin Desire War in 1938? A New Look at Soviet Behaviour during the May and September Crises', *Diplomacy & Statecraft* (March 1991).

4. Hitler's speech cited by M. Beloff, *The Foreign Policy of Soviet Russia, 1929–1941* (Oxford, 1949), vol. 2, p. 121.

5. *Dokumenty Vneshnei Politiki SSSR (DVPS)*, vol. 19, doc. 227.

6. Soviet foreign policy archives. Cited by V. Sipols, *Sovetskii Souz v Borbe za Mir i Bezopasnost 1933–1939* (Moscow, 1974), pp. 173–4.

7. Soviet foreign policy archives. Cited by *Soviet Foreign Policy 1917–1945* (Moscow, 1981), p. 328.

8. For Soviet press comment on the Austrian events see I. K. Koblyakov, *USSR: For Peace, Against Aggression 1933–1941* (Moscow, 1976), pp. 85–6.

9. *New Documents on the History of Munich* (hereafter *New Documents*) (Prague, 1958), doc. 4.

10. Ibid., doc. 7.

11. Ibid., doc. 8

12. Ibid., doc. 14 and *DVPS*, vol. 21, doc. 182.

13. On the 'May Crisis' see W. L. Shirer, *The Collapse of the Third Republic* (London, 1972), pp. 380–5. Also Lukes, 'Did Stalin Desire War', who argues that the May crisis was provoked by the Soviet Union. This is in line with his general interpretation of Soviet policy during the Czech crisis that it was designed to provoke a European war while the USSR stood on the sidelines. As the author himself admits, the argument is purely hypothetical and speculative. As far as I can see, it is entirely without foundation.

14. See J. Degras (ed.), *Soviet Documents on Foreign Policy*, vol. 3 (Oxford, 1953), pp. 282–94 for Litvinov's speech.

15. *New Documents*, doc. 20

16. *New Documents*, doc. 24. Also: *Documents Diplomatiques Français* (hereafter *DDF*), 2nd series, vol. 10, docs 5, 6, and 289; *DVPS*, vol. 21, doc. 300; *Documents on British Foreign Policy (DBFP)* 3rd series, vol. 2, doc. 637; and *Documents on German Foreign Policy*, series d, vol. 2, docs 381, 396 and 397;

17. *DDF*, 2nd series, vol. 11, doc. 511.

18. Ibid., doc. 534 and *New Documents*, doc. 25.

19. *New Documents*, doc. 26.

20. *DVPS*, vol. 21, doc. 325.

21. Ibid., doc. 330.

22. *New Documents*, doc. 27.

23. Ibid., doc. 30.

24. *DVPS*, vol. 21, doc. 343.

25. Ibid., doc. 348.

26. *New Documents*, doc. 33.

27. See Shirer, *Collapse of Third Republic*, pp. 402–5.

28. *Documents and Materials Relating to the Eve of the Second World War* (hereafter *Documents and Materials*), vol. 1 (Moscow 1948), doc. 22.

29. *New Documents*, doc. 36.

30. *Documents and Materials*, pp. 203–203; ibid., docs 38 and 39; and *Dokumenty i Materialy po Istorii Sovetsko-Chekhoslovatskikh Otnoshenii*, vol. 3, doc. 344, n. 1. Articles 16 and 17 of the League of Nations Covenant provided for sanctions against aggressors and military aid to the victims of aggression.

31. *Documents and Materials*, doc. 24.

32. Ibid., doc. 27, and Shirer, *Collapse of Third Republic*, p. 410.

33. See I. Maisky, 'The Munich Drama', *New Times*, no. 44 (1966), p. 27.

34. Degras, *Soviet Documents*, p. 303.

35. Ibid., pp. 304–5.

36. *Dokumenty i Materialy po Istorii Sovetsko-Chekhoslovatskikh Otnosheni*, vol. 3, docs 352, 354, and 374, n. 1.

37. See J. Haslam, *The Soviet Union and the Struggle for Collective Security in Europe, 1933–1939* (London, 1984), p. 189 and *DVPS*, vol. 21, doc. 366.

38. *DVPS*, vol. 21, doc. 370 and *DBFP*, 3rd series, vol. 2, doc. 1071.

39. See V. Sipols, *Diplomatic Battles Before World War 11* (Moscow, 1982), p. 181.

40. *DVPS*, vol. 21, doc. 369.

41. Telegram from Potemkin to Soviet ambassadors in Berlin, Warsaw, Rome, Budapest and Bucharest, 20/9/38, published in *Vestnik Ministerstva Inostrannykh SSSR*, no. 18, 1 October 1988, p. 45.

42. For an illuminating discussion of the September 1938 Soviet military mobilisation and the secrecy with which it was initially conducted see G. Jukes, 'The Red Army and the Munich Crisis', *Journal of Contemporary History*, 26 (1991).

43. Maisky, 'Munich Drama', p. 28.

44. See Hochman, *Failure of Collective Security 1934–8*, pp. 73–5 and Appendix C for the text of the Romanian proposal on Soviet rights of passage. For the background to these negotiations see Haslam, *The Soviet Union, 1933–9*, pp. 169–79. There appears to have been no Soviet reply to the Romanian proposals.

45. On this point see B. R. Posen, 'Competing Images of the Soviet Union', *World Politics* (July 1987), 586–8.

46. On Godesberg see L. Mosley, *On Borrowed Time* (London, 1971), pp. 46–55.

47. *New Documents*, doc. 55.

48. *Dokumenty i Materialy po Istorii Sovetsko-Chekhoslovatskikh Otnoshenii*, doc. 386. Also: I. Lukes, 'Stalin and Beneš at the End of September 1938: New Evidence from Prague Archives', *Slavic Review* (Spring 1993).

49. 'Notes on Events in Czechoslovakia in Late September and Early October 1938', *International Affairs* (Moscow) December 1988, pp. 125–32.

50. T. Taylor, *Munich: The Price of Peace* (London, 1979), pp. 452–6.

51. On the triple alliance negotiations of 1939 see G. Roberts, *The Unholy Alliance: Stalin's Pact with Hitler* (London, 1989), chs 6–7 and M. J. Carley, 'End of the "Low, Dishonest Decade": Failure of the Anglo-Franco-Soviet Alliance in 1939', *Europe–Asia Studies*, 45, no. 2 (1993). Also:

G. Roberts, 'The Fall of Litvinov: A Revisionist View', *Journal of Contemporary History* (October 1992), and 'The Failure of the Triple Alliance Negotiations 1939: The view from Moscow' (Unpublished, 1994).

5   FROM CONFRONTATION TO CONCILIATION: ORIGINS OF THE NAZI-SOVIET PACT, 1938–1939

1. See *God Krizisa, 1938–1939: Dokumenty i Materialy*, 2 vols (Moscow, 1990) (hereafter *God Krizisa*). Extensive extracts from the documents in this collection dealing with Soviet-German relations in 1939 are quoted by V. Ya. Sipols, 'Za Neskolko Mesyatsev do 23 Avgusta 1939 goda', *Mezhdunarodnaya Zhizn* (May 1989) (English translation: 'A Few Months Before August 23, 1939', *International Affairs* [Moscow], June 1989). A few of the documents are translated in full in 'Around the Non-Aggression Pact (Documents of Soviet-German Relations in 1939)', *International Affairs* (Moscow), October 1989. Some additional documents of interest were published in *Dokumenty Vneshnei Politiki 1939 god* (hereafter *DVP 1939*), 2 vols (Moscow, 1992). The events leading to the opening up of Soviet archives in 1989–1990 are discussed in G. Roberts, *The Unholy Alliance: Stalin's Pact with Hitler* (London, 1989), ch. 2 and T. J. Uldricks, 'Evolving Soviet View of the Nazi-Soviet Pact', in R. Frucht (ed.), *Labyrinth of Nationalism and Complexities of Diplomacy: Essays in Honor of Charles and Barbara Jelavich* (Columbus, OH, 1992).

2. See D. C. Watt's discussion in his 'The Initiation of the Negotiations Leading to the Nazi-Soviet Pact: A Historical Problem', in C. Abramsky (ed.), *Essays in Honour of E. H. Carr* (London, 1974).

3. *Soviet Peace Efforts on the Eve of World War II* (hereafter: *Soviet Peace Efforts*), part one (Moscow, 1973), doc. 47.

4. On Soviet foreign policy in the post-Munich period see Roberts, *Unholy Alliance*, ch. 6. The relevant Soviet diplomatic correspondence may be consulted in *SSSR v Borbe za Mir Nakanune Vtoroi Mirovoi Voiny* (Moscow, 1971) (English translation: *Soviet Peace Efforts on the Eve of World War II*, 2 vols [Moscow, 1973]); *God Krizisa*; and *DVP 1939*, vol. 1.

5. On the cancelled Schnurre trip see D. C. Watt, *How War Came: The Immediate Origins of the Second World War* (London, 1989), p. 121 and J. Haslam, *The Soviet Union and the Struggle for Collective Security in Europe, 1933–1939* (London, 1984), pp. 202–3.

6. Watt, 'Initiation of the Negotiations'.

7. *Documents on British Foreign Policy* (*DBFP*), 3rd series, vol. 4, p. 416.

8. J. Stalin, *Leninism* (London, 1940), pp. 619–30.

9. For Molotov's speech see J. Degras (ed.), *Soviet Documents on Foreign Policy*, vol. 3 (Oxford, 1953), pp. 308–11.

10. See references in note 4 above.

11. R. J. Sontag and J. S. Beddie (eds), *Nazi-Soviet Relations 1939–1941* (New York, 1948) (hereafter *NSR*), p. 2. A slightly different translation of Merekalov's statement will be found in *Documents on German Foreign Policy* (*DGFP*), series D, vol. 6, doc. 215.

12. E.g.Watt, 'Initiation of the Negotiations'.

13. *God Krizisa*, vol. 1, doc. 252.

14. *DVP 1939*, vol. 1, doc. 237. See also *DGFP*, series D, vol. 6, doc. 217.

15. *God Krizisa*, vol. 1, doc. 279.

16. *DVP 1939*, vol. 1, doc. 236. See also I. Fleischhauer, *Pakt: Gitler, Stalin i Initsiativa Germanskoi Diplomatii, 1938–1939* (Moscow, 1991), pp. 126–7 who cites a slightly different text of this report by Astakhov, dated 17 April 1939.

17. Watt, *How War Came*, p. 230.

18. *NSR*, p. 13.

19. For further exploration of this issue see G. Roberts, 'Infamous Encounter? The Merekalov–Weizsäcker Meeting of 17 April 1939', *Historical Journal* (December 1992). Merekalov was purged following his return to Moscow in April 1939.

20. R. Overy and A. Wheatcroft, *The Road to War* (London, 1989), p. 210.

21. The argument concerning Litvinov's dismissal is pursued in G. Roberts, 'The Fall of Litvinov: A Revisionist View', *Journal of Contemporary History* (October 1992). Some additional documents relevant to this issue were published in *DVP 1939*, vol. 1, espec. Litvinov's reports to Stalin in March–April 1939: docs 143, 150, 154, 156, 157, 206, 216, 223, 224, 228, 251, 267, 268.

22. A critique of Stalin and Molotov's stifling of informed discussion on foreign policy was one of the features of early glasnost debates in the USSR on pre-war Soviet foreign policy. See e.g. A. Chubaryan, 'Was an Earlier Anti-Nazi Coalition Possible?', *World Marxist Review* (August 1989).

23. *DVP 1939*, vol. 1, doc. 280; *NSR*, p. 3.

24. *God Krizisa*, vol. 1, doc. 329. Stumm's report of the meeting is in NSR, pp. 3–4. See also the memoirs of I. F. Filippov, *Zapiski o Tretiyem Reikhe* (Moscow, 1966), pp. 30–1, who was the Tass journalist being introduced by Astakhov.

25. God Krizisa, vol. 1, doc. 341. Among the rumours Astakhov was referring to in this letter was an AP report of 8 May 1939 that a Russo-German pact was imminent. See *Documents Diplomatiques Français (DDF)*, 2nd series, vol. 16, doc. 105.

26. Astakhov's report: *God Krizisa*, vol. 1, doc. 349; also: *DVP 1939*, vol. 1, doc. 318 for Astakhov's short telegram to Moscow on the meeting: Schnurre's report: *NSR*, pp. 4–5. According to the *God Krizisa* document the meeting took place on 15 May, whereas the telegram in *DVP 1939* indicates a date of 17 May (the same as that given by Schnurre).

27. *God Krizisa*, vol. 1, doc. 362. Schulenburg's account of the meeting is in *NSR*, pp. 5–9.

28. *NSR*, p. 6.

29. *God Krizisa*, vol. 1, pp. 482–3.

30. *DVP 1939*, vol. 1, doc. 342, and ibid., doc. 384 for a longer report by Astakhov of the same meeting. For Weizsäcker's report see *NSR*, pp. 15–18.

31. *Soviet Peace Efforts*, doc. 314.

32. On the German-Soviet economic negotiations see *DGFP*, series D, vol. 6 passim. Also *God Krizisa*, vol. 2, docs 388 and 412.

33. *NSR*, p. 21.

34. Bulgarian foreign policy archives, cited by S. A. Gorlov, 'Sovetsko-Germanskii Dialog Nakanune Pakta Molotova-Ribbentropa 1939g', *Novaya i Noveishaya Istoriya*, no. 4 (1993), 22.

35. *God Krizisa*, vol. 2, doc. 403.

36. *DVP 1939*, vol. 1, doc. 369.

37. Ibid., doc. 382.

38. *God Krizisa*, vol. 2, doc. 413, and *DVP 1939*, vol. 1, doc. 378.

39. *God Krizisa*, vol. 2, doc. 442. Schulenburg's account of the meeting, which puts a more optimistic gloss on it than Molotov's, is in *NSR*, pp. 26–30.

40. *God Krizisa*, vol. 2, doc. 485.

41. Ibid., docs 494 and 503. See also: *DVP 1939*, vol. 1, doc. 431. Also present at the meeting was E. Babarin, Soviet trade representative in Berlin. For Schnurre's account, which appears to conflate the meetings of the 24th and 26th, see *NSR*, pp. 32–6.

42. Soviet foreign policy archives, cited by Gorlov, 'Sovetsko-Germanskii Dialog', p. 28.

43. *God Krizisa*, vol. 2, doc. 510.

44. Ibid., doc. 511. See also Gorlov, 'Sovetsko-Germanskii Dialog', pp. 28–9.

45. A. J. P. Taylor, *The Origins of the Second World War* (Harmondsworth, 1964), p. 282.

46. *Soviet Peace Efforts*, doc. 376. The triple alliance negotiations are dealt with by Roberts, *Unholy Alliance*, ch. 7.

47. In this connection Alexander Yakovlev's report on behalf of the special commission on the Nazi-Soviet pact set up by the Congress of People's Deputies in June 1989 (*Pravda*, 24 December 1989) refers to the Soviet leadership's access to intelligence information that Germany planned to attack Poland in August/September. One of the sources was the reported remarks of Kleist, a Ribbentrop aide, in early May 1939. These were passed on to Stalin who wrote a note on the report asking for the name of the source. See *Izvestiya Tsk KPSS*, no. 3 (1990), pp. 216–19. Other remarks by Kleist, apparently from the same source and in the KGB archives, are cited in the notes to *DVP 1939*. See vol. 2, nn 131, 136, 169.

48. In relation to this last point one should note that in the KGB archives there is a report on remarks made by Kleist (see previous note) in mid-July 1939 in connection with Hitler's intentions towards the USSR. According to Kleist, Hitler told Ribbentrop that pending the resolution of the dispute with Poland he wanted a new Rapallo, a period of Soviet-German rapprochment and economic co-operation. However, this rapprochement would only be of a temporary character. See *DVP 1939*, vol. 2, n. 136, p. 559.

49. *God Krizisa*, vol. 2, doc. 504. Astakhov's letter to Potemkin is dated 27 July, but wasn't received in Moscow until either 29 July (Gorlov,

'Sovetsko-Germanskii Dialog', p. 28) or 31 July (*God Krizisa*, vol. 2, p. 139).

50. *God Krizisa*, vol. 2, doc. 523, and *DVP 1939*, vol. 1, doc. 445, for a longer report by Astakhov on the same meeting. For Ribbentrop's report of the meeting see *NSR*, pp. 37–9.

51. *God Krizisa*, vol. 2, doc. 525.

52. *NSR*, p. 41.

53. *God Krizisa*, vol. 2, doc. 528.

54. On the military negotiations see Roberts, *Unholy Alliance*; Haslam, *The Soviet Union, 1933–9*; M. Jabara Carley, 'End of the "Low, Dishonest Decade": Failure of the Anglo-Franco-Soviet Alliance in 1939', *Europe–Asia Studies*, 45, no. 2 (1993); and *Soviet Peace Efforts*, docs 315, 316, 317, 327, 328, 339 and 497. Additional documentary information includes the written instructions to the Soviet delegation on the conduct of the negotiations (*God Krizisa*, vol. 2, doc. 527) and a briefing document on tactics to be pursued in the negotiations (*DVP 1939*, vol. 1, doc. 453). Also of interest are the recollections of Alexander Ponomarev, a Soviet interpreter at the talks: 'Polkovnik perevel netochno? ...', *Novoye Vremya*, no. 33 (1989) (English translation in *New Times*, no. 34 [1989]).

55. *God Krizisa*, vol. 2, doc. 529.

56. Ibid., doc. 532.

57. Ibid., doc. 534.

58. Ibid., doc. 540.

59. *God Krizisa*, vol. 2, doc. 541. Astakhov was recalled to Moscow in September 1939. He was subsequently purged and died in a labour camp in 1942.

60. *DVP 1939*, vol. 1, doc. 465.

61. Ibid., doc. 556. For Schulenburg's report of the meeting see *NSR*, pp. 52–7. The telegram from the Soviet embassy in Rome at the end of June reporting on the so-called 'Schulenburg Plan' is doc. 437 in vol. 2, *God Krizisa*. The origin of these rumours concerning the Schulenburg Plan appears to have been Hans von Herwarth, Second Secretary of the German embassy in Moscow, who was passing confidential information about Soviet-German discussions to a contact in the Italian embassy. From there it found its way to Rome and then, via the Soviet embassy, back to Moscow. See H. von Herwarth, *Against Two Evils* (London, 1981), ch. 11.

62. *God Krizisa*, vol. 2, doc. 570. Schulenburg's report is in *NSR*, pp. 59–61.

63. *God Krizisa*, vol. 2, doc. 572. Schulenburg's report: *NSR*, pp. 64–5.

64. *God Krizisa*, vol. 2, docs 582 and 583. For the German record of the Stalin–Hitler exchanges see *NSR*, pp. 66–9.

65. On the discussions of 23 August see G. Hilger and A. G. Meyer, *The Incompatible Allies: A Memoir-History of Soviet-German Relations 1918–1941* (London, 1953), pp. 300–3; the testimony of Ribbentrop and Gaus at the Nuremberg Trials in *Trials of the Major War Criminals Before the International Military Tribunal*, vol. 10, pp. 268–9 and 310–13; A. Read and

D. Fisher, *The Deadly Embrace: Hitler, Stalin and the Nazi-Soviet Pact 1939–1941* (London, 1988), pp. 248–9; and Watt, *How War Came*, ch. 24.
66. *NSR*, p. 76.

6 THE NAZI-SOVIET PACT AND THE PARTITION OF POLAND

1. R. J. Sontag and J. S. Beddie (eds), *Nazi-Soviet Relations 1939–1941* (New York, 1948), pp. 76–8, for the text of the non-aggression treaty and the secret additional protocol. Although the secret protocols to the Nazi-Soviet pact were published in the west just after the war they were not officially admitted to exist or published in the USSR until 1989. In December 1989 the Soviet Congress of People's Deputies condemned the signature of the secret protocols as morally, politically and legally invalid. See L. Bezymensky, 'The Secret Protocols of 1939 as a Problem of Soviet Historiography' in G. Gorodetsky (ed.), *Soviet Foreign Policy 1917–1991* (London, 1994) and the appendix to the present book which reproduces the text of the resolution passed by the Congress of People's Deputies.

2. A. J. P. Taylor, *The Origins of the Second World War* (Harmondsworth, 1964), p. 318.

3. W. S. Churchill, *The Gathering Storm* (London, 1964), p. 346.

4. *Soviet Peace Efforts on the Eve of World War II* (Moscow, 1973), part 2, doc. 445.

5. Telegram, from Beck to Grzybowski in W. Jedrzejewicz (ed.), *Diplomat in Berlin 1933–1939* (New York, 1968). See also *Documents Diplomatiques Français*, 2nd series, vol. 18, doc. 374.

6. J. Degras (ed.), *Soviet Documents on Foreign Policy*, vol. 3 (Oxford, 1953), pp. 361–2.

7. See *Documents on Polish-Soviet Relations, 1939–1945*, vol. 1 (London, 1961), doc. 36; *Documents on British Foreign Policy*, 3rd series, vol. 7, doc. 694; and *Foreign Relations of the United States 1939*, vol. 1, pp. 348–9.

8. *The Polish White Book: Official Documents Concerning Polish-German and Polish-Soviet Relations 1933–1939* (London, 1940), p. 209.

9. *Dokumenty Vneshnei Politiky 1939 god* (*DVP 1939*), vol. 2 (Moscow, 1992), doc. 541.

10. Degras, *Soviet Documents*, pp. 363–71.

11. The treatment of Comintern policy is based on material from the Comintern archives reproduced in 'Komintern i Sovetsko-Germanskii Dogovor o Nenapadenii', *Izvestiya Tsk KPSS*, no. 12 (1989). See also the essay by the British scholar Monty Johnstone who was given access to Comintern archives for the same period: 'Introduction' to F. King and G. Matthews (eds), *About Turn: The Communist Party and the Outbreak of the Second World War* (London, 1990).

12. Cited by Alexander Yakovlev in his interview in *Pravda*, 18 August 1989.

13. On the change in line of the communist parties: P. Spriano, *Stalin and the European Communists* (London, 1985), ch. 10; F. Claudin, *The*

Communist Movement (London, 1975), pp. 294–304; F. Cremieux and J. Estager, *Sur Le Parti 1939–1940* (Paris, 1983); and J. Haslam, 'The Policy of the Communist International from August 1939 to June 1941', unpublished discussion paper, Birmingham University.

14. *Documents on German Foreign Policy* (*DGFP*), series D, vol. 7, docs 360, 382, 383, 387, 388, 413, 414, 424.

15. *NSR*, p. 86. See also Ribbentrop's telegram to Schulenburg on 15 September (*NSR*, pp. 93–4) and Schulenburg's report of 20 September that 'Molotov hinted that the original inclination entertained by the Soviet government and Stalin personally to permit the existence of a residual Poland had given way to the inclination to partition Poland.' (*NSR*, p. 101).

16. The quote is from a transcript unearthed from Schulenburg's personal archives by Ingeborg Fleischhauer. See *International Affairs* (Moscow), August 1991, pp. 114–29, p. 119 for the quote.

17. *NSR*, p. 87. Also *DVP 1939*, vol. 2, doc. 540, for the Soviet report on the meeting.

18. *DGFP*, series D, vol. 8, doc. 37.

19. See L. N. Kutakov, *Japanese Foreign Policy on the Eve of the Pacific War* (Florida, 1972), pp. 151–3.

20. *NSR*, pp. 91–6.

21. Degras, *Soviet Documents*, pp. 374–6.

22. N. Bethell, *The War Hitler Won* (London, 1972), pp. 306–7 and A. Werth, *Russia at War, 1941–1945* (London, 1965), pp. 74–6.

23. Bethell, *War Hitler Won*, pp. 311 ff. and Werth, *Russia at War*, pp. 76–8.

24. On the occupation, incorporation and sovietisation of the Polish territories see J. T. Gross, *Revolution from Abroad: The Soviet Conquest of Poland's Western Ukraine and Western Belorussia* (Princeton, NJ, 1988). For a record of some of the politburo's decisions on the organisation of the incorporation see *DVP 1939*, vol. 2, doc. 536.

25. *NSR*, pp. 105–7.

26. Ibid., p. 108.

27. Degras, *Soviet Documents*, pp. 388–92.

7   EXPANSION AND COEXISTENCE, 1939–1940

1. The USSR formally declared its neutrality in the European war on 17 September 1939. See J. Degras (ed.), *Soviet Documents on Foreign Policy*, vol. 3 (Oxford, 1953), p. 376.

2. Soviet-German economic and military relations during this period are dealt with by G. Roberts, *The Unholy Alliance: Stalin's Pact with Hitler* (London, 1989), ch. 10. Some further information on this subject has been gleaned from the Soviet archives by A. A. Shevyakov 'Sovetsko-Germanskiye Ekonomicheskiye Otnosheniya v 1939–1941 godakh', *Voprosy Istorii*, nos 4–5 (1991) and G. M. Ivanitskii, 'Sovetsko-Germanskiye

Torgovo-Ekonomicheskiye Otnosheniya v 1939–1941gg', *Novaya i Noveishaya Istoriya*, no. 5 (1989).

3. *Polpredy Soobshchayut: Sbornik Dokumentov ob Otnosheniyakh SSSR c Latviei, Litvoi i Estoniei, Avgust 1939g–Avgust 1940g* (hereafter: *Polpredy Soobshchayut*) (Moscow, 1990), doc. 59. A small selection from this volume of documents from the Soviet archives on Russian-Baltic relations during this period is available in English: 'The Baltic Countries Join the Soviet Union (Documents on the USSR's Relations with the Baltic Countries in 1939 and 1940)', *International Affairs* (Moscow), nos 3 and 4, March and April 1990.

4. On the background to Soviet concerns about security in the Baltic see: D. M. Crowe, *The Baltic States and the Great Powers* (Boulder, CO, 1993); J. Hiden and T. Lane (eds), *The Baltic and the Outbreak of the Second World War* (Cambridge, 1991); R. J. Misiunas, 'The Role of the Baltic States in Soviet Relations with the West During the Interwar Period', *Studia Baltica Stockholmiensia*, 3 (1988); and R. Ahmann, 'The German Treaties with Estonia and Latvia in June 1939', *Journal of Baltic Studies*, 20, no. 4 (winter 1989).

5. R. J. Sontag and J. S. Beddie (eds), *Nazi-Soviet Relations 1939–1941* (*NSR*) (New York, 1948), p. 78.

6. According to the documents in *Polpredy Soobshchayut* the only tangible Soviet move in the Baltic before the end of September 1939 was to respond positively to an Estonian proposal for trade negotiations between the two countries. See docs 12, 13 and 32.

7. B. J. Kaslas (ed.), *The USSR-German Aggression Against Lithuania: A Documentary History 1939–1945* (New York, 1973), doc. 48. The reference is to a statement by Molotov to the Lithuanian delegation in Moscow on 7 October 1939.

8. Ibid., for the Stalin quote and *Polpredy Soobshchayut*, docs 26, 34, 35, and 36 for reports from the Soviet legation in Kaunas.

9. On the circumstances surrounding Selter's trip to Moscow see *Polpredy Soobshchayut*, docs 12, 13 and 32; A. Rei, *The Drama of the Baltic Peoples* (Stockholm, 1970), p. 258; and *Report of the Select Committee to Investigate Communist Aggression and the Forced Incorporation of the Baltic States into the USSR: Third Interim Report of the Select Committee on Communist Aggression (House of Representatives)* (hereafter: *Committee on Communist Aggression*), p. 220.

10. *Committee on Communist Aggression*, p. 220. On the Soviet-Estonian negotiations and on the subsequent negotiations with Latvia and Lithuania see also Crowe, *Baltic States*, ch. 4.

11. *Ot Pakta Molotova-Ribbentropa do Dogovora o Bazakh: Dokumenty i Materialy* (Tallinn, 1990), pp. 139–40. On 26 September Voroshilov issued instructions on preparations for military action against Estonia and Latvia. See A. G. Dongarov and G. N. Peskova, 'SSSR i Strany Pribaltiki (Avgust 1939–Avgust 1940)', *Voprosy Istorii*, no. 1 (1991), p. 34.

12. *Ot Pakta Molotova-Ribbentropa do Dogovora o Bazakh: Dokumenty i Materialy* (Tallinn, 1990), p. 137.

13. *Committee on Communist Aggression*, p. 221.

14. Ibid., pp. 223–6 and Rei, *Drama of Baltic Peoples*, pp. 265–6.

15. *Committee on Communist Aggression*, p. 226.

16. For the Russian text of the Soviet-Estonian treaty see *Polpredy Soobshchayut*, doc. 44. An English translation is in *International Affairs* (Moscow), March 1991, pp. 141–2.

17. *Polpredy Soobshchayut*, doc. 58.

18. On the course of the Soviet-Latvian negotiations see: ibid., docs 58 and 59; A. Berzins, *The Unpunished Crime* (New York, 1963), pp. 45–8; and Dongarov and Peskova, 'SSSR i Strany Pribaltiki', pp. 35–7.

19. For the Russian text of the Soviet-Latvian treaty see *Polpredy Soobshchayut*, doc. 63. English translation in *International Affairs* (Moscow), April 1990, pp. 97–9.

20. On the Polish-Lithuanian dispute over Vilna, see F. P. Walters, *A History of the League of Nations* (Oxford, 1960), pp. 105–9, 140–3 and 398–400; P. J. Yearwood, 'Made to Look Ridiculous: The League of Nations and the Question of Vilna, 1920–1922', University of Jos, Nigeria, 1984. On Soviet support for Lithuania: S. A. Gorlov, 'SSSR i Territorialnye Problemy Litvy', *Voenno-Istoricheskii Zhurnal*, no. 7 (1990).

21. *NSR*, p. 107.

22. For the story of the Soviet-German agreement on the transfer of Lithuanian territory to Germany see B. J. Kaslas, 'The Lithuanian Strip in Soviet-German Secret Diplomacy, 1939–1941', *Journal of Baltic Studies*, iv (1973), 212.

23. This account of the Soviet-Lithuanian negotiations is based on *Committee on Communist Aggression*, pp. 312–17 and Dongarov and Peskova, 'SSSR i Strany Pribaltiki'. There is also J. Urbsys, 'Lithuania and the Soviet Union 1939–1940: The Fateful Year', *Litaunus*, no. 2 (1989).

24. *Committee on Communist Aggression*, p. 315.

25. Ibid., p. 316.

26. For the text of the Soviet-Lithuanian mutual assistance treaty and treaty on the transfer of Vilna see *Polpredy Soobshchayut*, doc. 73. In English: *International Affairs* (Moscow), April 1990, pp. 99–101.

27. Urbsys, 'Lithuania and the Soviet Union', p. 40.

28. J. Degras (ed.), *Soviet Documents on Foreign Policy*, vol. 3 (Oxford, 1953), p. 394.

29. The relevant documents are in *Polpredy Soobshchayut*, docs 93, 108, 110, 115.

30. Cited by Lev Bezymensky, 'What did Stalin and Hitler agree upon in 1939?', *New Times*, no. 37 (1991), 36.

31. On Soviet policy towards the Baltic States from autumn 1939 to spring 1940 see Crowe, *The Baltic States*, ch. 6 and A. N. Tarulis, *Soviet Policy Towards the Baltic States 1918–1940* (Notre Dame, Ind., 1959).

32. On the background to Soviet-Finnish relations see J. Haslam, *The Soviet Union and the Struggle for Collective Security in Europe 1933–1939* (London, 1984), pp. 207–9, 236–8 and appendix 2.

33. 'The Winter War (Documents on Soviet-Finnish Relations in 1939–1940)', *International Affairs* (Moscow), September 1989, doc. 7.

34. See V. Tanner, *The Winter War* (Stanford, Cal., 1957), chs 2–5.

35. The course of the Soviet-Finnish relations until the point of their breakdown in mid-November 1939 can be followed in ibid., the documents cited in note 2 above and *The Development of Finnish-Soviet Relations* (London, 1940).

36. See N. I. Baryshnikov, 'Sovetsko-Finlyandskaya Voina 1939–1940gg.', *Novaya i Noveishaya Istoriya*, no. 4 (1991), 33.

37. See Alexandra Kollontai's diary notes in ' "Seven Shots" in the Winter of 1939', *International Affairs* (Moscow), January 1990, pp. 185–6.

38. Cited by V. Mitenev, 'Archives reopen debate on the Winter War', *Soviet Weekly*, 3 June 1989.

39. Baryshnikov, 'Sovetsko-Finlyandskaya Voina', p. 34.

40. See Degras, *Soviet Documents*, pp. 401–3.

41. On the outbreak of the Soviet-Finnish war see D. W. Spring, 'The Soviet Decision for War Against Finland, 30 November 1939', *Soviet Studies* (April 1986).

42. *Khrushchev Remembers* (London, 1971), pp. 135–6.

43. For an account of the military aspects of the Soviet-Finnish conflict see J. Erickson, *The Soviet High Command* (London, 1962), pp. 542–52.

44. 'The Winter War (Documents on Soviet-Finnish Relations in 1939–1940)', *International Affairs* (Moscow), January 1990, doc. 20 and W. M. Carlgren, *Swedish Foreign Policy During the Second World War* (London, 1977), p. 29.

45. Degras, *Soviet Documents*, pp. 407–10.

46. On the Kuusinen government and Soviet policy see T. Vihavainen, 'The Soviet Decision for War Against Finland, 30 November 1939: A Comment', *Soviet Studies* (April 1987) and M. I. Meltukhov, ' "Narodny Front" dlya Finlyandii? (K Voposy o Tselyakh Sovetskogo Rukovodstva v Voine c Finlyandiei 1939–1940gg)', *Otechestvennaya Istoriya*, no. 3 (1993).

47. My general points on ideology were inspired mainly by C. Reynolds, *Modes of Imperialism* (London, 1981), ch. 4, 'Imperialism and Ideology' and J. Schull, 'What is Ideology? Theoretical Problems and Lessons from Soviet-Type Societies', *Political Studies* (1992), XL, 728–41. See also J. Schull, 'The Self-Destruction of Soviet Ideology' in S. G. Soloman (ed.), *Beyond Sovietology* (New York, 1993).

48. On these unofficial Soviet-Finnish contacts see Kollontai, 'Seven Shots', pp. 191 ff.

49. On the negotiations to end the war see Tanner, *The Winter War*, chs 7–11 and the Soviet documents he cites in n. 13. The text of the Soviet-Finnish peace treaty is appended to the Tanner book.

50. Soviet foreign policy archives. Cited by P. Sevostyanov, *Before the Nazi Invasion* (Moscow, 1981), p. 95. Soviet relations with Britain and France during the period of the Winter War are covered by G. Roberts, *The Unholy Alliance: Stalin's Pact with Hitler* (London, 1989), ch. 11. See also G. Gorodetsky, 'The Impact of the Ribbentrop–Molotov Pact on the Course of Soviet Foreign Policy', *Cahiers du Monde russe et soviétique*, XXXI (1) (January–March 1990).

51. On pre-pact Soviet policy towards Bulgaria and Turkey see Roberts, *Unholy Alliance*, pp. 167–8.

52. *God Krizisa 1938–1939*, vol. 2 (Moscow, 1990), docs 517 and 536; *Dokumenty Vneshnei Politiky 1939 god (DVP 1939)*, vol. 1 (Moscow, 1992), docs 451, 461, 471, and 499.

53. See Molotov's telegram to Terentev, the Soviet ambassador in Turkey, on 3/9/39 in *DVP 1939*, vol. 2, doc. 527. Also: docs 542, 545, 551, 560 and 578.

54. *NSR*, pp. 85–7, 97 and 120.

55. On the Soviet-Turkish negotiations see also Gasratyan and Moiseev, *SSSR i Turtsiya 1917–1941* (Moscow, 1981), pp. 157–60 and F. C. Erkin, *Les Relations Turco-Soviétiques et la Question des Détroits* (Ankara, 1968), pp. 160–70. There is also a memoir account by N. V. Novikov, *Vospominaniya Diplomata: Zapiski 1938–1947* (Moscow, 1989), pp. 28–34.

56. *DVP 1939*, vol. 2, doc. 654.

57. Soviet foreign policy archives. Cited by P. P. Sevostyanov, *Pered Velikim Ispytaniem* (Moscow 1981), p. 199.

58. *DVP 1939*, vol. 2, doc. 693.

59. On the Anglo-Turkish-French negotiations see L. Zhivkova, *Anglo-Turkish Relations 1933–1939* (London, 1976). On Russian protests about the Turkish accord with Britain and France: *DVP 1939*, vol. 2, docs 701, 725, 732 and 736.

60. A. L. Zapantis, *Greek-Soviet Relations 1917–1941* (New York, 1982), p. 382.

61. *Sovetsko-Bolgarskie Otnosheniya i Svyezi 1917–1944* (Moscow, 1976), docs 504 and 505.

62. Ibid., doc. 506; S. Rachev, *Anglo-Bulgarian Relations During the Second World War* (Sofia, 1981), p. 19.

63. *Istoriya Diplomatii*, vol. 4 (Moscow, 1975), p. 153.

64. Zapantis, *Greek-Soviet Relations*, p. 384, n. 27 and RIAA: *Survey of the Foreign Press 1939–1941*, vol. 2, no. 14.

65. *Sovetsko-Bolgarskie*, doc. 510.

66. *DVP 1939*, doc. 769.

67. Ibid., doc. 783.

68. For Molotov's speech see Degras, *Soviet Documents*, pp. 436–49.

69. See *Polpredy Soobshchayut*, docs 256, 273, 277, 285, 290, 293, 294, 295, 296, 297, 298, 299 and 300.

70. On the Soviet takeover of the Baltic States in summer 1940 see: Crowe, *The Baltic States*, ch. 7; D. Kirby, 'The Baltic States, 1940–1950', in M. McCauley (ed.), *Communist Power in Europe, 1944–1949* (London, 1977); R. J. Misiunas and R. Taagepera, *The Baltic States: Years of Dependence 1940–1980* (London, 1983); and L. Sabaliunas, *Lithuania in Crisis: Nationalism to Communism 1939–1940* (Bloomington, Ind., 1972). The specific interpretation of these events given in the text is developed in detail in G. Roberts, 'Soviet Policy and the Baltic States, 1939–1940: A Reappraisal' (unpublished, 1994). The main documentary basis for this interpretation is the new evidence from Soviet archives published in *Polpredy Soobshchayut*.

71. *NSR*, pp. 155, 160–3 and Degras, *Soviet Documents*, pp. 458–61.

8 CRISIS AND CONFLICT, 1940–1941

1. See G. Roberts, *The Unholy Alliance: Stalin's Pact with Hitler* (London, 1989), pp. 185–7.

2. Clause 3 of the secret additional protocol to the Nazi-Soviet pact stated: 'With regard to Southeastern Europe attention is called by the Soviet side to its interest in Bessarabia. The German side declares its complete political disinterestedness in these areas.' This is sometimes interpreted as an agreement that the Soviets could occupy this area if they wanted to. In truth what it amounted to was a restatement of a longstanding Soviet legal claim to this Romanian province and a keep-out message to the Germans.

3. On German foreign policy during this period see W. Carr, *Poland to Pearl Harbor* (London, 1985), pp. 112–27 and H. W. Koch, 'Operation Barbarossa – The Current State of the Debate', *Historical Journal*, 31, no. 2 (1988). Also: G. T. Waddington, 'Ribbentrop and the Soviet Union, 1937–1941', in J. Erickson and D. Dilks (eds), *Barbarossa: The Axis and the Allies* (Edinburgh, 1994).

4. R. J. Sontag and J. S. Beddie (eds), *Nazi-Soviet Relations, 1939–1941* (*NSR*), pp. 144 and 148.

5. See the telegram of the Soviet military attaché in Bulgaria (6/6/40) in *Izvestiya Tsk KPSS*, no. 3 (1990).

6. M. Toscano 'Italo-Soviet Relations 1940–1941: Failure of an Accord', in his *Designs in Diplomacy: Pages from European Diplomatic History in the Twentieth Century* (Baltimore, MD, 1970), pp. 146–56. For the back ground to Soviet-Italian relations see J. Calvitt Clarke's highly informative *Russia and Italy Against Hitler: The Bolshevik-Fascist Rapprochement of the 1930s* (Westport, CT, 1991).

7. Toscano, 'Italo-Soviet Relations', p. 157.

8. Ibid., p. 160.

9. J. Degras (ed.), *Soviet Documents on Foreign Policy*, vol. 3 (Oxford, 1953), pp. 457–8.

10. The Russians later claimed that they expected their statement to Rosso on 25 June to be transmitted to Berlin and that, in effect, it constituted a proposal to Germany as well as Italy. *NSR*, pp. 193–4. See also Molotov's complaints to Rosso on this score. Cited by Toscano, 'Italo-Soviet Relations', p. 203.

11. See Yehuda Lahav, 'Soviet Policy and the Transylvanian Question (1940–1946)', Soviet and East European Research Centre (Hebrew University of Jerusalem), Research Paper, No. 27, pp. 10–11; A. L. Zapantis, *Greek-Soviet Relations 1917–1941* (New York, 1982), p. 397, n. 60; D. Sirkov, 'Bulgaria's National Territorial Problem during the Second World War', *Bulgarian Historical Review*, no. 3 (1991), 5; and *Documents on German Foreign Policy* (*DGFP*), series D, vol. 10, pp. 132, 208–9.

12. Toscano, 'Italo-Soviet Relations', pp. 167–9.

13. See G. Gafencu, *The Last Days of Europe: A Diplomatic Journey in 1939* (London, 1947) ch. 2.

14. 'The Breach Between Germany and the Soviet Union', in *Survey of International Affairs 1939–1946*, p. 372.

15. *NSR*, pp. 180–3 and 190–6.

16. Soviet foreign policy archives. Cited by P. Sevostyanov, *Before the Nazi Invasion* (Moscow, 1984), p. 169.

17. *DGFP*, series D, vol. 11, pp. 296–7.

18. See *Khrushchev Remembers* (London, 1971), p. 115.

19. *DGFP*, series D, vol. 11, pp. 353–4.

20. A. M. Vasilevsky, *Delo Vcei Zhizn* (Moscow, 1973), p. 113.

21. Molotov to Stalin, 13/11/41 in *Mezhdunarodnaya Zhizn*, June 1991 p. 132. For full reference citation see note 23 below.

22. Degras, *Soviet Documents*, pp. 461–9 for Molotov's speech.

23. *NSR*, pp. 217–54; 'Nakanune: Peregovory V. M. Molotova v Berline v Noyabre 1940 goda', *Mezhdunarodnaya Zhizn*, June and August 1991.

24. *NSR*, p. 253.

25. V. M. Berezhkov, *S Diplomaticheskoi Missiei v Berlin 1940–1941* (Moscow, 1966), p. 33.

26. Stalin's telegrams are published in the collection cited in note 23 above. They are all businesslike in character and concerned with tactics in the negotiations with the Germans. None of them bears any remote resemblance to the message recalled by Berezhkov.

27. *NSR*, pp. 255–8.

28. Ibid., pp. 258–9

29. J. Erickson, 'Threat Identification and Strategic Appraisal by the Soviet Union, 1930–1941', in E. R. May (ed.), *Knowing One's Enemies* (Princeton, NJ, 1984), p. 414.

30. This point was brought to my attention by R. L. Garthoff, *Detente and Confrontation: American-Soviet Relations from Nixon to Reagan* (Washington, DC, 1985), p. 941, n. 152. Also of interest is Stalin's telegram to Molotov on 11/11/40 where he states that any reference to India in any Soviet-German declaration should be deleted on grounds that it could be a trick aimed at 'kindling war'. See *Mezhdunarodnaya Zhizn*, June 1991, p. 125.

31. *Mezhdunarodnaya Zhizn*, August 1991, p. 119.

32. According to Dmitri Volkogonov in his biography of Stalin, Molotov came back from Berlin convinced that Hitler was not about to attack the Soviet Union. However, he does not clarify the nature of Molotov's belief in this respect nor does he provide any evidence to support his assertion.

33. Soviet Foreign Policy archives. Cited by P. P. Sevostyanov, *Pered Velikim Ispytaniem* (Moscow, 1981), pp. 210–11. Sevostyanov's reference in the text is to a history of the Bulgarian communist party, but the same statement is partially cited by *Istoriya Diplomatii*, vol. 4 (Moscow, 1975), pp. 153–4, and here the reference is to Soviet archives.

34. *Istoriya Diplomatii*, p. 158, and S. Rachev, *Anglo-Bulgarian Relations During the Second World War* (Sofia, 1981), pp. 38–9.

35. *Istoriya Diplomatii*, p. 154, and *Sovetsko-Bolgarskie Otnosheniya*, vol. 1 (Moscow, 1976), docs 567, 569 and 588.

36. See A. L. Narochnitskii, 'Sovetsko-Ugoslavskii Dogovor 5 Apelya 1941g o Druzhbe i Nenapadenii', *Novaya i Noveishaya Istoriya*, no. 1 (1989), 4–5.

37. Degras, *Soviet Documents*, p. 449.

38. See V. K. Volkov, 'Sovetsko-Ugoslavskiye Otnosheniya v Nachalnyi Period Vtoroi Mirovoi Voiny v Kontekste Mirovykh Sobytii (1939–1941gg)', *Sovetskoe Slavyanovedeniye*, no. 6 (1990).

39. Soviet Foreign Policy archives. Cited by Sevostyanov, *Before the Nazi Invasion*, p. 190.

40. See J. Haslam, 'The Policy of the Communist International from August 1939 to June 1941' (unpublished paper, CREES, Birmingham University).

41. Soviet Foreign Policy archives. Cited by Sevostyanov, *Before the Nazi Invasion*, pp. 190–1.

42. Soviet Foreign Policy archives. Cited in *SSSR v Borbe Protiv Fashistskoi Agressii 1933–1945* (Moscow, 1986), p. 139.

43. *Sovetsko-Bolgarskie Otnosheniya*, doc. 56.

44. Degras, *Soviet Documents*, p. 482.

45. Ibid., pp. 482–3.

46. *Sovetsko-Bolgarskie Otnosheniya*, docs 581 and 582.

47. Degras, *Soviet Documents*, p. 483. *Sovetsko-Bolgarskie Otnosheniya*, doc. 583. See also *NSR*, pp. 277–9.

48. 'Mozhno li Bylo Predotvratit Aprelskuu Voiny? (Novye Dokumenty o Sovetsko-Ugoslavskom Dogovore o Druzhbe i Nenapadenii 1941g.)', *Vestnik Ministerstva Inostrannykh Del SSSR*, 15 August 1989, p. 58.

49. Ibid., pp. 59–60.

50. Narochnitskii, 'Sovetsko-Ugoslavskii Dogovor', pp. 13–14.

51. *NSR*, pp. 316–18 and Vestnik documents cited above, pp. 61–2 for the Soviet report of this meeting.

52. Degras, *Soviet Documents*, pp. 484–5.

53. *Foreign Relations of the United States 1941*, vol. 1 pp. 301–2 and 312–15. But see Narochnitskii, 'Sovetsko-Ugoslavskii Dogovor', pp. 18–19 who argues that any serious Soviet aid to Yugoslavia was ruled out by Stalin's determination to avoid provoking Hitler for as long as possible.

9 STALIN AND THE ROAD TO WAR, APRIL–JUNE 1941

1. On Soviet-Turkish relations see G. Roberts, *The Unholy Alliance: Stalin's Pact with Hitler* (London, 1989), ch. 14.

2. On the Soviet-Japanese neutrality pact see ibid. and J. Haslam, *The Soviet Union and the Threat From the East, 1933–41* (London, 1992), ch. 6.

3. On British-Soviet relations see Roberts, *Unholy Alliance*.

4. R. J. Sontag and J. S. Beddie (eds), *Nazi-Soviet Relations, 1939–1941* (*NSR*) (New York, 1948), p. 324.

5. Ibid., p. 336.

6. M. Beloff, *The Foreign Policy of Soviet Russia 1929–1941*, vol. 2 (Oxford, 1966), pp. 378–9; A. L. Zapantis, *Hitler's Balkan Campaign and*

the Invasion of the USSR (New York, 1987), p. 73; *NSR*, pp. 339–41; A. Nekrich, *June 22nd 1941*, ed. V. Petrov (Columbia, SC, 1968), pp. 166–7.

7. *NSR*, p. 344.

8. J. Erickson, *The Road to Stalingrad* (London, 1975), p. 77.

9. 'O Podgotovke Germanii K Napadeniu na SSSR', *Izvestiya Tsk KPSS*, no. 4 (1990).

10. 'Kanun Voiny: Preduprezhdeniya Diplomatov', *Vestnik Ministerstva Inostrannykh SSSR*, 30 April 1990; 'Fashistskaya Agressiya: O Chem Soobshchali Diplomaty', *Voenno-Istoricheskii Zhurnal*, no. 6 (1991); and *Izvestiya Tsk KPSS* no. 3 (1990), 220–1.

11. Vestnik source, note 10 above, p. 77.

12. It is traditional to attribute the Soviet military disaster following 22 June 1941 to a combination of German surprise and Stalin's purge of the armed forces in the 1930s. However, recent research indicates that the effects of the purges were more limited than previously thought and that the disaster was the result of a more complex set of factors than just that of surprise. See the Erickson and Tarleton articles cited in note 24 below and R. R. Reese, 'The Impact of the Great Purge on the Red Army', *Soviet and Post-Soviet Review*, 19, nos 1–3 (1992) and 'The Red Army and the Great Purges' in J. Arch Getty and R. T. Manning (eds), *Stalinist Terror: New Perspectives* (Cambridge, 1993).

13. A. Dallin, 'Stalin and the German Invasion', *Soviet Union/Union Soviétique*, nos 1–3 (1991), 35.

14. J. Haslam, 'Soviet Foreign Policy 1939–1941: Isolation and Expansion' in ibid., p. 120.

15. Cited by V. Khvostov, 'The Origins of the Second World War' in *Problems of the Contemporary World* (Moscow, 1970), p. 20, n. 3 (5).

16. Cited by A. Fontaine, *History of the Cold War* (London, 1968), p. 153.

17. See V. Anfilov, 'Ot Otstupleniya–K Pobede', *Literaturnaya Gatzeta*, 17/6/87 and D. Volkogonov, 'Nakanune Voiny', *Pravda*, 20/6/88; see also D. Ogden, 'Finding a Bitter Truth', *7 Days*, 22/8/87.

18. See S. Bialer (ed.), *Stalin and His Generals* (London, 1970), p. 145.

19. G. Zhukov, *Memoirs and Reminiscences*, vol. 1 (Moscow, 1985), p. 250.

20. Ibid. and V. D. Danilov, 'Sovetskoe Glavnoe Komandovaniye v Preddverii Velikoi Otechestvennoi Voiny', *Novaya i Noveishaya Istoriya*, no. 6 (1988).

21. L. Rotundo, 'Stalin and the Outbreak of War in 1941', *Journal of Contemporary History*, 24 (1989), p. 287.

22. Ibid., p. 290.

23. Ibid., p. 291.

24. On the question of Soviet war doctrine and its political effects see Rotundo, 'Stalin and the Outbreak of War'; J. Erickson, 'Threat Identification and Strategic Appraisal by the Soviet Union, 1940–1941', in E. R. May (ed.), *Knowing One's Enemies* (Princeton, NJ, 1984), pp. 416–23; and R. E. Tarleton, 'What Really Happened to the Stalin Line?', *Journal of Slavic Military Studies* (March 1993).

25. Cited by S. M. Miner, *Between Churchill and Stalin: The Soviet Union, Great Britain and the Origins of the Grand Alliance* (Chapel Hill, NC, 1988), p. 142.

26. C. Cruickshank, *Deception in World War II* (Oxford, 1981), p. 208.

27. On the German deception programme see ibid.; F. H. Hinsley et al., *British Intelligence in the Second World War*, vol. 1 (London, 1979), ch. 14; B. Whaley, *Codeword 'Barbarossa'* (Cambridge, Mass., 1973), pp. 170–87 and Appendix A; and V. T. Fomin, 'Iz Istorii Podgotovski Nemetsko-Fashistskoi Agressii SSSR', *Voprosy Istorii* (August 1966).

28. Rotundo, 'Stalin and the Outbreak of War', p. 291.

29. Whaley, *Codeword 'Barbarossa'*, p. 227.

30. See Hinsley, *British Intelligence*, ch. 14.

31. Whaley, *Codeword 'Barbarossa'*, p. 195.

32. Ibid.

33. Zhukov, *Memoirs*, pp. 272–3.

34. Ibid., p. 274.

35. Schulenburg's 'warning' reputedly came at a meeting with Dekanozov on 5 May 1941 (G. Kumanev, '22-go, Na Rassvete ...', *Pravda*, 22 June 1989, citing the recollections of trade minister and politburo member Mikoyan). However, Dekanozov's diary note-report on the meeting is reproduced in the *Voenno-Istoricheskii Zhurnal* source cited above, and this only records Schulenburg's expressions of concern about the state of Soviet-German relations. There was no warning of a German attack.

36. See A. Baidakov, 'Po Dannym Razvediki ...', *Pravda*, 8 May 1989.

37. See *Izvestiya Tsk KPSS*, no. 4 (1990), p. 221.

38. Cited by O. Gorchakov, 'Nakanune, ili Tragediya Kassandry: Povest v Dokumentakh', *Nedelya*, no. 44 (1988), 22. Note: there is some doubt about the authenticity of this quotation.

39. Dallin, 'Stalin and the German Invasion', p. 28.

40. On the Cripps memo and the Churchill warning see L. Woodward, *British Foreign Policy in the Second World War*, vol. 1 (London, 1970), p. 604; P. Sevostyanov, *Before the Nazi Invasion* (Moscow, 1984), pp. 141–2; Hinsley, *British Intelligence*, p. 453; and the various works of G. Gorodetsky on this subject, especially his *Stafford Cripps' Mission to Moscow* (Cambridge, 1984).

41. See J. Costello, *Ten Days That Saved The West* (London, 1991), ch. 17. Costello was given access to some KGB archives on the Hess affair.

42. I. Maisky, *Memoirs of a Soviet Ambassador* (London, 1967), pp. 145–7.

43. For the British reports of the Maisky–Eden meetings in June 1941 see Woodward, *British Foreign Policy*, pp. 616–17 and 620–2. Some extracts from Maisky's reports to Moscow on these meetings are cited by S. Gorlov and V. Voyushin, 'Warnings came not only from the German Ambassador', *New Times*, no. 21 (1991), from which the quote in the text comes.

44. Quoted by Gorlov and Voyushin, note 43 above.

45. Maisky's report on his meeting with Cadogan is reproduced in the *Vestnik* source cited above.

46. J. Degras (ed.), *Soviet Documents on Foreign Policy*, vol. 3 (Oxford, 1953), p. 489.

47. See D. Volkogonov, *Triumf i Tragediya*, book 2, part 1 (Moscow, 1989), pp. 122–4. Also Molotov's recollections concerning the Tass statement, as recorded by F. Chuev, *Sto Sorok Beced s Molotovym* (Moscow, 1991), pp. 42–3.

48. On this meeting see A. Read and D. Fisher, *The Deadly Embrace: Hitler, Stalin and the Nazi-Soviet Pact 1939–1941* (London, 1988), pp. 622–3.

49. *NSR*, pp. 355–6 and *Istoriya Diplomatii*, vol. 4 (Moscow, 1975), pp. 179–80.

50. *Istoriya Diplomatii*, p. 180; V. Berezhkov, *History in the Making: Memoirs of World War II Diplomacy* (Moscow, 1983), p. 76; and I. Koblyakov, 'On the Way Home From Berlin, June 1941', *International Affairs* (Moscow), May 1972.

51. *NSR*, pp. 356–7; Koblyakov, ibid., and Berezhkov, ibid., pp. 76–9.

52. Degras, *Soviet Documents*, pp. 490–1.

53. On this issue see, inter alia, V. Suvorov, *Icebreaker: Who Started the Second World War?* (London, 1990); G. Gorodetsky, 'Was Stalin Planning to Attack Hitler in June 1941', *RUSI Journal*, no. 3 (1986); and G. Ueberschar, 'Hitler's Decision to Attack the Soviet Union in Recent German Historiography', *Soviet Union/Union Soviétique*, nos 1–3 (1991).

54. There are various versions of Stalin's speech which make this suggestion (see Roberts, *Unholy Alliance*, pp. 259–60, n. 13). The best-known account along these lines is Alexander Werth's, which was based on discussions in Moscow during the war. See his *Russia at War 1941–1945* (London, 1965), pp. 132–3.

55. See L. Bezymensky, 'What did Stalin say on May 5, 1941', *New Times*, no. 19 (1991). Stalin said nothing about a pre-emptive strike but he made it clear to his audience that he had no doubt that war with Germany was coming. See also, D. Volkogonov, 'The German Attack, the Soviet Response, Sunday 22 June 1941', in J. Erickson and D. Dilks (eds), *Barbarossa: The Axis and the Allies* (Edinburgh, 1994).

56. See V. N. Kiselev, 'Upryamye Fakty Nachala Voiny', *Voenno-Istoricheskii Zhurnal*, no. 2 (1992).

10 CONCLUSION

1. R. K. Debo, *Revolution and Survival: The Foreign Policy of Soviet Russia 1917–1918* (Liverpool, 1979), p. 420. See also the same author's *Survival and Consolidation: The Foreign Policy of Soviet Russia, 1918–1921* (Montreal, 1992).

2. On the ideology of collective security and its role in foreign policy practice see G. Roberts, *The Unholy Alliance: Stalin's Pact with Hitler* (London, 1989), ch. 3.

3. See the Appendix for the text of the congress resolution on the pact. For background information: ibid. , ch. 2; T. J. Uldricks, 'Evolving Soviet

View of the Nazi-Soviet Pact' in R. Frucht (ed.), *Labyrinth of Nationalism, Complexities of Diplomacy* (Columbus, OH, 1992); L. Bezymensky, 'The Secret Protocols of 1989 as a Problem of Soviet Historiography', in G. Gorodetsky (ed.), *Soviet Foreign Policy, 1917–1991* (London, 1994); M. Hagen, 'History and Politics under Gorbachev', *Harriman Institute Forum* (November 1988); T. Sherlock, 'New Thinking on the Nazi-Soviet Pact', *Report on the USSR*, 28 July 1989; T. S. Szayna, 'Addressing "Blank Spots" in Polish-Soviet Relations', *Problems of Communism* (November–December 1988); V. Tolz and T. Sherlock, 'Latest Attempts to Review History of Soviet-Polish Relations', *Report on the USSR*, 23 June 1989; and A. Chubaryan, 'Revolution and Renewal in History: The Russian and European Experience', *Britain–USSR* (April 1990).

Select Bibliography

This is not a comprehensive bibliography on the subject of Soviet-German relations and the origins of the Second World War, or even a complete listing of all the works referred to in the notes to this book. Instead I have endeavoured to select those documents and secondary studies of most direct importance and interest. With regard to recent Russian/Soviet books and articles I have restricted myself to a few key contributions, with the accent on works available in English. For further bibliographical information see the present author's *The Unholy Alliance: Stalin's Pact with Hitler* (London, 1989) and T. J. Uldricks' essay on 'Evolving Soviet Views of the Nazi-Soviet Pact'. I would also like to draw the reader's attention to Jonathan Haslam's fine series of books on Soviet foreign policy in the 1930s. These can be read with profit as both a complement and an alternative to the present work.

DOCUMENTS (IN RUSSIAN)

Dokumenty i Materialy Kanuna Vtoroi Mirovoi Voiny 1937–1939, 2 vols (Moscow, 1981).
Dokumenty i Materialy po Istorii Sovetsko-Chekhoslovatskikh Otnoshenii 1934–1939 (Moscow, 1978).
Dokumenty i Materialy po Istorii Sovetsko-Polskikh Otnoshenii, vols VI–VII (Moscow, 1969 and 1973.
Dokumenty po Istorii Munkhenshogo Sgovora 1937–1939 (Moscow, 1979).
Dokumenty Vneshnei Politiki 1939 god, 2 vols (Moscow, 1992).
Dokumenty Vneshnei Politiki SSSR, vols XVI–XXI (Moscow, 1970–7).
'Fashistskaya Agressiya: O Chem Soobshchali Diplomaty', *Voenno-Istoricheski Zhurnal*, no. 6 (1991).
God Krizisa, 1938–1939: Dokumenty i Materialy, 2 vols (Moscow, 1990).
'Kanun Voiny: Preduprezhdeniya Diplomatov', *Vestnik Ministerstva Inostrannykh Del SSSR*, 30 April 1990.
'Mozhno Li Bylo Predotvratit Aprelskuyu Voinu? Novye Dokumenty o Sovetsko-Ugoslvaskom Dogovore o Druzhbe i Nenapadenii 1941g', *Vestnik Ministerstva Inostrannykh Del SSSR*, 15 August 1989.
'Nakanune: Peregovory V. M. Molotova v Berline v Noyabre 1940 goda', *Mezhdunarodnaya Zhizn*, nos 6 and 8 (1991).
'O Podgotovke Germanii k Napadeniu na SSSR', *Izvestiya Tsk KPSS*, no. 4 (1990).
'Osobaya Missiya Davida Kandelaki', *Voprosy Istorii*, no. 4–5 (1989).
Ot Pakta Molotova-Ribbentropa do Dogovora o Bazakh: Dokumenty i Materialy (Tallinn, 1990).
Polpredy Soobshchayut: Sbornik Dokumentov ob Otnosheniyakh SSSR c Latviei, Litvoi i Estoniei, Avgust 1939g–Avgust 1940g (Moscow, 1990).
Sovetsko-Bolgarskie Otnosheniya i Svyezi 1917–1944 (Moscow, 1976).

'Sovetsko-Germanskoe Voennoe Sotrudichestvo v 1920–1933 godakh', *Mezhdunarodnaya Zhizn*, no. 6 (1990).

SSSR v Borbe za Mir Nakanune Vtoroi Mirovoi Voiny (Moscow, 1971).

'Zapiska M. M. Litvinova I. V. Stalinu, 3 Dekabrya 1935g', *Izvestiya Tsk KPSS*, no. 2 (1990).

'Zimnyaya Voina: Dokumenty o Sovetsko-Finlandskikh Otnosheniyakh 1939–1940 godov', *Mezhdunarodnaya Zhizn*, nos 8 and 12 (1989).

1940 God v Estonii: Dokumenty i Materialy (Tallinn, 1990).

DOCUMENTS (IN ENGLISH)

'Around the Non-Aggression Pact (Documents of Soviet-German Relations in 1939)', *International Affairs* (Moscow), October 1989.

'The Baltic Countries Join the Soviet Union (Documents on the USSR's Relations with the Baltic Countries in 1939 and 1940)', *International Affairs* (Moscow), March and April 1990.

The Development of Finnish-Soviet Relations (London, 1940).

Documents on German Foreign Policy, series C, vols I–VI and series D vols I–XII.

Documents and Materials Relating to the Eve of the Second World War, 2 vols (Moscow, 1948).

'Documents: The Struggle of the USSR for Collective Security in Europe during 1933–1935', *International Affairs* (Moscow), June, July, August and October 1963.

'The Molotov–Ribbentrop Pact: The German Version', *International Affairs* (Moscow), August 1991.

'Moscow and the Nazis', *Survey* (October 1963).

'Munich: Witnesses Account', *International Affairs* (Moscow), December 1988.

Nazi-Soviet Relations 1939–1941, ed. R. J. Sontag and J. S. Beddie (New York, 1948).

New Documents on the History of Munich (Prague, 1958).

'The New Version of the Tukhachevsky Affair: Declassified Documents from the USSR Foreign Policy Archives', *New Times*, no. 13 (1989).

'On the Eve: V. M. Molotov's Discussions in Berlin, November 1940', *International Affairs* (Moscow), July 1991.

Report of the Select Committee to Investigate Communist Aggression and the Forced Incorporation of the Baltic States into the USSR: Third Interim Report of the Select Committee on Communist Aggression (House of Representatives) (Washington, 1954).

Soviet Documents on Foreign Policy, 3 vols, ed. J. Degres (Oxford, 1951–3).

'Soviet-German Military Co-operation 1920–1933', *International Affairs* (Moscow), July 1990.

Soviet Foreign Policy 1928–1934: Documents and Materials, 2 vols, ed. X. J. Eudin and H. F. Fisher (Pennsylvania, 1967).

Soviet Peace Efforts on the Eve of World War II (Novosti Press, 1973).

'The Winter War', *International Affairs* (Moscow), August 1989 and January 1990.

MEMOIRS, SPEECHES, AND STATEMENTS

V. Berezhkov, *History in the Making: Memoirs of World War II Diplomacy* (Moscow, 1983).

F. Chuev, *Sto Sorok Beced c Molotovym* (Moscow, 1989).

R. P. Drax, 'Mission to Moscow', *Naval Review* (November 1952 and February 1953).

I. F. Filippov, *Zapiski of Tretiyem Reikhe* (Moscow, 1966).

E. Gnedin, 'V Narkomindele: 1922–1939', *Pamyat: Istoricheskii Sbornik*, no. 5 (Moscow, 1981; Paris, 1982).

E. Gnedin, *Katastrofa i Vtoroye Rozhdeniye* (Amsterdam, 1977).

E. Gnedin, *Iz Istorii Otnoshenii Mezhdu SSSR i Fashistskoi Germaniei* (New York, 1977).

G. Hilger and A. G. Meyer, *The Incompatible Allies: A Memoir-History of Soviet-German Relations 1918–1941* (London, 1953).

Khrushchev Remembers (London, 1971).

A. Kollontai, 'Sem Vystrelov Zimoi 1939 god', *Mezhdunarodnaya Zhizn*, no. 12 (1989); (English translation in *International Affairs* (Moscow), January 1990).

M. Litvinov, *Against Aggression* (London, 1939).

I. Maisky, *Who Helped Hitler? Spanish Notebooks, Memoirs of a Soviet Ambassador 1939–1943* (London, 1964–7).

I. Maisky, 'The Munich Drama', *New Times*, nos 42–4, 46–7, 49 (1966).

V. Molotov, *Soviet Peace Policy* (London, 1941).

N. V. Novikov, *Vospominaniya Diplomata* (Moscow, 1989).

A. Ponomarev, 'Has the Colonel Made an Error in Translation: An Eyewitness Account of Military Talks between Britain, France and the Soviet Union on the Eve of World War II', *New Times*, no. 34 (1989).

J. V. Stalin, *Leninism* (London, 1942).

W. Strang, *Home and Abroad* (London, 1956).

W. Strang, 'The Moscow Negotiations 1939', in D. Dilks (ed.), *Retreat from Power*, vol. 1 (London, 1981).

V. Tanner, *The Winter War: Finland Against Russia 1939–1940* (Stanford, Cal., 1957).

J. Urbsys, 'Lithuania and the Soviet Union 1939–1940: The Fateful Year', *Litaunus*, 35, no. 2 (1989).

G. Zhukov, *Memoirs and Reminiscences* (Moscow, 1985).

SECONDARY STUDIES

Falsifiers of History (Moscow, 1948).

R. Ahmann, 'Soviet Foreign Policy and the Molotov–Ribbentrop Pact of 1939: An Enigma Reassessed', *Storia delle relazioni Internazionali*, no. 2 (1989).

M. Beloff, *The Foreign Policy of Soviet Russia*, 2 vols (Oxford, 1966).

L. BEZYMENSKY, 'Alternatives of 1939', *New Times*, nos 23, 24, and 34 (1989).

L. BZEYMENSKY, 'The Secret Protocols of 1939 as a Problem of Soviet Historiography', in G. Gorodetsky (ed.), *Soviet Foreign Policy, 1917–1991* (London, 1994).

J. CALVITT CLARKE, *Russia and Italy Against Hitler: The Bolshevik-Fascist Rapprochement of the 1930s* (Westport, CT, 1991).

M. J. CARLEY, 'Down a Blind Alley: Anglo-Franco-Soviet Relations, 1920–1939', *Canadian Journal of History* (April 1994).

M. J. CARLEY, 'End of the "Low, Dishonest Decade": Failure of the Anglo-Franco-Soviet Alliance in 1939', *Europe–Asia Studies*, 45, no. 2 (1993).

E. H. CARR, *German-Soviet Relations 1919–1939* (Baltimore, 1951).

E. H. CARR, *A History of Soviet Russia* (London, 1950–78).

E. H. CARR, *The Twilight of Comintern 1930–1935* (London, 1982).

F. L. CARSTEN, 'The Reichswehr and the Red Army, 1920–1933', *Survey*, no. 5 (1962).

A. CHUBARYAN, 'Was an Earlier Anti-Nazi Coalition Possible?', *World Marxist Review* (August 1989).

B. M. COHEN, 'Moscow at Munich: Did the Soviet Union Offer Unilateral Aid to Czechoslovakia?', *East European Quarterly*, 7, no. 3 (1978).

R. CRAIG NATION, *Black Earth, Red Star: A History of Soviet Security Policy, 1917–1991* (Ithaca, NY, 1992).

D. M. CROWE, *The Baltic States and the Great Powers* (Boulder, CO, 1993).

A. DALLIN, 'Stalin and the German Invasion', *Soviet Union/Union Soviétique*, nos 1–3 (1991).

D. J. DALLIN, *Soviet Russia's Foreign Policy 1939–1942* (New Haven, Conn., 1942).

A. DASHICHEV, 'Stalin in Early 1939', *Moscow News*, 27 August 1989.

S. DULLIN, 'Les diplomates soviétiques à la Société des Nations', *Relations Internationales* (autumn 1993).

H. L. DYCK, *Weimar Germany and Soviet Russia 1926–1933* (London, 1966).

J. ERICKSON, *The Soviet High Command* (London, 1962).

J. ERICKSON, *The Road to Stalingrad* (New York, 1975).

J. ERICKSON, 'Threat Identification and Strategic Appraisal by the Soviet Union, 1930–1941', in E. R. May (ed.), *Knowing One's Enemies* (Princeton, NJ, 1984).

J. ERICKSON and D. DILKS (eds), *Barbarossa: The Axis and the Allies* (Edinburgh, 1994).

I. FLEISHCHHAUER, *Pakt: Gitler, Stalin i Initsiativa Germanskoi Diplomatii* (Moscow, 1991).

G. GINSBURGS, 'The Soviet Union as a Neutral 1939–1941', *Soviet Studies* (July 1958).

S. A. GORLOV, 'Sovetsko-Germanskii Dialog Nakanune Pakta Molotova-Ribbentropa 1939g', *Novaya i Noveishaya Istoria*, no. 4 (1993).

G. GORODETSKY, 'The Hess Affair and Anglo-Soviet Relations on the Eve of "Barbarossa"', *English Historical Review* (April 1986).

G. GORODETSKY, 'The Impact of the Ribbentrop Pact on the Course of Soviet Foreign Policy', *Cahiers du Monde russe et soviétique* (Jan–Mar. 1990).

G. GORODETSKY (ed.), *Soviet Foreign Policy, 1917–1991* (London, 1994).

G. GORODETSKY, *Stafford Cripps' Mission to Moscow* (Cambridge, 1984).

G. GORODESTSKY, 'Was Stalin Planning to Attack Hitler in June 1941?', *Journal of the Royal United Services Institution*, no. 3 (1986).

A. A. GROMYSKO (ed.), *History of Soviet Foreign Policy*, 4th edn (Moscow, 1981).

J. T. GROSS, *Revolution from Abroad: The Soviet Conquest of Poland's Western Ukraine and Western Belorussia* (Princeton, NJ, 1988).

R. H. HAIGH et al., *German-Soviet Relations in the Weimar Era* (Aldershot, 1985).

R. H. HAIGH et al., *Soviet Foreign Policy, The League of Nations and Europe 1919–1939* (Aldershot, 1986).

R. H. HAIGH et al., *The Years of Triumph? German Diplomatic and Military Policy 1933–1941* (Aldershot, 1986).

J. HASLAM, 'The Soviet Union and the Czechoslovakian Crisis of 1938', *Journal of Contemporary History* (July 1979).

J. HASLAM, *Soviet Foreign Policy, 1930–1933* (London, 1983).

J. HASLAM, *The Soviet Union and the Struggle for Collective Security in Europe, 1933–1939* (London, 1984).

J. HASLAM, 'Soviet Foreign Policy 1939–1941', *Soviet Union/Union Soviétique*, nos 1–3 (1991).

J. HASLAM, *The Soviet Union and the Threat from the East, 1933–1941* (London, 1992).

J. HIDEN, *Germany and Europe, 1919–1939* (London, 1977).

J. HIDEN and T. LANE (eds), *The Baltic and the Outbreak of the Second World War* (Cambridge, 1992).

M. HITCHENS, *Germany, Russia and the Balkans* (New York, 1983).

J. HOCHMAN, *The Soviet Union and the Failure of Collective Security, 1934–1938* (Ithaca, NY, 1984).

M. JAKOBSON, *The Diplomacy of the Winter War* (Cambridge, Mass., 1961).

G. JUKES, 'The Red Army and the Munich Crisis', *Journal of Contemporary History* (April 1991).

B. J. KASLAS, 'The Lithuanian Strip in Soviet-German Secret Diplomacy', *Journal of Baltic Studies*, IV (1973).

D. KIRBY, 'The Baltic States 1940–1950', in M. McCauley (ed.), *Communist Power in Europe 1944–1949* (London, 1977).

V. N. KISELEV, 'Upryamye Fakty Nachala Voiny', *Voenno-Istoricheskii Zhurnal*, no. 2 (1992).

I. K. KOBLYAKOV, *USSR: For Peace, Against Aggression 1933–1941* (Moscow, 1976).

H. P. KROSBY, *Finland, Germany and the Soviet Union 1940–1941* (Wisconsin, 1968).

J. A. LARGE, 'The Origins of Soviet Collective Security Policy, 1930–1932', *Soviet Studies* (April 1978).

J. LEAMAN, 'The Treaty of Non-Aggression between Germany and the USSR, August 1939 – Old Myths, New Myths and Reinterpretations', *German History*, 12, No. 2 (1994).

I. LUKES, 'Did Stalin Desire War in 1938? A New Look at Soviet Behaviour during the May and September Crises', *Diplomacy & Statecraft* (March 1991).

I. LUKES, 'Stalin and Beneš at the End of September 1938: New Evidence from Prague Archives', *Slavic Review* (Spring 1993).

I. F. MAKSIMYCHEV, *Diplomatiya Mira protiv Diplomatii Voiny: Ocherk Sovetsko-Germanskikh Diplomaticheskikh Otnoshenii v 1933–1939* (Moscow, 1981).

R. MEDVEDEV, 'Diplomatischeskiye i Voennye Proschety Stalina v 1939–1941gg', *Novaya i Noveishaya Istoriya*, no. 4 (1989).

S. M. MINER, *Between Churchill and Stalin: The Soviet Union, Great Britain and the Origins of the Grand Alliance* (Chapel Hill, NC 1988).

R. J. MISIUNAS and R. TAAGEPERA, *The Baltic States: The Years of Dependence, 1940–1980* (London, 1983).

A. NEKRICH, *June 22nd 1941* (Columbia, SC, 1968).

B. NEWMAN, *The Captured Archives* (London, 1948).

L. N. NEZHINSKII (ed.) *Sovetskaya Vneshnyaya Politika, 1917–1945* (Moscow, 1992).

R. OVERY and A. WHEATCROFT, *The Road to War* (London, 1989).

V. PETROV, 'The Nazi-Soviet Pact: A Missing Page in Soviet Historiography', *Problems of Communism* (Jan.–Feb. 1968).

H. D. PHILLIPS, *Between the Revolution and the West: A Political Biography of Maxim M. Litvinov* (Boulder, CO, 1992).

O. PICK, 'Who Pulled the Trigger? Soviet Historians and the Origins of World War II', *Problems of Communism* (September 1960).

I. PLETTENBERG, 'The Soviet Union and the League of Nations', *in The League of Nations in Retrospect* (New York, 1983).

B. R. POSEN, 'Competing Images of the Soviet Union', *World Politics* (July 1987).

R. C. RAACK, 'Stalin's Plans for World War II', *Journal of Contemporary History*, 26 (1991).

L. RADICE, *Prelude to Appeasement: East Central European Diplomacy in the Early 1930s* (New York, 1981).

P. D. RAYMOND, *Conflict and Consensus in Soviet Foreign Policy 1933–1939*, PhD thesis, Pennsylvania State University 1979.

P. D. RAYMOND, 'Witness and Chronicler of Nazi-Soviet Relations: The Testimony of Evgeny Gnedin (Parvus)', *The Russian Review*, no. 44 (1985).

A. READ and D. FISHER, *The Deadly Embrace: Hitler, Stalin and the Nazi-Soviet Pact 1939–1941* (London, 1988).

R. REESE, 'The Impact of the Great Purge on the Red Army', *The Soviet and Post-Soviet Review*, 19, nos 1–3 (1992).

R. REESE, 'The Red Army and the Great Purges', in J. Arch Getty and R. T. Manning (eds), *Stalinist Terror: New Perspectives* (Cambridge, 1993).

G. ROBERTS, 'Collective Security and the Origins of the People's Front', in J. Fyrth (ed.), *Britain, Fascism and the Popular Front* (London, 1986).

G. ROBERTS, *The Unholy Alliance: Stalin's Pact with Hitler* (London, 1989).

G. ROBERTS, 'The Soviet Decision for a Pact with Nazi Germany', *Soviet Studies* (January 1992).

G. ROBERTS, 'The Fall of Litvinov: A Revisionist View', *Journal of Contemporary History* (October 1992).

G. ROBERTS, 'Infamous Encounter? The Merekalov–Weizsäcker Meeting of 17 April 1939', *Historical Journal* (December 1992).

G. ROBERTS, 'Military Disaster as a Function of Rational Political Calculation: Stalin and 22 June 1941', *Diplomacy & Statecraft* (July 1993).

G. ROBERTS, 'A Soviet-Bid for Co-existence with Nazi Germany, 1935–1937: The Kandelaki Affair', *International History Review* (August 1994).

K. ROSENBAUM, *Community of Fate: German-Soviet Diplomatic Relations 1922–1928* (Syracuse, NY, 1965).

A. ROSSI, *The Russo-German Alliance* (London, 1950).

L. ROTUNDO, 'Stalin and the Outbreak of War in 1941', *Journal of Contemporary History*, 24 (1989).

G. L. ROZANOV, *Stalin-Gitler: Dokumentalnyi Ocherk Sovetsko-Germanskikh Diplomaticheskikh Otnoshenii 1939–1941gg* (Moscow, 1991).

L. SABALIUNAS, *Lithuania in Crisis: From Nationalism to Communism, 1939–1940* (New York, 1972).

P. SEVOSTYANOV, *Before the Nazi Invasion* (Moscow, 1984).

W. E. SCOTT, *Alliance Against Hitler: The Origins of the Franco-Soviet Pact* (Durham, NC, 1962).

M. I. SEMIRYAGA, *Tainy Stalinskoi Diplomatii, 1939–1941* (Moscow, 1992).

A. SELLA, ' "Barbarossa": Surprise Attack and Communication', *Journal of Contemporary History*, no. 13 (1978).

Z. SHEINIS, *Maxim Litvinov* (Moscow, 1990).

A. SHTROMAS, 'Soviet Occupation of the Baltic States and their Incorporation into the USSR', *East European Quarterly* (September 1985).

V. SIPOLS, *Diplomatic Battles Before World War II* (Moscow, 1982).

V. SIPOLS, 'A Few Months Before August 23, 1939', *International Affairs* (Moscow), June 1989.

D. W. SPRING, 'The Soviet Decision for War Against Finland', *Soviet Studies* (April 1986).

V. SUVOROV, *Icebreaker: Who Started the Second World War?* (London, 1990).

A. N. TARULIS, *Soviet Policy Towards the Baltic States 1918–1940* (Notre Dame, Ind., 1959).

A. J. P. TAYLOR, *The Origins of the Second World War* (London, 1964).

T. TAYLOR, *Munich: The Price of Peace* (London, 1979).

M. L. TOEPFER, 'The Soviet Role in the Munich Crisis', *Diplomatic History*, no. 4 (1977).

N. TOLSTOY, *Stalin's Secret War* (London, 1981).

M. TOSCANO, *Designs in Diplomacy* (Baltimore, MD, 1970).

T. J. ULDRICKS, *Diplomacy & Ideology: The Origins of Soviet Foreign Relations 1917–1930* (London, 1979).

T. J. ULDRICKS, 'Russia and Europe: Diplomacy, Revolution and Economic Development in the 1920s', *International History Review*, no. 1 (1979).

T. J. ULDRICKS, 'A. J. P. Taylor and the Russians', in G. Martel (ed.), *The Origins of the Second World War Reconsidered* (London, 1986).

T. J. ULDRICKS, 'Evolving Soviet Views of the Nazi-Soviet Pact', in R. Frucht (ed.), *Labyrinth of Nationalism, Complexities of Diplomacy* (Columbus, OH, 1992).

T. J. ULDRICKS, 'Soviet Security Policy in the 1930s', in G. Gorodetsky (ed.), *Soviet Foreign Policy, 1917–1991* (London, 1994).

A. B. ULAM, *Expansion and Coexistence: A History of Soviet Foreign Policy* (New York, 1968).

D. VOLKOGONOV, *Triumf i Tragediya, I. V. Stalin: Politicheskii Portret*, 4 vols (Moscow, 1989).

S. V. VOLKOV and U. V. EMELYANOV, *Do i Posle Secretnykh Protokolov* (Moscow, 1990).

D. C. WATT, 'The Initiation of the Negotiations Leading to the Nazi-Soviet Pact', in C. Abramsky (ed.), *Essays in Honour of E. H. Carr* (London, 1974).

D. C. WATT, *How War Came: The Immediate Origins of the Second World War, 1938–1939* (London, 1989).

D. C. WATT, 'Who Plotted Against Whom? Stalin's Purge of the Soviet High Command Revisited', *Journal of Soviet Military Studies* (March 1990).

G. L. WEINBERG, *Germany and the Soviet Union 1939–1941* (Leiden, 1954).

G. L. WEINBERG, *The Foreign Policy of Hitler's Germany: Diplomatic Revolution in Europe 1933–1936* (Chicago, 1970).

G. L. WEINBERG, *The Foreign Policy of Hitler's Germany 1937–1939* (Chicago, 1980).

A. WERTH, *Russia at War 1941–1945* (London, 1965).

B. WHALEY, *Codeword 'Barbarossa'* (Cambridge, Mass, 1973).

A. YAKOVLEV, 'Soobshcheniye Komissii po Politicheskoi i Pravovoi Otsenke Sovetsko-Germanskogo Dogovore o Nenapadenii ot 1939 goda', *Pravda*, 24 December 1989.

UNPUBLISHED WORK

G. ROBERTS, 'The Failure of the Triple Alliance Negotiations, 1939: The View from Moscow' (1994).

G. ROBERTS, 'Soviet Policy and the Baltic States, 1939–1940: A Reappraisal' (1994).

Appendix

RESOLUTION OF THE CONGRESS OF PEOPLE'S DEPUTIES OF THE USSR:
'ON THE POLITICAL AND LEGAL EVALUATION OF THE SOVIET-GERMAN
TREATY OF NON-AGGRESSION OF 1939'

1. The Congress of People's Deputies of the USSR notes the conclusions of the Commission for the political and legal evaluation of the Soviet-German Treaty of Non-Aggression of 23 August 1939.
2. The Congress of People's Deputies of the USSR agrees with the opinion of the Commission that the non-aggression treaty with Germany was concluded in a critical international situation, under conditions of a threat of growing fascist aggression in Europe and of Japanese militarism in Asia, and that one of its aims was to deflect the threat of approaching war from the USSR. In the event this aim was not achieved and miscalculations in connection with the commitment of Germany to its obligations to the USSR aggravated the consequences of the treacherous Nazi aggression. At this time the country was faced with a difficult choice.

The obligations arising from the treaty came into force immediately after it was signed, although the treaty was subject to ratification by the Supreme Soviet of the USSR. The resolution on its ratification was adopted in Moscow on 31 August and instruments of ratification were exchanged on 24 September 1939.

3. Congress considers that the contents of this agreement did not conflict with the norms of international law and the treaty practices of states, which were acceptable for similar settlements. However, when the treaty was concluded a 'secret additional protocol' was also signed – a fact concealed during the ratification process. The protocol delineated the 'spheres of interest' of the contracting parties from the Baltic to the Black Sea, from Finland to Bessarabia.

The originals of the protocol have not been found in either Soviet or foreign archives. However, expert graphological, photographic and lexical examination of copies, maps and other documents and the correspondence of subsequent events with the contents of the protocol confirm the fact of its signature and existence.[1]

4. The Congress of People's Deputies of the USSR hereby affirms that in accordance with the norms of international law the non-aggression treaty of 23 August 1939, the friendship and frontier agreement between the USSR and Germany signed on 28 September of the same

year, and the other Soviet-German agreements lost their force the moment Germany attacked the USSR on 22 June 1941.

5. Congress states that the protocol of 23 August 1939 and other secret protocols signed with Germany in 1939–1941 deviated from the Leninist principles of Soviet foreign policy, in both method of composition and content. The delineation of 'spheres of interests' between the USSR and Germany and other actions were from the juridical point of view in contradiction with the sovereignty and independence of a number of third countries.

Congress notes that in this period the USSR's relations with Latvia, Lithuania and Estonia were regulated by a system of treaties. In accordance with peace treaties of 1920 and treaties of non-aggression concluded in 1926–1933 the participants committed themselves to respect, regardless of the circumstances, each other's sovereignty and territorial integrity and inviolability. The Soviet Union had similar obligations to Poland and Finland.

6. Congress states that the negotiations with Germany for the secret protocols were conducted by Stalin and Molotov without the knowledge of the Soviet people, the central committee and the party, the Supreme Soviet, and the government of the USSR. These protocols were excluded from the process of ratification. Thus the decision to sign them was in essence an act of personal power and in no way reflected the will of the Soviet people, who were not responsible for that deal.

7. The Congress of People's Deputies of the USSR condemns the signing of the 'secret additional protocol' and other secret agreements with Germany. Congress accepts that the secret protocols are judicially invalid and were null and void from the moment of their signing.

The protocols did not create a new legal basis for the mutual relations between the Soviet Union and third countries, but were used by Stalin and his circle to present ultimatums and to pressurise other states, in breach of legal obligations undertaken before.

8. The Congress of People's Deputies of the USSR proceeds from the fact that awareness of a complicated and contradictory past is part of the process of perestroika, whose mission is to ensure each people of the Soviet Union the possibility of free and equal development, an integrated world, and increasing mutual understanding.

Izvestiya, 27 December 1989.

1. The originals of the secret protocols have since been found in the Soviet archives and published.

Index

DATE DUE